PIER GIORGIO FRASSATI

CRISTINA SICCARDI

PIER GIORGIO FRASSATI

A Hero for Our Times

~

Translated by Michael J. Miller

IGNATIUS PRESS   SAN FRANCISCO

Original Italian edition:
Pier Giorgio Frassati: Il giovane delle otto beatitudini
© 2002 Edizioni San Paolo s.r.l., Cinisello Balsamo, Italy

Cover art and design by Carl E. Olson

© 2016 by Ignatius Press, San Francisco
ISBN 978-1-62164-000-4
Library of Congress Control Number 2014949948
Printed in the United States of America ∞

Dedicated to you,
my little Pier Giorgio,
darling nephew,
and to you, Laura,
dearly beloved sister

CONTENTS

Preface 9

1. In the Coffeehouses of Turin. 15
2. A House without Flowers and without Fire 29
3. His Mark on History. 47
4. An Odd Rebellion 63
5. Great Ideals. 94
6. Like a Castaway 111
7. Pluralism in One Creed. 127
8. His Hymn to Charity 149
9. Politico-Social Commitment 166
10. Friends 205
11. Berlin 216
12. Laura 231
13. "A Tremendous Mountain Climber" 258
14. The Vigil 275
15. Sister Death 291
16. The Triumph 313
17. "Now Everything Is Clear to Me". 328

Appendix 347
Bibliography 355

PREFACE

A new biography of Pier Giorgio Frassati? But what else can be said about him?

Faced with the mass of documents, volumes, questionnaires for the canonization process, and testimonies old and new, we felt like castaways, just as Pier Giorgio felt when faced with books and lecture notes. Thousands upon thousands of pages have been written about this Blessed, who is loved so much yet sometimes not understood: recollections and memoirs that we have examined attentively in order to try to understand who this young man was who lived scarcely twenty-four years but was capable of leaving an indelible impression of sanctity. The famous theologian Karl Rahner, whose works Pier Giorgio knew, writes: "God does not grant to all the grace to die young, when everything is morning promise and immaculate beginning. And not every early death is the fulfillment of this beginning."

What we tried to do was reconstruct, in a sea of papers, not only the personality of Pier Giorgio, which was by no means simple, but also a set of very complex and contradictory family relationships: the story of souls in search of ties that were established only at the end.

Pier Giorgio, proclaimed Blessed on May 20, 1990, is the only saintly young man in whose name the younger generations gather in prayer in various parts of the world. He is a figure who remains extraordinarily relevant, and for this reason, too, people never tire of talking about him. He was a forerunner of the apostolic laity, an interpreter of Vatican Council II *ante litteram* [before the conciliar documents were written]. In the letter *Operosam diem* by John Paul II, we read: "It is characteristic of the saints mysteriously to remain contemporaries with every generation: this is the result of their profound rootedness in the eternal present of God."

Marked by the sign of Christian joy, Pier Giorgio, who repeatedly experienced a lack of understanding in his own family that was as serious as the sense of remorse and self-blame of those immediately involved, was not the son of his father, who went no farther than to donate to charities. Pier Giorgio was quite different; his charity was the mature fruit of his ongoing interior work, of his boundless love for his neighbor and in a very special way for the poor: he shared in their sufferings while seeking to alleviate them, and into the attics and slums of Turin in the second and third decades of the twentieth century he brought the light of his person, his unabashed smile, and his overflowing vitality.

On the day of his funeral, the eyes of his father, his mother, and his sister were opened to a totally unknown reality: thousands of persons arrived to pay their last respects to the friend of the poor and their own, touching his coffin as though it belonged to a saint. The youth who, instead of studying, "lounged around" with his friends from the Church of San Vincenzo, from FUCI [Federazione Universitaria Cattolica Italiana, the Association of Italian Catholic University Students], from the People's Party of Don Sturzo, in the friary of the Dominican Fathers, in the sacristies of churches, "wasting his time" in prayer, Eucharistic celebrations, reading Saint Paul, Saint Augustine, and Saint Thomas, and who at the diplomatic mission in Berlin, where his father was ambassador, used to "steal" the flowers in the meeting rooms so as to put them on the graves of poor people, now drew a crowd, not because of the famous name he bore, but because of the good works he had performed. His success was not of the earthly sort continually pursued by the Frassati family, but rather an eternal accomplishment that will never fade or tarnish.

The civil engineer Pier Giorgio Frassati, endowed with a lively practical intelligence, whose university degree was conferred *post mortem* in 2001, a hundred years after his birth, was truly ahead of his time, living out the lay apostolate in a missionary spirit and with tireless commitment; he was a champion of charity, speaking, acting, and thinking in the name of Christ and of the Gospel in a way consistent with a marvelous life of integrity.

Self-taught in the faith, although he grew up in a materialistic, sterile, and spiritually arid environment, he had a soul as wide as an ocean and let it emerge in all its radiance. A strong, extremely intense call from God led him along a very personal, sweeping path: it not only gave meaning to his life but also fired him up and opened limitless vistas.

His proverbial cheerfulness diminished in the last phase of his life, when signs of his premature end appeared. It was dampened by a series of conditions that were suffocating him: his love for Laura Hidalgo, his father's plan to involve him professionally in *La Stampa*, the daily newspaper that he himself had founded and now edited, and fear that his beloved parents would separate. These were trials to which the Blessed responded with a personal maturation that is clearly evident from his writings but also from his face, which gradually lost its last boyish features.

Pier Giorgio's education in sanctity is fascinating: he did not renounce his privileged status but made of it an instrument of charity, demonstrating that the rich young man in

the Gospel failed to do the will of God, not because he had
a lot of money, but because he was full of himself, proud
and seemingly self-sufficient. Pier Giorgio, on the contrary,
set out humbly but resolutely on the path shown to him by
the Savior, and his was an *Imitation of Christ* that always put
God first, ahead of everything and everyone.

In parallel with the earthly career of Pier Giorgio, we
have conducted an investigation of his father, Senator Alfredo Frassati, a supremely gifted individual: endowed with
an astonishing intellect, he was not only a magisterial journalist but also an expert in politics and an entrepreneur on
a grand scale. Extremely proud of his successful position
within the middle-class society of the major world powers, his life broke down when death carried off his son, for
whom he had feelings of pride and respect and whom he
wanted to make his worthy heir. It broke down, but a new
prospect opened up to him: the material goods on which he
had spent his energies for fifty-seven years were replaced,
year by year with ever greater intensity, by spiritual reflection. This, in our judgment, was the first miracle of Blessed
Pier Giorgio. The two men of the Frassati household, as
unlike as they were and however different their earthly ideals, were reunited in their full understanding of the soul:
the son led the father to Christ. This aspect of the story
emerges quite clearly through an investigation of the facts,
but also through precious unpublished documents. We are
talking about correspondence, which is now published in
this book, between Cardinal Giovanni Battista Montini, the
future Paul VI and then-archbishop of the principal city in
Lombardy, and Senator Frassati. It is a story of spiritual pain
and conversion that is in turn forceful, passionate, and—as
we must say without exaggeration—moving.

Another story, never told before, is the one about the

relationship between Pier Giorgio and Laura Hidalgo, with whom he fell in love. In biographies of the Blessed, Laura always has remained hidden in the shadows, mentioned and then nothing more. Now we finally know who she was, her origins, and her life experience after the departure of the young man of the beatitudes.

A modern Christian Siegfried, Pier Giorgio performed bold feats of mountain climbing in the Alps that he loved and longed to conquer; very handsome, vigorous, charming, he was the embodiment of vital energy, the center of attraction of his friends, both male and female. He made friendship, which for him had an irreplaceable value, one of the foundations of his life, to the point of creating a close-knit, spirited confraternity resembling those of medieval university students that was dubbed the Society of the Sinister Types, made up of *lestofanti e lestofantesse*, "swindlers both male and female", who were united by their mutual harmony, by their faith, and by prayer above and beyond the demands of the time.

The Blessed, with a rosary in one hand and a cigar in the other, was not a bigot whose faith is rhetorical, unctuous, and hypocritical, but rather a young man who firmly believed in Christ's words and did not stop at communicating them but also lived them twenty-four hours a day.

Often we have heard people ask: But what did Pier Giorgio do to have been raised to the honor of the altars? He was a capable fellow, like many others in his day, yet he did not build churches or found religious institutes or hospitals or schools. . . . Well, his sanctity is modern: it is the extraordinary grafted onto the ordinary; it is fallen human nature renewed in spirituality; it is simple daily living in God, in his light; it is man who unconditionally allows himself to be shaped by revealed truth.

It is strange to observe that people talk about him in the United States and in Poland, in Germany as well as in Australia, while in the streets of middle-class La Crocetta the memory of him is fleeting and inconstant, except in the parish of La Beata Vergine delle Grazie (Our Lady of Grace), where Pier Giorgio went every day to recharge his hyperactive mornings with the Body of Christ and where today pilgrims arrive from afar to visit him and to rediscover the atmosphere that he breathed, to see through his eyes, and to ponder his thoughts.

IN THE COFFEEHOUSES
OF TURIN

Leafing through the photograph album of Pier Giorgio Frassati, a veritable biography in images, we are struck particularly by two snapshots. The first is from May 17, 1925: Pier Giorgio, on the Rocca Sella, is mountain climbing in a roped party together with three young friends. And it is remarkable that the first one is Giuseppe Grimaldi, who would be the executor of his will, which would be for the benefit of the poor. Here, by way of a metaphorical interpretation of the scene, the smiling, athletic youth, who died at the age of twenty-four and was declared Blessed on May 20, 1990, lifts up to the spiritual heights his contemporaries, present and future.

In the other picture, dated 1913, his father, Alfredo Frassati, is celebrating his appointment as senator with the twelve-year-old Pier Giorgio. In the parent's look we can discern how proud he is of his male child and his assurance that he will include him in the management of his daily newspaper, *La Stampa*, of which he is publisher and editor.

These two moments from the life of a Blessed do not fit into the usual hagiographic patterns. The two photographs show two loves, paternal and Alpine, that would influence and mark the life of the only son, the saintly layman, who is now in a position to charm a multitude of Catholic youths.

No one could imagine for the scion of the Frassati family a future so far removed from the life-style pursued in that residence in Turin, where a distinguished, respected, powerful, and liberal upper-middle-class family lived in the first years of the twentieth century.

When Pier Giorgio was born, the Frassati family was living in a spacious apartment of a manor house at 33 via Legnano, facing the corso Siccardi (the main street) and the large expanse of the Piazza d'Armi (which was completely open before the aristocratic villas were built), where old men, mothers, nannies, and children added local color to everyday scenes in the foothills of the Alps. It was April 6, 1901, Holy Saturday, when the little boy came into the world, two years after the death of his sister Elda, at the age of only eight months, and one year before the birth of his sister Luciana.

In January, Giuseppe Verdi had died in Milan, and April 22 would be the date of the death of Gaetano Bresci, the anarchist who had assassinated King Umberto I on July 29, 1900. The criminal's death, officially passed off as a suicide, was in reality caused by several prison guards, as it was later explained. Meanwhile, Guglielmo Marconi sent the first radio-telegraphic transmission between Europe and America, thus starting the revolution of the global communication of sounds and images.

The general census determined that the number of people residing in Italy was 33,778,000. Giovanni Giolitti, minister of the interior in the Zanardelli government that had formed in February after the resignation of Giuseppe Saracco, introduced a liberal approach in the government's policy in labor conflicts, both in agriculture and in industry, promoting the growth and the organization of labor unions. The government thus succeeded in winning the support of the Socialist deputies, who predominantly took the reformist approach theorized by Filippo Turati and disputed by other Italian Socialist Party leaders.

A law instituted the General Emigration Commission: many Italians were seeking their fortune abroad, especially in America, and their numbers were increasing. Some of the major problems of the country, in particular the "Southern Question" and the abolition of excise duties, were again getting attention in the legislative chambers and in public opinion. Leo XIII, the pope of the social encyclical *Rerum novarum*, addressed the question of the autonomy of the Christian Democratic movement, which arose in Europe and Latin America beginning in the late nineteenth century in the wake of his Magisterial teaching. In a short message addressed to the eighteenth Catholic Congress in Taranto, the pontiff ruled out the possibility of the movement transforming itself into a political party and required that Christian Democrats belong to the second section of the *Opera dei congressi* [Work of the Conferences].[1] By subordinating the

---

[1] The Work of the Conferences [*Opera dei congressi*] was an organization that assembled the most uncompromising Italian Catholics; its first public manifestation was the conference in Venice in 1874, followed by another eighteen until the year 1903. It fostered intense activism by the Catholic movement, while claiming to represent the "real country" as opposed to the liberal State and coordinating all sorts of Catholic initiatives: social, cooperative, educational, and journalistic. The Work of the Conferences reached its high point with the presidency of Paganuzzi (1889–1902), whose rigid conservatism collided with the authorities of the new Christian-Democratic generation of Romolo Murri, a priest from the Marches, founder of the Federation of Catholic University Students and of the magazine *Vita nuova*, which were absorbed into the Work of the Conferences. Murri went so far as to ask Catholics to commit themselves to the defense of fundamental liberties and of the common people, while also supporting some of the militant causes of the extreme left, for the purpose of creating an autonomous political party. In order to thwart that plan, Leo XIII issued the encyclical *Graves de*

activity of the Christian Democratic movement to the official organization of Italian Catholicism, the pope intended
to ensure that the ecclesiastical hierarchies would control
the movement itself, thus checking autonomous tendencies.
Leo XIII, moreover, sent a new bylaw to the Work in which
he also assumed formally the title of president of the Work
itself.

The mother, Adelaide Ametis, did not experience much joy
at the birth of her second-born child: she would have preferred another girl. During her first pregnancy, she had written to her husband: "Actually I would be afraid of a boy,
and even though you would always be there to help me,
what would you, who have no religion, be able to tell him
someday to encourage him to resist his passions?"

It was a problem of upbringing, therefore, and the fear of
being unable to watch over a male child as she wished, in
keeping with strict Catholic morality. "Dodo", as Pier Giorgio was called by his family (and sometimes also *Sonntags-*
kind, German for "Sunday child", because he had brought
back smiles after the death of his sister who had preceded
him), appears in some photographs dressed and with his hair
styled as though he were a baby girl: his mother dolled him
up in this way, pretending that she had a new daughter. For
a few years, in memory of her first-born, Adelaide used to
say to Pier Giorgio: "You are my little baby girl."

His cousin, Rina Maria Pierazzi, seeing the newborn lying

---

communi (1901), whereby he forbade Catholics to give the Christian Democratic movement a political character. Murri and some of his followers nevertheless continued their activity, winning the support of Giovanni Grosoli,
the new head of the Work of the Conferences. But because of the internal
conflicts that logically resulted, in 1904 Pius X decided to dissolve the authority of the Work itself.

in the white cradle, did not hesitate to exclaim: "He looks like a fly that fell into the milk!" And he certainly does look like that, with his fine little head of black hair and his two big dark brown eyes.

Pietro Giorgio Michelangelo was born in the third degree of asphyxia, and therefore it was decided to have him baptized the following day, Easter Sunday, by Monsignor Alessandro Roccati, the priest who, as the pastor of the Chiesa della Beata Vergine delle Grazie (Our Lady of Grace), the church in the prestigious La Crocetta district in which the Frassatis lived, would minister to Pier Giorgio from his birth until his death.[2] It seems that we can see the young Pier Giorgio immersed in prayer and meditation at the place in the church where he is commemorated pictorially in a mosaic, together with Don Bosco and Saint Joseph Benedict Cottolengo, and where there is a large inscription that tells about him:

> Pier Giorgio Frassati, Apostle of Charity, who in prayer and daily Eucharistic union drew light and strength to fight the good fight, to finish the race of this life, and to respond serenely to God's unexpected call as a good soldier of Christ. May he be a reminder and an incentive for young people.

Pier Giorgio had merely to cross the street, and suddenly he found himself in the church, which was austere on the outside but sumptuous inside, combining various styles: from the late Byzantine era in the floor plan in the form of a Greek cross to the Romanesque style of the bell tower, from the friezes ornamented in the Ravenna style

[2] The term "Crocetta" is derived from the name of the little seventeenth-century church, Santa Croce, which had been enlarged by Pier Giorgio Frassati's pastor, Monsignor Roccati. His bust can be found in the church today in the first chapel on the right.

to the paleo-Christian form of the apse, from the solemn vestibule reminiscent of the ancient narthex to the ceiling with its wooden rafters.

The baby boy, named Pietro at Alfredo's insistence, in memory of his father, and Giorgio because it pleased Adelaide, in honor of the saint and knight who slew the dragon, succeeded in winning his battle to survive and was baptized officially on September 5, the third wedding anniversary of Adelaide and Alfredo, in the Church of Saints Fabian and Sebastian in Pollone, in the province of Biella so loved by Alfredo Frassati and later also by Pier Giorgio.

The baptismal ceremony was performed by the bursar of the Shrine in Oropa, Father Clemente Zovetto. The godparents were the grandparents Francesco Ametis and Giuseppina Frassati.

In 1904 the family moved to 55 corso Siccardi (today called corso Galileo Ferraris), and in 1917 they would go to live in a large, aristocratic two-story villa that is still beautiful today and can be seen (as the headquarters of Banca Fideuram) at number 70 along the same street, across from the parish church of Our Lady of Grace and a few steps from the stadium that many years later would be replaced by the modern Polytechnic School.

The life of the two children was made up of prohibitions and isolation; there was no opportunity for friendships with others their own age, and there was no room for any weakness. It was a rigid, almost military education, the purpose of which was to teach physical and moral strength, habits of discipline and obedience, and the acceptance of continual sacrifices, while overcoming obstacles, sorrows, and fatigue by a Spartan method. Obedience and sacrifice were permanently engraved in the heart and mind of Pier Giorgio.

Shut off from the outside world, segregated in a house of "do not do, do not say, do not think", Pier Giorgio and Luciana never experienced familial warmth, and despite their continuous squabbles and quarrels that ended in blows, as often happens between brothers and sisters, they were very fond of one another; indeed, in their mutual affection they sought the maternal warmth that was often lacking. The two little children were constrained to live in a suffocating atmosphere and sought comfort and support in each other.

Their parents forbade them not only to play with other children but also to have visits from adults, and so they spent all their free time alone. The only pleasant break was after dinner, when their father kept his children company, taking part in their games. But being a highly capable man of action, Alfredo Frassati would be thinking about his work and always returned to the great passion of his life: *La Stampa*. He was capable of assuming major responsibilities and seeing onerous tasks to completion, and so for him, his daughter, Luciana, maintained, life was a problem to be solved, economically as well, with efforts that were intense and flexible at the same time.

Adelaide imposed on her children a Spartan education and at the same time employed the clever feminine art of emotional blackmail: she postured as a victim and gave them to understand that anything contrary to her wishes broke her maternal heart, causing bouts of prostration.

Pier Giorgio, being big-hearted and surprisingly sensitive, loved his parents intensely and never blamed them or expressed disappointment in their regard. His filial love remained unchanging and to the very end preserved its freshness and initial liveliness, as we can tell from his letters.

On July 19, 1922, he wrote as follows to his mother:

Dear Mama,

I regret, and it has caused me a lot of pain, that you should think such things that are not true.[3] A mother's advice is always the wisest, and it is always good, even when someone is already old. This year you were very far from me, and I was able to appreciate what it means not to have our mother close by, who scolds us once in a while but in the evening gives us a kiss and her blessing. Unfortunately, dear Mama, I cannot be with you in Pollone; rather serious studies are to blame in part. The third year is tough, and it is necessary to make many sacrifices in order to arrive safely at the goal. But let us not lament the fact, because in this life there are greater misfortunes. Dear Mama, excuse me also for all the little displeasures I have caused you, yet be sure that if at times I have failed you, in the future I will try to do better, because I think of you often and pray to God that he will give you the consolations that I because of my faults cannot give you, although I wish you the best. Kisses to you and to my aunt.

Pier Giorgio

This letter recalls the simplicity, sincerity, and tone of the eight-year-old boy who wrote on December 19, 1909:

My heart is very sorrowful to see you sick. Get well, dear Mama. . . . When you are well again my heart will be glad, but now it is sad. Good little Mama, I wish you a quick recovery. I will pray to God that he may make you well, and God will listen to my prayers.

Although it had traumatically lost the title of capital of the united Kingdom of Italy (someone was so desolate as to commit suicide over it), Turin with its "fine Parisian manners", as Guido Gozzano put it, remained a prestigious

---

[3] This is a letter replying to a remark made by his mother that had grieved him: "Well, now you are grown up and no longer need me."

city of nobles and notables. Elegant, refined historic Savoy residences served as the artistic cornerstone for a city that was being industrialized, with the resulting social tensions. After the loss of its leading role in Italy, the capital of Piedmont made some specific decisions in the urban reconstruction and the topographical reshaping of the ancient heart of the city. Pressures exerted by interested landowners converted whole residential areas for the poor into better-quality housing or for higher-level services such as banks, real estate agencies, and financial institutions. While streets were being redesigned and new major arteries were being laid out, lower-class housing became concentrated in the vicinity of the chain of factories and smoking chimneys that logically enough had been built outside the center of the city.

Turin, one of the best qualified European capitals, deprived of its leading position, managed to pick itself up energetically. It was no accident that it opened its doors to the *art nouveau* that, over a span of fifteen years, involved artisans and customers, for whom the floral vocabulary continued to be used even after the decline of that style, which quietly survived until the 1930s, when *art deco* had already triumphed and there were clear signs of the dictates of rationalism in art and architecture.

After espousing "liberty" for their urban and hillside residences, the *haute bourgeoisie* [upper middle-class] and the entrepreneurial class demonstrated their fidelity to these artistic choices by employing them also for industrial buildings. This new, cheerful style could be an effective advertisement for the various manufacturing firms. After the regulatory plan of 1908, even in the peripheral zones in which the quality of life was declining, the new artistic style made its appearance in municipal buildings (especially schools). The city had grown tremendously because of the continual immigration of farmers arriving from the countryside, and the demand for housing was enormous. Lower-class houses, which later would be visited by Pier Giorgio Frassati, had no toilets or washrooms, and therefore the municipality promoted the construction of a series of public baths, which are remarkable not only artistically but also for their functionality.

Turin was the city that, within the course of a few decades, saw sanctity flourish in social services that became the pride of the Church in that subalpine region and beyond: Giuseppe Cafasso, the Marquess Giulia and the Marquis Carlo Tancredi Falletti di Barolo, Giuseppe Benedetto Cottolengo, Francesco Faà di Bruno. . . . John Bosco had been dead for just thirteen years, and Pier Giorgio did not live to see 1929, the year of the beatification of the teacher and father of youth, the founder of the Salesian family.

It was also in Turin that the younger generations were formed on the pages of the book *Cuore* (1886). The city mapped out in the book was still crisscrossed by charcoal dealers, carpenters, chimney sweeps, and soldiers. And through this urban microcosm, which was depicted in chiaroscuro tones, passed laborers, poor people, and beggars.

Cuore, which successfully inaugurated a new phase in educational publishing,[4] has been described as a "dull" book that, despite its edifying optimism, accurately reflects the harsh reality of everyday life in those very difficult years after Italian unification, when, in a massive willful effort, the young nation aspired to make arduous civil progress that was attainable, according to its author, Edmondo De Amicis

[4] *Cuore*, an illustrated newspaper for boys that cost 20 centesimi and was published in Milan, was still being read in the 1920s.

(a brilliant journalist and an accomplished writer),[5] only by dint of an indiscriminate acceptance of the ethics of sacrifice and solidarity.

Enrico Bottini, one of the main characters in the book, hears his father tell him: "Think about it: you lack nothing, and they [the poor] lack everything; while you want to be happy, they are content not to die. Think how horrible it is that in the midst of so many palaces, along the streets where carriages and children clothed in fine velvet pass, there are women and children who have nothing to eat."

Little Pier Giorgio would wear velvet clothes and would ride in carriages and in the first automobiles that came out of the factories on the corso Dante; he would live in those palaces and would pass in front of the little tables of the famous cafés in Turin. Here the intelligentsia and the common folk met: the coffeehouses of Turin, then the only place where the different classes could socialize, were the setting for major decisions and historic deeds. In the Caffè Alfieri in the winter of 1860, Garibaldi, Bixio, and Crispi set up an office to recruit for the Expedition of the Thousand. They were also a cultural landmark: Camasio and Oxilia wrote their hit comedy *Addio giovinezza!* on the outdoor tables of the Caffè Molinari; Ernesto Ragazzoni, who was also an employee of Alfredo Frassati's newspaper, *La Stampa*, wrote most of his nocturnal verses on those tables; at the Caffè delle Alpi, at the corner of the via Dora Grossa and the via Consolata, Edmondo De Amicis penned the unforgettable pages of *Cuore*. Nor can we overlook the birth of the manufacturing firm Fiat. The social circle where the entrepreneurial ideas of the owners of Fiat developed was the Caffè Burello

[5] In 1890 Edmondo De Amicis (1846–1908) joined the Socialist movement, in which he was a militant reformer of the school of Turati.

on the corso Vittorio Emanuele, which is decorated with plaster figures and gilded ornaments; it was frequented by two rather different groups of patrons: the travelers coming from the nearby station of Porta Nuova and the elite of the bourgeoisie who met there to discuss politics and business on red velvet sofas. Landaus, traveling carriages, and coupés stopped in front of this café, and the roar of the motorcars drew the curious, who formed colorful groups of onlookers.

At the Caffè San Carlo, Francesco Crispi convinced his friends from the left wing in parliament to launch the African colonial adventure, which ended unhappily at Adua. Again at the San Carlo, Antonio Gramsci, at a separate table, wrote his theater gossip columns after attending the premieres of Alfieri and Carignano. Benedetto Croce and Luigi Einaudi also made their appearances in that locale.

Giovanni Giolitti, a good friend of Senator Frassati, as we will see, after arriving from Rome and while waiting for the connecting train to his destination, Cavour, used to stop at the San Carlo in the company of Alfredo or else read the *Illustration*. Almost every day Piero Gobetti passed by deep in thought, his pockets bulging with books and manuscripts. Alongside the intellectual, well-to-do social classes, there were people who lived in poverty and unhappiness.

In that Turin, where the bleakest misery coexisted with the *belle époque*, amidst political and cultural debates, high fashion that competed with Paris and simple dressmakers (called *caterinette*), laborers and captains of industry, concerts and cabarets,[6] Alfredo Frassati, born in Pollone on September 28, 1868, felt that he was more a son of Biella than of Turin. He himself declared:

[6] Turin held the record in Italy for the largest number of cabarets and ballrooms. The city became a magnet for the greatest stage artists: Petrolini, Pasquariello, Maldacea, Villani, Fregoli.

Every so often, when someone asks me about my birthplace, I answer, "I am Biellese", and I feel within me a dignity and pride as though I had said that I belonged to the most ancient aristocratic family. In our soul we hold high the feeling of dignity and independence that animated our ancient commune, which caused it to rise up against the bishop of Vercelli and prompted it to give itself freely to the House of Savoy, to which it remained stubbornly faithful.[7]

The region around Biella was known not only for its intense entrepreneurial and manufacturing activity, but also for its religious indifference, which Alfredo Frassati himself acquired, an indifference that Pier Giorgio by his charm would try to counteract among the young people of Pollone.

The first biographer of Pier Giorgio Frassati, the Salesian priest Antonio Cojazzi,[8] was acquainted with the Blessed for a long time and wanted to make him known with a book that had great success and was translated into several languages; the Polish edition was read by the young Karol Wojtyła, who was immediately fascinated by Pier Giorgio, experiencing "his beneficial influence". In the biography, Cojazzi wrote:

[7] Marcello Staglieno, *Un santo borghese: Pier Giorgio Frassati* (Milan: Bompiani, 1988), 12.

[8] Don Antonio Cojazzi (1880–1953) composed his work, which was published by SEI in 1928, by relying on his own acquaintance with Pier Giorgio and on a long series of testimonials. The book was a great success among Catholics, selling more than 200,000 copies, and was the first stone in the enormous edifice of books and journalism constructed to present the example of Pier Giorgio Frassati to various Catholic movements and circles. A second edition of the volume appeared in 1977, edited by a committee of friends who retouched some features connected with the author's initial personal interpretations, and there was a third edition in 1990, again from SEI, with a preface by Francesco Traniello.

He [Pier Giorgio] had his faults. Not major ones in themselves, but a serious list of them: an impulsive temperament, a truly Biellese stubbornness, carelessness about his use of time, and little love of order. He was no prodigy of innate virtue, therefore. He, too, knew those moments of irritability and apathy that are part of any childhood. Hence the quarrels with his little sister, his fellow student and playmate, which were often resolved by force. He loved her, however, with intense affection; her name was always on his lips; he did nothing, made no decision, without her opinion; his sister was, all told, his counsel and comfort in all uncertainty.[9]

Initiative, seriousness, candor, honesty, obstinacy, and consistency. His family called him "Hardheaded". A Biellese temperament, therefore, just like his father's.

---

[9] Antonio Cojazzi, *Pier Giorgio Frassati: Il libro che lo ha fatto conoscere e amare* (Turin: SEI, 1990), 17.

2

A HOUSE WITHOUT FLOWERS
AND WITHOUT FIRE

A spacious corner room, fitted out with large pieces of furniture in the Piedmontese baroque style, accommodated us every day at mealtimes. Two windows looked out over the street . . . and over the old Piazza d'Armi, which had already been invaded by villas and small houses, making it impossible to see the ponderous monument to Vittorio Emanuele II. A dark walnut mantelpiece with the carved angels of that style occupied the whole wall adjacent to the door leading to the studio. The terrace without flowers that joined it to the dining room and the fireplace without a fire seemed to be the symbol of our family.

This is Luciana speaking, who left the most blunt and detailed testimony about their family life, which she called "an ill-defined nightmare",[1] a nightmare shared with her brother, whom she understood very little at first and loved very much after his departure.

Luciana Teodolinda Maria came into the world on August 18, 1902, in Pollone. When they presented the newborn to Pier Giorgio, the child rejected her and, pointing to the door, told his mother to take her away. "This selfish, jealous gesture of the little boy, who nevertheless was

---

[1] Luciana Frassati, *I giorni della sua vita* (Rome: Studium, 1975), 18.

destined to become a man of charity, can serve as proof that saints are not born but are made day by day by dint of the will and correspondence with God's graces."[2]

Life in the Frassati house was anything but calm and relaxed. Relations among the family members were cold, forbidding, and arid; everything seemed to be measured in terms of material things rather by the spirit; according to ambitions, power, success, and public opinion rather than the philosophical, religious, and psychological standards of the human mind. Yet in this environment, silently but productively like leaven, the prodigious, extraordinary sanctity of Pier Giorgio matured and emerged.

Despite the mask put on to confront the outside world, many aspects of that problematic household atmosphere did not remain hidden, and there are plenty of testimonies in this regard. "Upon entering that house I always felt an indescribable sense of coldness. Everything was beautiful, everything was elegant, but everything was icy, too; and I had no illusions about that iciness",[3] wrote Rina Maria Pierazzi, the cousin of Adelaide Ametis.

Let us read also what the postulator of the cause of beatification, Father Paolo Molinari, wrote:

> Between the children and their parents there was no real trust or closeness: the family setting, apparently unimpeachable, masked an emotional chill that weighed heavily on the little children. In fact, there was a split between the two parents, even though superficially family relations were always deceptively clear and sound. A silent battle over the

[2] M. Codi, *Pier Giorgio Frassati: Una valanga di vita* (Casale Monferrato [AL]: Portalupi, 2001), 36.

[3] R. M. Pierazzi, *Così ho visto Pier Giorgio* (Brescia: Queriniana, 1955), 197–98.

years brought sadness to the house and wordless sorrows that were poured out primarily on Pier Giorgio and Luciana. Because of the children, the split between the parents never resulted in open separation [which did take place after the death of the son]; but it is understandable that henceforth their respective centers of interest were outside the walls of the home, in paintings and social life for the one and in editing *La Stampa* for the other.

While the children were minded by their governess, Caterina Bianchetti, Adelaide Ametis, who liked to feel emancipated, was chiefly intent on "self-affirmation", proud that she had attained success that was independent of her husband's fame and power. She openly showed her lack of prejudice and struck poses as she did so: she used to smoke cigars, and her "frequent visits in the upper-class circles of the city started a constant stream of gossip".[4]

Adelaide maintained that she could face all the dangers that threaten a woman without being deflowered by them. . . . For this reason, she knew no limits in her friendships both with men and with women; and perhaps this was why she did not spare herself many an unpleasant rumor that ran around Turin, in which, however, I believe there was nothing truly bad.

Proud and authoritarian, more used to giving orders than to discussions, [Alfredo] accumulated a set of misunderstandings with Adelaide that—perhaps also combined with romantic adventures—ended up distancing him from her, while she drew close, probably too close, to the painter Alberto Falchetti.[5]

---

[4] M. Staglieno, *Un santo borghese: Pier Giorgio Frassati* (Milan: Bompiani, 1988), 18.

[5] Ibid.

A brilliant artist and a friend of John Sargent and of Segantini, Falchetti was one year younger than Adelaide Ametis (she was born in Turin on February 17, 1877); he distinguished himself as a vigorous colorist, although he did not have the same degree of talent as his father, Giuseppe. Adelaide wrote letters to the painter, confidentially calling him in English "my dearest Bertie".[6] But the artistic interests of young Signora Ametis led her to keep company with other painters: an attitude that was sometimes considered outrageous by public opinion, which craved gossip and scandals. Adelaide, however, paid no attention to them, intent as she was on perfecting her art, to the point of being admitted in 1912 to the Biennial Exposition in Venice (she would return again in 1920 and in 1922), where she had the unexpected satisfaction of seeing King Vittorio Emanuele III purchase one of her oil paintings.

A friend of the family, Giuseppe Borioli, left testimony

---

[6] Here is the text of the letter from Holy Thursday 1918: "My dearest Bertie, *mio carissimo*, time has flown by in work, courses, washing paintbrushes, erasing, seeing the sights (a little), and in the evening, in the brief moments of rest around the 'quiet oil lamp', someone is chatting, another chats, somebody is shouting verses from Tasso or Storia, and the setting is not conducive to writing. . . . I was in Oropa on Tuesday—we arrived with Pier Giorgio, who brought me my bags. . . . The valley of Oropa was bathed in the most beautiful sunlight—rose-colored in the dark blue sky—dazzling snow and such peace and quiet! Everything here moves me. The profile of Mount Mucrone and Mount Tovo, the streams, the children walking to kindergarten, the sight of an old man who was acquainted with my father and spoke the same unrefined dialect. . . . As I strolled alone, I thought that I am indeed my father's daughter! When he left the country at the age of seventeen, maybe he already had a dream about this house. And the thought of returning gave him the strength to remain in that foreign land, to work and to save, and then to return to make this wonderful site for himself! I fear that my children will no longer feel this love for their hometown. But I digress—I wanted to tell you about the painting (so much to finish, and today it is cloudy!) and to hear from you about the small portrait."

that is important in understanding the very difficult relations between the Frassatis, a crucible of tensions and conflicts that started from the first years of their marriage:

> The husband and the wife remained together only because
> of their preoccupation with a higher social status for their
> family, and it is only logical that this state of mind did not
> produce unity and serious affection between them. I had
> to say this, although . . . it was painful, because I am con-
> vinced that this split in the family is the key to many of
> the things that Pier Giorgio did later. . . . Of course [Ade-
> laide's] wordless battle with the senator over the years, the
> lack of any glint of light and love, ended up drying out the
> hearts of both. The venom of hatred constantly passed from
> her to him, year after year, never submitting to any solu-
> tion whatsoever that might resolve everything one way or
> the other. . . .
>
> From the earliest days, it was not difficult to notice a
> state of muted tension between Signora Adelaide and her
> husband. Being very discreet by nature, I never made any
> inquiries about the matter, but even though I did not seek
> it, quite a bit of news reached me in this connection from
> various parties, and I understood that there was a serious
> rift between them and that only their children, their reli-
> gious scruples, and worldly reasons kept that rift from de-
> veloping into a clean break. In those days, the views of
> the nineteenth century prevailed; anything could serve as a
> pretext for an attempt to overthrow the Frassatis' fortune!
> And a hundred and one reasons existed, therefore, to galva-
> nize a union that was little more than a formality. I some-
> times had the impression that Signora Ade had to prove
> that even though physically she was not one of the most
> fortunate women, because she was little, rather solid, with
> a short neck, she nevertheless could arouse interest and be
> courted and deemed an elite woman. All this was not the
> result of feminine flirtatiousness and emulation, but out of a

desperate attempt to win back her husband by arousing his jealousy or out of sheer spite, in order to taunt him. But he never said a thing about it. It is obvious that he for his part had some secret, given his position, his charm, his wealth, the lack of consolation from his wife for his labors. He always controlled himself, and if there were ever any bitter, sharp words, they were spoken only by Signora Ade.[7]

Alfredo and Adelaide were cousins; both of them grew up in well-to-do households. He was the third son of Pietro, a physician, and of Giuseppina Coda Donati. In his parents' house, a tragedy occurred that left its mark on him for the rest of his life: his dearest sister, Emma, was killed by her fiancé. Although he tried to persuade her to call off the wedding that was scheduled for June 20, 1889, Alfredo had no way of knowing the criminal nature of Luigi Pizzetti, who on June 9, blinded by jealousy when his fiancée refused to marry him (she had found out about his disorderly, dissolute life), threw her out of the window, two steps away from the room of the young woman's mother. The murderer was sentenced to eight years in prison, and the famous criminologist Cesare Lombroso, founder of the Italian positivist school, even though he was the lawyer for the Pizzetti family at the young man's trial, declared: "It is my conviction that Pizzetti has no moral sense and is mentally enfeebled: he may be a moral madman or a born delinquent."[8]

Benito Mussolini, in the issue of *Il Popolo d'Italia* dated April 14, 1919, maliciously wrote in one of his customary jabs at Frassati: "Privately he began his financial fortune through the mysterious defenestration of one sister"; or else he devised nasty labels for him: "Tyrolean Senator", "Gio-

[7] Staglieno, *Un santo borghese*, 19–20.
[8] Luciana Frassati, *Un uomo, un giornale: Alfredo Frassati*, vol. 1 (Rome: Edizioni di Storia e Letteratura, 1978), 13–14.

litti's cowboy", "the enemy within", "one of the worst national threats". Frassati did not react to these provocations so as not to fuel useless polemics, which Italy certainly did not need.

The wound that he suffered through the loss of his beloved sister did not heal even with the passage of time, and it became more acute when Alfredo received news of the death of his twenty-year-old cousin Emilia Ametis from a heart attack. Let us read carefully this letter addressed to the same Ametis family, dated November 2, 1894:

> A very sad day of the dead. I was thinking of another beautiful young woman, as pure and good as your Emilia, and more unfortunate than your Emilia. I thought today of my dearest, unforgettable Emma, cut off in the flower of her youth by an assassin's hand. My thoughts, my tears fly to the cemetery in Oropa, . . . but I hoped to be the only one to weep. . . . Poor mother, think of the God in whom you believe and bow your head before him. God gave her to you, God took her from you; may his will be done.

Can a truly convinced atheist write these words? Certainly he was not a practicing Catholic, but from the documents that have been recovered, we cannot rule out the possibility that he yearned for the infinite and the Almighty. Dejected and "searching", Frassati speaks about the immortality of the soul.

Unlike Giovanni Giolitti, who *l'era nen da tonbe*, as they would say in the Piedmontese dialect (or, in standard Italian: *non era per le tombe*, "he was not one for visiting graves"), so much so that he could not identify the place where his grandparents were laid to rest, Senator Frassati went to the cemetery every year on the anniversary of his father's death and, when he was the ambassador of the kingdom to Berlin, charged Pier Giorgio with continuing the pious custom in his stead. He appreciated the tranquility of the graveyard in Oropa. On August 14, 1922, he wrote to his wife from Berlin: "At least there everyone is equal; a cross, a stone that recalls who is buried there."

His was therefore a stifled faith that would be liberated gradually, through a surprising personal *rapprochement* with men of the Church, beginning on July 4, 1925, with the tragic and very painful death of his son, Pier Giorgio.

His yearning for the infinite, which he would attain at the end of his long life, always led him to a rigorous ethical code that accompanied him throughout his public life. On September 8, 1887, Celestina Bertolini, his acquaintance, wrote to him:

> I have come across so many people who boasted of having faith and did not even know the name of love, because they attributed to it a meaning that seems to me to be a profanation, that I am almost tempted to cheer myself up with you. When someone has an immense, infinite love in his heart, there are plenty of sparks to light the torch of all the virtues, whereas what good is faith with a cold heart?[9]

Aware of his own limits, he wrote:

> Happy are they [the dear departed]! If I knew with certainty that in dying I would leave as much mourning as those good souls left, dying would matter little to me. But I am not good like they were, and certainly the thanks and tears that we pour out today for our dead would not follow me to the grave.[10]

So present was the memory of them to him that it prompted him to write: "The remembrance of the living is the life

[9] Ibid., 1:17.
[10] Ibid., 1:15.

of the dead." He used to say and to keep in mind: "Affection must conquer even death."

Frassati completed a law degree in Turin in 1890. From his boyhood, he showed an interest in journalism, contributing to several papers: *Gazzetta piemontese, Gazzetta letteraria, Perseveranza.* Alfredo was a born journalist but also an entrepreneur. At the age of twenty-three, he founded the biweekly *La Tribuna biellese.* He had a knack for new initiatives and outstanding organizational skills. Meanwhile, he developed his own liberal views and completed his studies of law in Germany, in the city of Heidelberg, where he perfected his knowledge of German. After a further period of improvement in Berlin, he wrote various essays on legal themes, and, at the age of twenty-seven, he obtained a position as lecturer in law and penal procedures at the University of Sassari.

On June 29, 1899, he wrote to his wife, Adelaide:

> [Thanks to *La Stampa*] I earned 10,000 [lire] last year besides my salary [again from *La Stampa*]. Adding up the salary, the university, and the *Tribuna*, I earned about 18,000 last year: a more than reasonable income for my age. I think, though, that I deserved it, partly because of my ability and partly because of my persistence. Of these 18,000 lire, at least 10,000 are in savings for Elda [the first daughter, who died young], for the others who will arrive, and for us when we are old. We do need to think about and provide for our old age, for emergencies and misfortunes. As you see, from the material perspective as well, you can be rather content with your husband, who knows the right time to spend and also knows the right time not to spend. . . .

But his love for journalism led him to Turin, where he capitalized on his managerial talents by taking over the *Gazzetta piemontese*, which had been founded in 1867 by Casimiro Farale. Intelligent and dynamic, Alfredo was a twentieth-century man; leaving the previous century behind him, he had a typically modern personality: far-sighted, a lover of truth, honesty, and consistency in his thoughts and actions.

Having grown up in the Biellese school of sobriety and thrift, Alfredo passed all these values on to Pier Giorgio, including his love of literature. Alfredo, despite his work in journalism, did not abandon his literary studies. He wrote about Dante, Sudermann, Ibsen, and even an original essay on "Hamlet's Will", written in the 1930s in order to transform the anemic, paranoid Hamlet into a very astute man who was conscious of his own actions. The work, which met with both criticism and approval, including that of Benedetto Croce, was dedicated to the memory of Pier Giorgio in the heartrending words of an inconsolable father: "To your memory, my dear, handsome, holy Giorgetto, I wish I could dedicate, not whatever there is of mine in this little work, but rather my life, had it not become such a wretched thing since your death. Your Papa."

On November 13, 1913, at the age of forty-five, Alfredo Frassati became the youngest senator in the kingdom, and he was the one who

> first turned to the entrepreneurial middle class so that it might do the work of renewal, replacing the old orientations of the nobility and the moneyed aristocracy, which had not yet disappeared from the scene, with other broader directions inspired by a dynamic, progressive liberalism. . . . He was an admirer of the English model, of a system based on the firmness and stability of governments and on an orderly, efficient parliamentary system.[11]

---

[11] V. Castronovo, *Torino* (Bari: Laterza, 1987), 154–55.

He had a strong sense of the State, confidence in liberal democracy, and an abhorrence of all oppressive regimes; he was true to the Piedmontese tradition of the absolute independence of journalists from any governmental interference:

> [And] as a logical consequence, [independence] from every effort by a party to influence men in power directly. I had supported the policies of the Honorable Giolitti, which I understood as a renewal of political-social custom, so as to call more classes of citizens, with broader rights and freedoms, into the orbit of public life and public interests; but this had been a direct encounter of ideals that was due to confidence in methods that placed the State above the interests of the privileged classes and, for that very reason, promoted by their impartiality the free development of political and social forms. But each one in the field of its own activity.[12]

He was considered a man who was "all of a piece", as they say, and people declared: "*La Stampa* is Frassati", and no one could deny that he harbored the categorical imperative in his conscience: his faith in secular values.

A certain existential malaise permeated Alfredo's conscience, as this letter to his fiancée dated September 14, 1896, may show:

> I write cold, ugly letters: but if you knew, too, how much conflict and controversy there is in my life, you might not be surprised if sometimes I feel utterly exhausted and would give the world for an hour of peace. I have a deep, physical melancholy, which perhaps poisons everything for me and makes me unfair to others and even to myself.

A sentimental, passionate, impetuous romantic, Alfredo wrote to his female cousins in the Ametis family on June

[12] A. Frassati, *Giolitti* (Florence, 1959), 8.

29, 1896: "Words are to affection what dew is to a flower.
And a flower without dew dies." Being a deep thinker, he
experienced the malaise of existential uneasiness; he himself said that he felt that he was involved in a Hamletesque
battle between being and nonbeing, a malaise caused by the
thought of evils endured and by the presentiment of future
ills:

> Speaking about the malaise of certain souls, Geiger writes:
> "A desperation resulting from the contrast between the
> peace enjoyed by others and the uneasiness that torments
> our mind, a form of discouragement born of the awareness
> that all our efforts will never attain the desired goal, and
> finally the persuasion that man's life is an everlasting vi-
> cious circle in which the worst men triumph and the best
> men succumb. Whatever you may call such a state—and
> instead of *acedia*, people like to call it by a modern name
> such as pessimism, melancholy, or hypochondria—no one
> will ever succeed in fully expressing this painful feeling that
> eludes all precise definition, and it cannot be avoided, be-
> cause it is closely connected with the nature of man, who is
> always restless and subject to error, which means the desire
> to help people but to remain distant from them, to occupy
> the highest position and yet to be content with a golden
> mediocrity, to strive actively and nevertheless to lead a con-
> templative life." Now you know me.[13]

A complex, meditative person, he used to reflect deeply
with his keen mind: "How egotistical are those who have
never really suffered, those who have found life easy! They
can understand nothing, respect nothing."

---

[13] See L. Frassati, *Un uomo, un giornale*, 1:28.

Adelaide was the younger daughter of Francesco Ametis and Linda Copella. She had felt the appeal of painting since her childhood, when she dreamed of attaining the high artistic standards set by Lorenzo Delleani, a famous painter from Biella. She remained very close to her sister Elena even after her marriage and made her her most intimate confidante, as well as the family administrator, and Alfredo never objected to that bond; indeed, he admired his sister-in-law's talent for running a household. She acted toward Pier Giorgio as a foster mother, whose sermons were quite similar to Adelaide's: "Do not waste time; do not be disorderly; study", and the perpetual "Go shave!"

An interesting analysis was made of the handwriting of Pier Giorgio's mother in the *Positio* of the Blessed:

> Vibrant, the writer needs to live a fast-paced life and becomes agitated if the life around her is not active and if her day is not full. Two words are enough for her to get to the bottom of any question; no frills; no turns of phrases; she is definitely a modern woman, ahead of her time, too, because of the extreme liberality of her ideas. . . . Cool in her reactions, and so she is truly capable of never losing her head and of seeing, if one can say so, more accurately than anyone else. Presumptuous, she does not hesitate to consider herself more up-to-date than anyone else about anything. She basically feels that she is an intellectual, and even before her interlocutor has opened his mouth, she has already judged him—whether correctly or unfairly does not matter.

While they were still engaged, Alfredo wrote to her in 1896:

> We have characters that are too similar to avoid these squalls: I would need a kindly woman who was able to forgive my

moments of ill humor, an occasional harsh word of mine, someone who would smile calmly at me: not someone who increased my sorrows and the reasons for my anguish. And you would need a gentle man who was able to forgive you quickly.

Alfredo "desperately" thought of the disagreements "that would be repeated even more frequently in the future".

So strong was the bond that joined Adelaide to her sister Elena that Alfredo often addressed them both, considering them as one, and in fact the two sisters no longer were separated after Elena went to live in the Frassati house. Alfredo used to reprimand his future wife without sugarcoating what he said, as in his letter dated September 24, 1897:

> Be a lady, make me admire you not only as a sympathetic and always adorable friend, but as a high and noble companion for a life of work, as a companion who is aware of my toils and my sorrows. . . . Go for a stroll, certainly, go to the mountains, amuse yourself . . . but, along with the amusement, the work that God has assigned to us and that we must do in order to be worthy of our mission.

He expressed forthrightly his brilliant observations about beauty and character:

> The head is the characteristic feature *par excellence*: it immediately tells you a person's character: a head born to command, to impress: full of brains and strong will: the same sort of forehead, very sympathetic, because everything that reveals strength is beautiful . . . you have such a prominent forehead, which tells someone who looks at you either to submit or to be broken . . . even your nose says that your will must be of iron . . . anything in your face that is not beautiful disappears perfectly in the splendor of two little intelligent eyes, vivacious, full of life, spirit, and cunning . . . a complete lack of knowledge about thrifty living, en-

thusiasm for everything that is beautiful or appears to be such. You are too intelligent to have a restricted horizon. Sensitive: the misfortune of a friend makes you sad; fortunately, though, you are very easily distracted; in speaking about someone else you completely forget the sorrowful impression, and you are again able to wear a sincere smile. . . . Your chief defect: superficiality in your sentiments; your chief virtue: a heart of gold for everyone.[14]

The education of Pier Giorgio and Luciana was Adelaide's prerogative, and she paid attention to the rules and the formalities and very little to the sensibilities, moods, and feelings of her children. Alfredo Frassati returned home for the midday meal and for supper like any father of a family. Pier Giorgio and Luciana were educated more strictly than the children of the poor. It was imperative to convey to them an austere sense of life, of duty, respect for money, things, and persons, even by controlling what they ate, so that they would be accustomed, not to luxury and comforts, but to severity and order, to composure and moderation in speech, to the utmost seriousness in their attire. They were to rise every morning at seven to wash in cold water, and their day concluded at eight-thirty in the evening. They gathered at table at half past noon and at seven-thirty in the evening, always with the correct posture, back perfectly straight, wrists on the edge of the table and arms at the sides. Some families, in order to get better results, used to put coins under their children's armpits on Sunday.

The household cook, Carolina Masoero, left us this priceless testimony:

Pier Giorgio and Luciana helped each other as much as they could, but they always lived somewhat in fear. I remember

[14] Ibid., 1:26.

little Miss Luciana crying once because her Papa was late
coming back; when her Mama told her to stop, she continued instead even more noticeably. Once I heard the senator
say to my lady: "You are always away; at least treat these
children well." And Signora Frassati really was away all the
time: she did not return until seven in the evening, and you
might say that she was there only to scold.

The angry scenes between the father and the mother were
very frequent, and the children often witnessed them, cowed
into silence by their respect for their parents. Only once did
Pier Giorgio, upset by the tension of yet another clash between the two, shout a word, just one, but it cracked like a
whip: "Enough!"

Normally boys bond more with the maternal figure and
girls with the paternal figure, and so it seemed to happen in
the Frassati household. Often Pier Giorgio took his mother's
side, perhaps to protect her from the senator's authoritarian
and sometimes despotic behavior; but in reality he had great
love and the highest esteem for him and was very proud of
him; one illustration of this was his dedication to his studies,
which he never liked but which he pursued with determination so as not to disappoint his father's expectations.

Pier Giorgio always put his family ahead of his own
choices: first came his parents' desires, then his own, but
if his parents opposed the latter, then the young man of
the eight beatitudes, as John Paul II described him, would
obey in silence and suffering. His love for them appears even
more surprising and heroic to us if we think of the setting
in which he was nurtured. Then it seems incredible, more
than his lively sympathy and cheerfulness could bear, that
after growing up in such a tense, sad environment, his filial
love should remain strong, as unshakable as granite, despite
the incompatibility and the rift that were being created be-

tween the spiritual, political, and social choices of Pier Giorgio and the ideas and life-style of his parents. The only areas to which his parents had no access—the "islands" on which Pier Giorgio expressed himself fully—and which they were not capable of obstructing in any way were his life of faith, manifested in prayer and the constant thought of Christ; his life of charity, expressed by an irrepressible love for the poor; and his exuberance and energy. It was a veritable "avalanche of life", capable of seizing the fullness and essence of human existence, so as to transmit it to those around him and particularly to his friends; the intervals dedicated to hiking and mountain climbing: in the mountains he breathed deeply the rarefied air of the infinite and transcendence.

On June 1, 1925—Pier Giorgio would die one month later—Senator Frassati added to the editorial board of *La Stampa* his friend Giuseppe Cassone (1877–1953), a reporter who had dedicated forty years of his life to the newspaper, for the purpose of starting his son on the difficult task of serving as general manager. Alfredo did not dare to meet his son's eyes as he revealed his arrangements to him, the fact that he was using his friend. But listen to the account of Cassone himself

> Senator Frassati wanted to make Pier Giorgio his successor at *La Stampa*, to entrust at least the administrative management to him. But how could he tell him this if Pier Giorgio, who was nearing graduation, had decided to become a mining engineer? It was his dream to live among the miners, a plan that he had preferred to an initial vocation to the priesthood. I had the job of convincing Pier Giorgio to give up his plan.
>
> One day when he had come to visit me at my office, I seized the opportunity. I spoke to him as though to a wise, dear son. He listened to me in silence, with his beautiful

boyish eyes fixed calmly and searchingly on me, and then he asked: "Cassone, do you really think that if I come here to *La Stampa*, Papa will be happy?" I told him yes. He no longer hesitated. "Tell Papa that I accept." Appreciating the fact that it was a big sacrifice for him, I was moved, and I embraced him.[15]

---

[15] Codi, *Pier Giorgio Frassati*, 46–47.

3

HIS MARK ON HISTORY

Who were the six million Italians who from 1896 to the first half of the year 1900 emigrated to the cities or left the country in search of fortune? Generally they all came from the countryside, from the lands where people worked hard but struggled to survive. In Alfredo Frassati's newspaper, *La Stampa*, they talked about it, just as on page one, under gigantic headlines, they reported the tragedy of the *Titanic*: only 706 of the 2,300 passengers of the legendary transatlantic ship were rescued. The tragic aftermath profoundly troubled public opinion, as though it were an omen of much more serious catastrophes.

On April 16, 1913, the theologian and physician Albert Schweitzer arrived at Lambarené, on the west coast of Africa, in present-day Gabon, and with profound love and Christian charity built a hospital for the local populations. With his groundbreaking studies of the life of Jesus, his name had become well known in cultural and scholarly circles. In the autumn of 1904, he had read an appeal from the mission in Congo seeking personnel, and thus he discovered a new, profound professional vocation: "I wanted to become a physician so as to be able to intervene physically, without having to make speeches." The following year he started his studies in medicine, which he concluded in 1913 with a thesis on *The Psychiatric Evaluation of Jesus*. His work in Africa was interrupted because of the outbreak of the First World War. In 1917 he traveled in Europe to practice his profession on the war fronts and for about a year was detained in various French concentration camps. He did not return to Africa to resume work in his hospital until 1924, and two years later he obtained funds for the construction of a leprosarium. He was a theologian and a musician, passionately interested in the technique of musical instruments and co-editor of Bach's organ works, which he interpreted in an innovative way. Schweitzer was a genial, complex person, the "physician of the jungle", who loved other people deeply, especially the weak and the needy, for whom he developed in this context his theory of "respect for life".

The only important events in the summer of 1914 were national matters: Great Britain addressed the crisis in Ulster; France followed attentively, with bated breath, the murder trial of the wife of a minister; in Germany, conservatives and social democrats were involved in a lively debate about the recession. At first not even the assassination in Sarajevo on June 28, 1914, led anyone to suspect that a very serious crisis was looming, so that in early July the leaders of all the European countries tranquilly went on vacation.

Driving the world toward what would be described as the "mother of all twentieth-century catastrophes" was a set of antagonisms among nations that at the time were caught up in a foolish arms race because of their greed for expansion: Germans and British vied for dominion on the high seas, while the gigantic Russian empire desired free access to the Bosporus and the Dardanelles.

The causes of the conflict were exacerbated by one prevailing force: nationalism. Combined fatally with the aspirations for the autonomy and sovereignty of peoples articulated by the French Revolution in 1789, nationalism proved to be a dangerous, two-edged weapon, which, amalgamated with patriotism, was wielded directly against all who happened to be identified as enemies: in Berlin the windows of the British Embassy were broken, whereas in Paris and London the people threw stones at the display windows of German shopkeepers.

Young men all over Europe, influenced by the hate-filled speeches of political and military leaders, threw themselves with wild enthusiasm into the horror of war. Politicians emphatically and rhetorically praised "the hero's death", while philosophers wrote that the war served to "temper steel", strengthening and exalting the manly spirit. There was no room for neutral voices; only that of Alfredo Frassati was heard widely, thanks to the columns of his newspaper.

On the morning of January 1, 1895, the daily paper was at the newsstands with a new masthead, *La Stampa* (The press), in a typeface that has remained unchanged to this day, with the subtitle *Gazzetta piemontese*, which later disappeared on August 13, 1908. Thanks to Alfredo Frassati, the independent political daily had outgrown its role as a local newspaper and taken on national proportions. "Create something, it matters little whether it be great or small, according to our abilities, but create." That was his motto.

Frassati had taken the gasping, debt-ridden newspaper off the hands of Senator Luigi Roux, a very bad administrator, and, like a good Biellese, had first put the paper back in the black and then led it to prosperity by his rigorous management. On December 31, 1894, he had taken the reins of the newspaper that was destined to play a leading role in the political and cultural life of Italy; nevertheless, the one who created it saw in it his own destiny: "In five minutes I will sign the agreement that may be my life or my death. . . . If

I were a Roman, I would sign gladly and contentedly: as an Italian, I sign it calmly and confidently."[1]

Having understood the highly influential role of the printed page on public awareness, in a programmatic editorial in the issue dated February 7–8, 1895, he wrote:

> The press in the modern State . . . is a new force . . . that sees no boundaries on its horizon, has no limits to its mission, and has no end to its journey. Although little noticed at first, little by little it has conquered the world; a few decades ago, when it already seemed very powerful, it was described as the fourth estate; but it aims to become in fact the first, because having made itself the spokesman of this immense force of public opinion, it implicates all the other estates and powers, exerts influence over them all, and dominates in a mysteriously irresistible way. . . .
>
> We picture the press also as the priestess of that exalted moral law which is found in the public conscience; which the interests, passions, or special influences of the moment may cause to waver or go astray but which nevertheless, by gathering in a supreme synthesis the voice and the aspiration of all humanity, guides the nations to the acquisition of the common good. . . .
>
> The new title also represents our aspirations, even though we do not proudly presume to embody all that the press is and can be. This title allows us physically to cross over the boundaries of our old, beloved Piedmont region.

At the age of only thirty-two, Alfredo Frassati found himself at the head of one of the most important newspapers with political and administrative responsibility on his shoulders, and he even devised joint subscriptions with other periodicals alongside the daily paper: *La Stampa sportiva, La*

[1] Luciana Frassati, *Un uomo, un giornale: Alfredo Frassati*, vol. 1 (Rome: Edizioni di Storia e Letteratura, 1978), 79.

Donna, La Stampa agricola. But now his uneasiness returned, despite the successes that he had achieved:

> Many of my dreams are coming true even earlier than I expected, but others, alas: how far off they still are! Maybe they will be far away for my whole life. I sense the ideals that I lack much more than those I have already attained, and my all-too-anxious mind cannot savor the present moment but only becomes embittered thinking of the future.[2]

Pietro Frassati, an engineer to whom life, in the opinion of his brother Alfredo, did not give the career that he deserved, was involved in building and developing *La Stampa.* Pietro brought the utmost expertise and meticulousness to his work. It was not uncommon to see him on Sunday strolling around the headquarters of the daily paper, skirting the wall, as though to protect the creation of his brother; he was so different from him in his humility and simplicity, but also in his zeal to economize as much as possible: for example, the flooring material in the managing and editorial offices was obtained from the rotunda of a public ballroom.

He was called "Giacchettina" (little jacket) because of his way of dressing: a short, black-and-white checkered coat worn over tight trousers. He issued only one pen nib at a time to the editors, and eventually this irritated Alfredo, too; once, after obtaining his pen nib and failing to get it to work, he peremptorily ordered a hundred pen nibs. They were hidden in the director's drawer and thereafter circulated noiselessly in the realm of the wise administrator. At the end of every month, the typesetter Antonio Cavalletto, who used kerosene to clean lead type, appeared at Pietro Frassati's office with an empty kerosene can. The administrator, horrified, pointed to the red 27 on the calendar that

[2] Ibid., 1:96.

loomed over his shoulders and declared, "There are still three days until the end of the month!"

His thriftiness was proverbial—he even collected pieces of string so as to reuse them—and Pier Giorgio himself had the opportunity to experience it directly: one day the administrator visited the newspaper's linotype machine with his nephew and there advised Pier Giorgio to use the back of the printer's proofs for the records of his charitable organization.

The headquarters of the daily newspaper were at the corner of the via Stampatori and the via Davide Bertolotti, across from the building where Guido Gozzano was born.[3] An unassuming staircase led to the mezzanine floor, where the administrative offices were located; following them farther, one arrived at the first floor and the editorial offices. On the left, a little room was used to welcome visitors, who were more inclined to wait in the long corridor, which from 1913 on would lead to the larger offices at piazza Solferino 20. The editorial department was open to everyone; among the visitors was the tall, imposing, and elderly Prime Minister Giolitti, who, as he usually did upon arriving in Turin, after a stop at the Bologna Inn on the corso Vittorio Emanuele II, in front of the station at the corner of via XX Settembre, would go unceremoniously, alone, to tell the editor-in-chief that he was there.

In the basement of the building, the presses were set up. Alfredo wrote to his wife on July 11, 1902: "I am in the

---

[3] The memorial plaque, along the via Davide Bertolotti where it intersects with the piazza Solferino, dedicated on May 21, 1971, the tenth anniversary of the death of Senator Alfredo Frassati, reads as follows: "Here Alfredo Frassati / brought *La Stampa* into the world / and waged his battles, / but when the sign of silence arrived / and Pier Giorgio's dear face had departed, / here he saw that free voice break, / shackled by events."

workshop a lot, often with my machines. And I rather like to think that my soul, my energies have left and will leave a lasting imprint on them. Can I say as much about the world?" In this sense, the one to leave an imprint on the world would be his son, Pier Giorgio . . .

In the "workshop" of the Turin daily newspaper lived an ancient tribe of stern lineage, members of the rough-hewn laboring aristocracy: the typesetters. Any journalist who walked into *La Stampa* immediately had to deal with this group, and from them he received his first examination. Typesetters worked with lead and seemed to have derived from it some of its hardness, solidity, and severity. From it one learned that words were truly stones that would not decay with time; individual letters took on the weight of the strong metal and thus acquired greater value and weight than they have today. Their aprons were black, their hands and faces were black, and even the editors' white collars were black, left on the benches while they cooked and stirred the newspaper with the linotype operators, the proud practition-ers of an excellent trade, with background music provided by the persistent hammering of the linotype machine. Alfredo Frassati, conductor of that orchestra (which included also the new, efficient, and revolutionary apparatuses that were part of the international system of communication, such as the rotary machine and the telephone), walked amid the lead type and the galley sheets with the pride, dignity, and great satisfaction of someone who is making his dream come true.

The four-page edition of *La Stampa* grew to six; the best mechanical and technical instruments available on the mar-ket were acquired, and remarkable improvements were made to the telegraph and telephone services. And so the news-paper had print runs of 100,000 by the year 1906. In that same year, *La Stampa* obtained the right to publish, at the same time as giants of the world press such as *The Times* and *Le Matin*, telegrams that arrived from all parts of the world. Thus the daily could present every day four columns of news that no other Italian newspaper was capable of providing. *La Stampa* became the second most widely read newspaper in Italy after *Il Corriere della Sera*. The war in Libya, the earthquake in Messina, and the 1911 World's Fair in Turin, which put the former capital of Italy in the European spotlight, fabulously increased the paper's circulation until, in 1915, it had reached a print run of 300,000 copies. Alfred himself often took charge of the distribution, as he often did with occasional inspections of the newsstands, while his brother battled with the railroad lines.

"I always, always need something great to attract me, something noble to sustain me, something pure to save me: some faith in a banner under which to fight", the senator wrote in 1895. Pier Giorgio found greatness in the Gospel, nobility in the poor, and purity in his genuine Christian youth, and his banner would be Christ, the standard of grace and perfect happiness.

While Pier Giorgio felt satisfaction in acting directly in the social and political struggle, his father got his gratification from the newspaper, the pages of which he inked with contemporary history. "It is a rare pleasure to hear the heartbeat of history throbbing in one's own work."[4]

At the turn of the century, he clearly expressed his dream of greater Italian influence in the Mediterranean in his article "Time for Daring", and he would never abandon it.[5]

---

[4] A. Frassati, "Ci siamo!", *La Stampa*, October 6, 1911.

[5] In an article entitled "Austria and Italy" published in *La Stampa* on October 23, 1912, Alfredo Frassati writes: "Italy is a Mediterranean power, and therefore it has confronted the great African enterprise, but it still remains

When the First World War broke out, there was such intense general excitement that an enormous rift was caused between the interventionists and those who wished to remain neutral. Frassati's decision to defend neutrality, side by side with Giovanni Giolitti, elicited vulgar, hysterical reactions, accompanied of course by a few who agreed with him, and therefore he had to face unpopularity and ill will. As early as 1910 Frassati wrote: "Nothing serious is happening on the surface, but beneath the stuffy tranquility a gigantic accumulation of adverse forces is slowly simmering." Around the two great powers, England and Germany, the sympathies, passions, and ambitions of the other powers were coalescing.

Interventionism and neutralism clashed not only in the columns of newspapers, with *La Stampa* and *Il Corriere della Sera* taking opposite sides, but also on the public square and in the workplace and, violently, at the Teatro lirico in Rome,

---

an Adriatic power, and therefore it cannot ignore the Balkans, which have their most important coastline precisely on the Adriatic. The Austro-Italian alliance absolutely cannot exclude the question of the Balkans. . . . Together with the Balkan question there is a Mediterranean question. . . . It affects all of European politics. In this regard, Italy can contribute to the Triple Alliance many new essential elements. Above all: a complete freedom of action, now that the obligations that had tied her to France and England have expired. . . . Moreover, Italy has a new, formidable naval base that multiplies the potential of its navy . . . , which now has a force of 200,000 men who are already battle-tested, a navy . . . that has dispelled many legends that are bitter to our country about State finances and public morale that stubbornly resist the anxious vicissitudes of war. . . .

"Therefore, there is a possibility of a definitive understanding between Austria-Hungary and Italy in the area of their material interests. There is also clear proof that an alliance with Italy, passively and actively, can create great positive benefits for Austria. But not everyone realizes this yet. . . . What is needed is a vital, real policy of loyalty, guarantees, and compensations. . . . Italy, which is emerging from the war in Tripoli stronger, more mature, and more aware, has the right to ask for it: Austria can reasonably grant it."

where reformist socialists had gathered to hear an incendiary harangue by Bissolati, a patriot from the Five Days in Milan who was making a comeback. That meeting concluded with a dilemma: "Either war or revolution." Italy did not go so far as revolution, but it experienced the paralysis of the general strike and then the war.

Public opinion followed the dictates of the political minority, which managed to impose its own ideas: the outcry against Giolitti and neutrality became ever more deafening. On December 18, 1917, Frassati, in a debate with the *Gazzetta del Popolo*, wrote: "For the fatherland we fight the powerful and stand manfully by those who have suffered for the fatherland: but the Honorable Giolitti has appeared greater to us ever since he has been alone."

Both Alfredo and Pier Giorgio, who was sixteen years old then, had a negative opinion about the war, with a consistency and a lucidity that many followers of Giolitti lacked. Pier Giorgio's classmate, the interventionist Mario Attilio Levi, received a shower of blows from him because he had thrown a few coins at him and shouted "Soldino", in other words, "sell out to Germany".

Pier Giorgio fully shared his father's opinions as well as many of his political judgments: about Fascism, about the Franco-German crisis in 1923, or about the concept of the value of freedom and democracy, in a sort of "familial continuity"[6] that until now has remained in the shadows because too many writers and journalists have been intent on pointing out the contrasts between the Blessed and his father. In this way, Pier Giorgio swam against the general interventionist current of the young men of his class and of his age who yearned for war and conquests. Several times he said

[6] Cf. D. Veneruso, "Pier Giorgio Frassati e l'azione cattolica", in *Sociologia: Rivista di Scienze Sociale* (Rome: Istituto Luigi Sturzo, 1990), 175.

that he would gladly offer his life for the cessation of the immense tragedy at the front, for an end to the holocaust of soldiers from the mountain regiments.

Before it turned into an enormous slaughter, the Great War was welcomed by many people as a revolutionary event capable of bringing about new, attractive scenarios: the conflict was considered salutary, destined to sweep away the old, decadent bourgeois world and finally to open the doors to the new man of the twentieth century. Orators declared this from podiums all over Europe, and from their desks schoolteachers invited students to write patriotic compositions in which love for their own country coincided with the necessity of intervening as soon as possible in the war.

And it was precisely the young men who played an essential role in the country's intervention in the conflict: having grown up amid liberal politics and its deep-seated resistance to political change in the early years of the century, they had experienced the advantages of a nation with a growing economy, and, in the secondary schools and at the universities, they had been fed romantic, anti-middle-class ideals. For them the war was a sort of redemption, a suitable means of overturning the traditional positions of the generations so that they could feel more alive and active than their parents, who were accustomed to a comfortable, placid existence. While the Italian Parliament remained undecided about its own positions and Pope Benedict XV spoke out explicitly against the cruelties of the conflict, the "war party" was born. Its adherents were teachers, clerks, professionals, in short, those on the lower rungs of the middle class who were severe and impatient; they had found their demagogue and spokesman in "il Vate" (the Bard), Gabriele D'Annunzio.

Patriotic impatience, which had remained muted for almost fifty years, returned and seethed in the veins of the populace. It expressed itself in intolerance and violence: trades and businesses run by non-interventionist citizens were attacked and destroyed. The bellicose euphoria and enthusiasm got the better of moderation and prudence. On May 23, 1915, Italy declared war on Austria, breaking off diplomatic relations with Germany. The next day the first military operations began along the borders. Vittorio Emanuele III became the soldier-king.

From the very first battles, World War I was a trench war. The infantry, the machine gun, and the trench were the three key factors in an unprecedented conflict. While industries increased the pace of their work and their productivity so as to address the new demands of the technological conflict, the military authorities and medical science had to resolve the problem of how to train and deploy a new type of combatant, the "mass-produced soldier", who was suddenly thrown from civil life into the horror of war at the front lines to face bombs and deadly gas.

The slow, cumbersome infantry proved to be the decisive weapon, even though the collective imagination was fascinated by the cavalry and the airplane pilots: aviation captured the fancy of civilians and made a good showing on propaganda posters, calming the worries of the modernists and satisfying the nostalgia of the traditionalists.

Rifles, hand grenades, flamethrowers, machine guns, cannons, the availability of networks of roads and railways, and means of communication certainly varied from one combatant nation to the next. Indeed, when they did intervene, Germany, Great Britain, France, and the United States were capable of deploying more advanced weapons and better-equipped, more modern armies.

Citroën received an order for a million instruments of war. The State advanced financing so as to strengthen existing manufacturing firms and to foster the rise of new ones. All the factories that produced war materiel increased the pace of their work, their productivity, and their profits at dizzying rates. In Tolosa, a gunpowder factory that had one hundred workers before the war was employing four thousand in June 1914 and twenty thousand a year later. The futurist poet Filippo Tommaso Marinetti celebrated a literary triumph with his praise of technological beauty, while asphyxiating gases were used in action, causing such great hazards to humanity that they were then banned by the League of Nations. Submarines, airships that bombarded cities, poison gases and "tanks", the code name assigned to the precursor of the modern armored vehicle, signaled the technological revolution of the new weapons of mass destruction. But the new weapons did not always guarantee effective results. Only the armored vehicles proved to be decisive, and by deploying them the Allies won priceless victories against the armies of the Central Empires.

At the end of the conflict, of the sixty-five million men who had been mobilized, there were nine million dead and six million disabled. Once the false hopes of a short war had vanished definitively, disillusionment, bitterness, suffering, and privations weighed on the minds of combatants and civilians alike. Discontent crept in among the soldiers of all the armies, and insubordination and mutinies proliferated despite severe measures to repress them.

In August 1917, Pope Benedict XV sent to all the powers involved in the war a diplomatic note fraught with significance and containing a forceful judgment on the conflict, which it described without any political hypocrisy as "useless carnage". The judgment had the effect of a lashing, but it ran the risk of delegitimizing in the eyes of the people the good reasons that every government made sure to give for its own decision to go to war and of backing displays of insubordination.

While in the Russian Empire the disastrous October Revolution covered history with the pall of death, Italy experienced the shame of the Battle of Caporetto, for which Pietro Badoglio and Luigi Cadorna bore serious responsibility. The retreat caused enormous losses for the army: thirty thousand men were wounded or killed, 300,000 were taken prisoner, and just as many left the ranks of the army and fled. After the general retreat behind Mount Grappa and the Piave River, in 1918 General Armando Diaz replaced Cadorna: he managed to reorganize the army and to lift spirits, rallying the forces, and, after blocking the progress of the enemy advance, reversed the rout and went on the offensive until the final victory of Vittorio Veneto.

When the war finally ended on November 4, 1918, Pier Giorgio joyfully ran to sound the bells of his municipality of Pollone continuously. Fearlessly and without diplomatic nuance, Senator Frassati unhesitatingly denounced the absenteeism of those who could and should have avoided the terrible conflict. On July 15, 1920, he resolutely wrote to Giolitti's daughter Enrichetta: "If you had had one ounce of power in 1914–1915, I assure you, *Signora*, that the war would not have been waged: *it would not have been waged*." He had foreseen the developments and consequences with pained lucidity: "It was the work of his [Giolitti's municipality of] Cavour that collapsed, it was the anguish of his inability to avert Italy's tragedy, it was the confirmation . . . that he could not delay the war by a single day, by one hour", and did not manage to bring a single soldier to safety.[7]

[7] L. Frassati, *Un uomo, un giornale*, 1:346.

On November 4, 1918, *La Stampa* exulted over the liber-
ation of Trent and Trieste, while the Italian flag waved over
Buon Consiglio castle and the tower of San Giusto:

> The dream of the poets, the hope of the martyrs, the con-
> suming desire of every Italian soul is now a reality. Over the
> castle in Trent, where the gallows of the Hapsburgs stifled
> Cesare Battisti's last cry to the fatherland: over the tower
> of San Giusto, in the sunny sky of Trieste, flies the ban-
> ner of Italy. The glorious Communes of Venice, which so
> many times over the centuries stopped the invading waves
> of Teutons, Hungarians, and Turks, saw the Austrian flag
> retreat. . . . The people of Italy have risen to the heights
> of their history. In order to rise, they had to suffer, and
> they did suffer. . . . However, a new story has begun, and
> inasmuch as the light of democracy and liberty can illu-
> mine the world, Trent and Trieste will eternally remain
> milestones thereof. . . . And the words of the women and
> children coming out festively to greet the soldiers of the
> fatherland will be repeated down through the centuries:
> *Benedetti, benedetti.* Yes, blessed are all those who bring free-
> dom. Blessed are those who fight to preserve and consoli-
> date it.

This is history, in real time, throbbing in the columns
of Frassati's daily newspaper, whose ink sings the praises of
liberty, democracy, and justice. On November 12, in his
"Epilogue of the great drama", he again writes:

> The whole lifetime of the men who are present would not
> be enough to dry the tears shed during sleepless nights by
> millions and millions of mothers and widows. . . . Not to
> have understood this and to have believed that they could
> attain world hegemony at the cost of so many sorrows,
> to have thought that, for the sake of economic interests,
> they could break through the barriers of nations without

respecting nationalities, is the crime that history will not forgive the rulers of Germany. They believed that they could bypass modern history, which has as its foundation the work of past generations to win national freedoms and, as the logical consequence thereof, the aspiration to achieve these liberties fully throughout Europe. . . . Economic expansion cannot cross national boundaries and bind men into a community of work and commerce unless nations are not only respected but restored to their full liberty. The Germans, who on the fields of Leipzig had once affirmed this idea, were misled by a materialistic world view and believed that economic value had surpassed all other values. Such a materialistic concept of life cast them headlong into error and into their worst crime, namely, to have failed to understand how much moral values weigh in the world, how respect for these values serves to uplift a populace and make it progress. . . . The values of life are infinite, and they all want to live alongside each other. The wisdom of the new political man consists of knowing how to observe and respect them all so as to do work that is advantageous to his own people and to the world. . . . What the language of the poets and the ruminations of the philosophers have been unable to do will be accomplished by the need that urges everyone to save himself. . . . Truly *magnus saeculorum nascitur ordo* (A great world order is being born).

4

AN ODD REBELLION

Once the war was over, no one felt tranquil in the peace that had been won so dearly. In Italy, as in France and Germany, many powerful veterans' associations were formed, whose reason for being was the common past that united them but also a present and an immediate future of presumed peace: yet in that same postwar period, the foundations for the Second World War were laid.

The conflict that ended in 1918 swept away old friendships of the Frassati family, some because they had close ties with Gabriele D'Annunzio, others because they were acquainted with and esteemed General Cadorna, or else because they were affiliated with the interventionist newspaper *Corriere della Sera*. To compensate, they made new acquaintances, such as the Honorable Mario Chariaviglio, Giovanni Giolitti's son-in-law. His Honor was anxious to reassure Adelaide Ametis that he no longer belonged to the Freemasons and was no longer affiliated with any sort of lodge. Pier Giorgio's mother replied decisively: "No matter; that does not matter; it still leaves an imprint on your character."

Meanwhile, Pier Giorgio was growing up. He was a healthy, handsome, robust youth, but also very kind. As it happens in all lives of the saints, his hagiographers traced back to his infancy the early signs of a character dedicated to holiness. For this reason, they mention several episodes that highlight his generosity, altruism, and selflessness. The first occurred when he was of preschool age. It was lunchtime at the kindergarten. The children had already sat down at table. Pier Giorgio saw one, sitting at a distance, who had been isolated because of an eczema on his face. Instinctively he stood up and went to keep him company, calmly using his spoon. The nun who was supervising, worried about the risk of contagion that Pier Giorgio was running, tried in vain to send him away.

The second occurred at home. He and the housemaid were alone. Someone rang the doorbell. Pier Giorgio went to open the door and found himself facing a poor woman with a barefoot child on her arm. Without hesitation he took off his shoes and socks and gave them to the little boy's mother.

The third incident happened in Villa Ametis in Pollone: a novice was picking flowers for the kindergarten chapel. Pier Giorgio picked a red rose and ran up to her, saying, "Sister . . . ," but the young woman replied, "I am not a Sister." He then fervently said, "Sister, bring this rose to Jesus for me . . ."

One day he saw his father at the door of the house arguing with a poor man who was asking for alms. The lawyer immediately understood that the individual was drunk and quickly sent him away. Pier Giorgio ran to his mother in tears: "Mama, there was a poor man who was hungry, and Papa did not give him something to eat." Father Cojazzi relates that his mother ordered him to go and call the man back, so that they could provide him with some food. Later on, after inquiries were made, they found out that the man had lied, giving a false address, and Papa Frassati explained to the boy why that individual deserved no help.

The tenderhearted boy was trained to practice charity and the love of God, but that did not alter the fact that his temperament made him determined to find his own way, his own field of action and thought, especially along the vertical dimension of spirituality.

The special and pronounced sensitivity of Pier Giorgio Frassati in his early youth can be observed in other contexts as well, for instance when he came down with chicken pox and endured thirst and sleeplessness for an entire night because he did not want to wake his mother. This sensitivity found expression also in religious matters: at the end of his catechism lessons, he used to ask Don Cojazzi to tell him some stories from the life of Jesus. If what the Salesian priest described was of a doctrinal nature, the boy's face lit up. But if the priest told about a work of charity, a healing, a miracle, or aid given to the suffering, then his face became serious: two big tears ran down his cheeks because of the emotion he felt.

It is that same Don Cojazzi who helps us make Pier Giorgio real, and not some ethereal angel, when he truthfully explains:

> When . . . I try to sum up Pier Giorgio, I cannot help describing him as follows: a primitive or elementary individual. . . . He was impetuous, impulsive, absolute, and categorical in his convictions and decisions, so that he became on several occasions truly obstinate and stubborn. These were not serious things: little incidents, which still could sadden his mother, however, who had to bend him to the requirements of everyday life or of his situation. These and other shadows, however, accentuate the many highlights in the picture of his life.[1]

[1] A. Cojazzi, *Pier Giorgio Frassati: Testimonianze* (Turin: SEI, 1928), 32–33.

What did Don Cojazzi mean by "primitive"? Simply that social conventions never took hold in Pier Giorgio's character: he took nothing for granted, and for him life was not a series of customary rules. He was genuine and forthright, without masks or dissimulation. Dodo showed signs of what he would be later on, but his amusing "defects" help to bring his sanctity closer to our paradigms. The Blessed wrote to his friend Isidoro Bonini on February 27, 1925:

> My life is monotonous, but every day I understand better what a grace it is to be Catholic. The poor people who have no faith are wretched: to live without any faith, without a heritage to defend, without upholding the truth in a continual battle, is not living but struggling to make ends meet. We should never struggle to make ends meet but rather live, because even amid disappointments we must remember that we are the only ones who possess the truth, we have a faith to uphold, a hope to attain: our [heavenly] homeland. And therefore we should banish all melancholy, which can exist only when faith is lost. Human sufferings affect us, but if they are seen in the light of religion and, hence, of resignation, they are not harmful but salutary, because they cleanse the soul of the small, inevitable stains with which we men, because of our fallen nature, are often stained. . . . Ever onward for the triumph of Christ's reign in society.

Pier Giorgio and Luciana were not happy children: their parents' badly strained marital relations, which the children noticed and which affected them intensely, along with their rigid education were the factors that determined their mood: sometimes sad, sometimes pensive, and a bit frightened and alarmed. Theirs was the valiant education generally provided by the middle class in that era, which incidentally is described also on the pages of Natalia Ginzburg's famous book *Lessico famigliare* (*Family Sayings*) and in Susanna Agnelli's *Vestivamo alla marinara* (*We Always Wore Sailor Suits*). The pedagogical objective was to give children an austere sense of life, training them to be dignified. Their diet was strictly controlled: few vegetables and fruits and only if cooked, meat three times a week, no rolls, only bread; no salted meat and no sweets. All spirit of initiative and independence was stifled. Giuseppe Borioli testifies:

> Just as the clothes of that time were inspired by rigidity and formalism, so too the children had to be raised with good manners, moderation in all things, and governed by hundreds and hundreds of prohibitions. . . . It was forbidden to be present at the conversations of adults: around them one must always show due reverence and then with the governess, too, in rooms that were not very cheerfully lit. . . . When you watched on the terrace for Papa's return, you would run to Mother and say, "Mama, slap us; Papa is coming." This was so that our cheeks would look redder; it may have been done in jest a few times, but then it became routine. Papa certainly could not take you with him, but Mama and Auntie[2] had countless worldly things that absorbed them: parties, conferences, visits, etc., and so you remained a lot of the time with Dalla,[3] and sometimes they left you with Grandmother. Although your parents loved you dearly. But there was none of the ongoing affectionate physical and spiritual closeness that children want and that attaches them to their mother and father.[4]

Not a very pleasant atmosphere, then, where the needs of the heart were neglected and, instead, more attention was paid to discipline. Nevertheless, Pier Giorgio always felt

---

[2] Aunt Elena, the sister of Adelaide Ametis, who remained single.

[3] This was the governess, Dadà.

[4] M. Staglieno, *Un santo borghese: Pier Giorgio Frassati* (Milan: Bompiani, 1988), 22.

indebted to that family, sincerely proud of the intelligence, the dynamic qualities, the honesty, and the uprightness of his parents. During the years of his childhood and adolescence in Pollone, whenever his father was to arrive from Turin on Saturday evening, Pier Giorgio savored those magical moments and awaited him anxiously; then, upon his arrival, great rejoicing, screaming, and running through the garden and the rooms of the house. In Turin, Pier Giorgio and Luciana used to go to meet him at the newspaper offices, "and the return trip was a continual chase along the avenues, with the children hiding behind trees and front gates; and after lunch, how they ran through the rooms! And wrestled! Mama pursued all three from room to room, in order to save the furniture and the windowpanes from the ruckus."[5] It is nice to observe through the peephole of a door Pier Giorgio and his father, so calm and smiling, ready to capture the best aspects of life such as the undying love between father and son, or to eavesdrop on their customary greeting at mealtimes, so simple and so imbued with affection: "Ciao, Giorgetto bello!" (Hello, handsome Georgie!) "Ciao, pappo!" At that time they could not have imagined what would happen a few years later: from those rooms and from that house a coffin would proceed that was able to attract thousands of persons to participate in an unexpected, deeply moving funeral procession: they were there not only because Senator Frassati's son had died, but because Pier Giorgio shone with a light that was exclusively his own.

The father had a sort of intuition about the marvelous character of his Pier Giorgio, especially in the last years of his son's life. In the first biography composed by Don Cojazzi, which Laura Hidalgo—the girl loved by Pier Giorgio

---

[5] Cojazzi, *Pier Giorgio Frassati*, 37.

about whom we will speak later on—read and annotated, thus giving us an invaluable testimony of her own reminiscences,[6] there is one incisive word: *Vero* [true] that corroborates the author's statement: "The father's tenderness kept increasing until it became a sort of veneration in the final years."[7]

Alfredo Frassati wrote to Pier Giorgio in 1922:

> From the few lines that you wrote to Luciana I understand you completely. I see that you have a fine, honest mind, as I dreamed you would. Whatever happens, do not change. I am very proud of you, my dear Pier Giorgio: and with pride I see that the little bit of good that is in my character has not been lost. Never before as in this moment, I embrace you, with greater faith and courage.

Alfredo tried to see himself reflected in Pier Giorgio, but that was only the beginning.

For his mother, Pier Giorgio had a special love; "he doted on her", according to one of the Blessed's biographers, Marino Codi, and for her he was ready to sacrifice everything. By virtue of and in the name of that filial love, he performed the great acts of self-denial that would change the course of his life.

Introduced by his mother to a love for beauty and art, Pier Giorgio attentively observed the world of colors and loved flowers. At the same time, he was very interested in classical music and, in particular, operas, attending many performances. Verdi and Wagner were his favorite composers. Among the countless associations in which he enrolled was the Gioventù universitaria musicale (Musical union of

---

[6] It was possible to consult the copy of Cojazzi's book belonging to Laura Hidalgo thanks to her daughters, Beatrice and Stefania.

[7] Ibid., 38.

young university students). When he was far from home, Pier Giorgio, who visited half the museums and art galleries in Europe, never failed to write to his Mama to describe to her the works of art he had seen and the interesting exhibitions he had visited: he used to include a wealth of details in his observations. One of his companions on his last excursion, Guido Unterrichter, relates that on June 7, 1925, at the Lunelle di Lanzo in Turin, they happened to walk through an expanse of magnificent rhododendrons in full bloom. Faced with that enchanting sight, he thought of his mother: "If only my mama were here to see these colors!" he exclaimed. He did not hesitate to gather a handful to bring to her. But when he arrived in Turin, several children, fascinated by the vivid hues of the flowers, immediately asked for them, leaving the young man with very little to bring home . . .

He was grateful to his mother for the advice that he had received and strove to put it into practice. "It is no exaggeration to state that he revered her. Blind obedience to her orders accompanied him from his earliest years until his adolescence, which is to say, practically until his death."[8] He was eight years old when one day, while playing in front of the house, he was seized by a fit of coughing. His great-aunt, who was nearby, offered him some hard candy to soothe it, but the child did not accept it: "No, Mama does not allow it."

The most welcome presents were the ones that came from his "dear distant Mama". On September 22, 1921, Adelaide wrote to her son in Germany: "Your dear mother carries you with her in her heart all day long; she sends you a kiss when you go to sleep; may your first thought be of her when

[8] M. Codi, *Pier Giorgio Frassati: Una valanga di vita* (Casale Monferrato [AL]: Portalupi, 2001), 41–42.

you awake." Whenever Pier Giorgio saw his mother's hand-writing, he experienced "an immense joy", as he himself admitted. During his stay in Germany with his father, who had been appointed ambassador of the kingdom to Berlin, Pier Giorgio had rejoiced to receive a photograph of his mother, which he prized so dearly that he used to hold it tight in order "to feel that she was closer and to be able to look at her every evening" (October 7, 1921). When a mother is near, "you do not sufficiently appreciate her company; but when she is far away, even for a short time, you immediately feel the enormous void that her absence leaves."

And she, Adelaide, at Easter of 1925 in Pollone, as though foreseeing what would happen a few months later, wrote to her daughter, Luciana, in Aja, where she had gone to live with her husband:

> How many dear people there were here! And now they are dead or gone, which amounts to the same thing. I go back to that dream, that nightmare, when I will walk alone through the rooms and there will no longer be any of those whom I have loved. This year for the second time, Pier Giorgio, the silent son who is the blessing of this house, will no longer be here.[9] Grandmother and he are the cornerstone of it. . . .

And that grandmother and Pier Giorgio, "the silent son" within the walls of their home, would depart in the month of July, just a few days apart from each other.

Pier Giorgio often mentioned his mother, and from her he got his tastes, attitudes, and gestures, with an involuntary mimicry that was caused primarily by his intense, profound affection. A female friend of the family later testified that she was accustomed to hearing Pier Giorgio repeat whole

---

[9] If Pier Giorgio had not died, he would have had to serve in the military.

sentences and habitual opinions of his mother, and he prefaced many statements with her name: "Mama says that. . . . Mama wants. . . . My mother does it this way. . . ." Then, when he found himself looking at masterpieces of nature or art, he would come out with a revealing exclamation: "If only Mama were here!"

Sometimes, after a meal, he liked to take a sip of Marsala wine from his mother's glass, and he learned to prize Tuscan cigars, in particular Garibaldis, from his mother's habit of smoking them. He jokingly explained his passion for cigars and his pipe: "My mother smoked a pipe for me back when I was nursing!"

Pier Giorgio's schooling was designed primarily for classical studies. The formative value of the classics consisted in the acquisition of linguistic, logical, historical, and cultural tools, but above all in the opportunity and ability to confront the fundamental questions of life.

The questions being debated in the early 1900s in the field of education concerned the structure and management of the school in every aspect, the contents of courses, the curriculum, teaching methods, and the function of the instructors. In particular, there was an attempt to popularize primary school by making it in effect obligatory and by setting up schools throughout the nation.

Augusto Monti (1881–1966), a disciple of the radically liberal, anti-Fascist Pier Gobetti, became a famous educator who influenced a whole generation of secondary school students in Turin. Monti wrote:

> In this sense the real school, the important, fundamental, essential, complete school, is one that immediately follows the home and the family, namely, the elementary school. Elementary school, which teaches reading, writing, and arithmetic, puts into your hands the first tools for "earn-

ing a living"; while teaching you these three things, it also teaches you to "behave like a gentleman", in other words, to live well.[10]

The establishment of the Italian school system went back to the Casati law of 1859, which was designed to unify the school systems of Lombardy and Piedmont and then extended to the entire kingdom. It provided for obligatory public elementary instruction that was entrusted to the communes (municipalities) and a secondary school system based on the French model, which considered technical subjects marginally useful. The obligation to attend school until the age of nine was confirmed by the Coppino law in 1877, and then the Daneo-Credaro law of 1911, making the elementary schools the responsibility of the State, resolved the problems in many communes that could not afford instruction, thus beginning to overcome illiteracy, which still affected 38 percent of the population at the time when it was passed.

The Gentile reform in 1923 introduced the principle of the State examination and, in keeping with an idealistic approach to education, reinforced the primacy of humanistic formation. At the same time, it also instituted the scientific secondary school and systematized the formation of elementary school teachers in pedagogical institutes. Besides the school curriculum that led to secondary school instruction and admission to university studies, provisions were also made for a specific, abbreviated course to prepare students for the working world.

It is curious and at the same time interesting to learn that Don Antonio Cojazzi, the Salesian priest who enormously esteemed his pupil Pier Giorgio, in the 1920s sided

[10] A. Monti, *Il mestiere di insegnante: Scritti sulla scuola 1909–1965* (Cuneo: Araba Fenice, 1994), viii.

with the Church in fighting for an anti-positivistic, Christian culture and promoted a campaign against the philosophy textbooks used in the secondary schools and pedagogical institutes of Turin. He wrote to Archbishop Gamba on February 25, 1925, that he had carefully investigated the authors in the fields of philosophy and pedagogy—Hegel, Kant, Hume, Locke, Spinoza, Rousseau, Berkeley, Schopenhauer, Giordano Bruno—who were studied in many non-private schools in Turin and had encountered commentaries that confirmed or aggravated the philosophical errors of the authors themselves; therefore, Don Cojazzi requested authorization to publish textbooks containing assessments that could neutralize "the poison".

Fascism observed the formative task of the schools attentively and scrupulously and started organizations with which to recruit from among the ranks of young people, such as the Opera Nazionale Balilla, the Piccola Italiana for girls, and the Avanguardisti; it often collided or came into conflict with the world of Catholic education.

In November 1907, elementary instruction for Luciana and Pier Giorgio began at home, with Rosina Buratto as their teacher; the instruction ended with examinations in July 1910 at the Salesian institute in Alassio.

During that same year, Freemasonry had unleashed a universal persecution against religious orders and congregations throughout Italy. Of all people, the Salesians were the target of disgraceful calumnies: the anticlerical association had spread reports about the alleged corruption of minors in the college in Varazze. Alfredo Frassati, who was indeed secular in his mind-set but respected the Church highly, submitted the case to Giovanni Giolitti and put Giuseppe Cassone, the editor-in-chief of *La Stampa*—which was not merely an informative newspaper but also an operation capable of engaging in politics and influencing it—in charge of conducting a careful investigation of it. The August 24 issue of Frassati's daily paper read: "The Honorable Giolitti, knowing the facts as they are from administrative investigations that had been ordered, decided to transfer the subprefect in Savona (who was chiefly responsible for the spread of the rumors) to a less important post, as a true and proper punishment." The Salesians were quite satisfied with that and were always very grateful to the publisher of *La Stampa*. They asked the senator what they could do for him in return, and that is how Don Antonio Cojazzi entered the Frassati household as an educator.

Accustomed by now to a strict regimen, the little Frassati children were not surprised if they were expected every morning to wash themselves in cold water, even in midwinter. Pier Giorgio was hardly eight years old when he and his family participated in an excursion outside the commune. They left from Fiery d'Ayas and headed for the Schwarzsee through the hills of Teodulo (more than 10,000 feet in elevation). The hike required ten and a half hours of walking. They made only two or three brief stops: they ate "a cutlet and two raw eggs", drank a gulp of fresh water, and then continued their march.

They stayed at the Schwarzsee for two days. Here is the continuation of Pier Giorgio's excursion, as his mother tells it:

> The morning of our departure, there was no way to wake him up. I called him, I washed his face, nothing worked. Then I dressed him and together with Elena [the aunt] carried him to breakfast, but he scarcely opened his eyes to eat. To me and Alfredo, it seemed cruel; it was a long way, and it was necessary to leave in the dark. Dodo returned with Alfredo and with Albert and Antonio Fosson by way

of Furggen . . . whereas I went up to Zermatt with Elena, and we returned by train.

Even after that, Pier Giorgio continued to lead a Spartan, rigorous life. He tremendously enjoyed swimming in the Alpine streams and lakes. In the summer, Pier Giorgio and Luciana loved to plunge repeatedly into the cold water and then to warm up again by running along the meadows until they were out of breath.

In September 1911, he undertook ascents that were unthinkable for a boy of his age: he crossed the Bettaforca and Mount Furggen and climbed Mount Castor (13,800 feet) along with Mount Rosa. Again his mother recalls: "The boy, tied with the rope, was often dragged along by the quick pace of the men. He got a little angry because they did not let him 'jump over the crevasses right'."

He was familiar with the mountains, but also with the sea. His initial encounter with the water was traumatic, but afterward it became easy for Pier Giorgio to go for long, exhausting swims, even when the water was choppy. With his friends at the country residence, he used to organize competitions to see who could stay underwater the longest or dive the deepest. He would jump out of the boat far from the shore and then surface again with a handful of sand, thus proving that he had reached the bottom. Alassio, Albisola, Forte dei Marmi, and Francavilla are some of the country towns in which he was the hero of adventures and showed prowess in sports (recall that he was also adept at fencing, skiing, sailing, and horseback riding), accomplishments that excited his friends, as his second cousin Mario Gambetta testifies:

> I see you again in the passage of years, when you used to come and spend a few hours with us; you would run up and

embrace me very affectionately, and every time I found that you had grown physically and morally! How strong you were, well-proportioned and physically tough! During the summer that you spent here in Albisola, your exceptional physical fitness was a revelation to me; I saw you make efforts while swimming and rowing that only exceptionally gifted and especially trained men could have made, but you were not training in those sports at all.

When evening came, Pier Giorgio turned into another person. He did not join the others who walked around outdoors but looked for a place suited for recollection. For example, when he was at Alassio, staying together with his family as a guest of the pension Gregorovius—where he made the acquaintance of the writer Maxim Gorky—he used to visit the church of the Capuchins as a spiritual refuge.

Spending the summer in the country was then the prerogative of the privileged few, and Pier Giorgio, although saintly, was a middle-class youth of his day and did not renounce what was offered by the society to which he belonged. Although more pensive than Luciana and quick-witted, Pier Giorgio would throw himself into games, or sometimes altercations, with his sister; this happened especially in Pollone, where the children had greater freedom of movement. At the Villa Ametis, under the careful supervision of their grandmother Linda Copello, it was not possible to jump on the beds, nor could they run in the elegant salons, amid the precious antique Louis XV-style furniture covered with doilies and knickknacks. As portraits of their ancestors looked down on them, bearing witness to the efforts they had made, generation after generation, to ensure the family's economic well-being and social prestige, the brother and sister were allowed to walk through the whole villa: from the spacious kitchens with its wood stoves to the cellars and then up to the attic that Adelaide had converted into an *atelier* where honey and lavender mingled with perfume and where the children were admitted only after they had knocked.

In Pollone, together with the gardener, Giuseppe Gola, Pier Giorgio used to hoe, dig, sow, fertilize, water plants, mow, gather grapes, press them, pick vegetables. . . . Gola was a former soldier who, after serving his country, now worked on the extensive grounds of the villa in Pollone and in the stable. Pier Giorgio learned many secrets from him and built a relationship of true friendship both with him and with his sons, who were his own age. With the *gnere* [pronounced like the last two syllables of *giardiniere*], as Gola was familiarly called, Pier Giorgio bedded out plants, flowers, and vegetables and carried wood, baskets of fruit, jars, and manure. Watering the plants and flowers in the garden was the last chore of those work-filled days: he filled around one hundred twenty watering cans each evening.

During the war years, to make himself useful, he attended the agricultural courses of the Istituto Bonafous, earning a diploma: the final examination consisted of reaping grain, bundling it, and arranging it in the hayloft. Since he knew how to ride a horse, they let him direct the field work, but he started to work also as a simple laborer so as to help the gardener's wife, who was left alone after her husband was sent to the front. Pier Giorgio devised a unique alarm clock to wake him early in the morning: a rope tied to the drawer of his nightstand, which descended from the window of his room and was pulled from below at dawn; once, though, the little bureau fell over because the rope had been pulled too much. Then they chose a long bamboo pole, the one that was used to knock nuts down from the trees.

With his constant activity, he developed strength and endurance, and he was capable of bicycling the fifty-three miles from Turin to Pollone and then returning without batting an eye. On those trips, he was accompanied most times by his friend Carlo Bellingeri. At the end of such an enormous effort, instead of throwing himself down on his bed or taking a nice invigorating bath, he would start pacing back and forth in the house declaiming verses from Dante or passages from *Hamlet*. In Ravenna, his friends heard him recite whole cantos from *The Divine Comedy* at the tomb of the immortal poet. In the house in Turin, only family members and the domestic servants heard the verses that he recited aloud, but in Pollone everyone recognized the unmistakable voice of Pier Giorgio: the less educated thought that he was speaking in Latin, and many people learned some of the verses by heart. His voice, which had become familiar, was the signal for the beginning of the daily work: "Il mat del senator parla già fort", they would say in the local dialect ("The senator's son is already speaking loudly.") When the voice was no longer heard, the people of Pollone started to say: "The one who always used to sing has died."

The roads in those days were precarious, dusty in the summer and full of holes and puddles in the winter. Once he ventured on a bicycling expedition that could be considered madness: leaving from Turin, he traveled via Genoa and went as far as Albisola and then returned home.

Soon Pier Giorgio began to drive the automobile. His mother relates the story:

> At the age of fourteen, he drove me from Turin to Pollone. . . . He was scarcely a youth when he began to drive. I was the first victim. I held on with all my strength, ready to jump through the roof at every crossing along the road; sudden stops followed by lightning-quick starts, and sometimes I was thrown against the side at curves in the road.

At the Villa Ametis, his father enjoyed the tolerant disdain of his wife, who often called him "Madama di Tebe"
[a comic character from an operetta] because his forecasts
were so off the mark. There he was received, Luciana Frassati insists, as a guest. The children, on the other hand, were
always welcome. The earliest photographs portray the two
children on the terrace in the arms of their great-grandmother
Antonia Copello, who later died in 1905, or else in the spacious park, near the great sequoia. Extremely rare in Italy,
the tree had been transplanted by Francesco Ametis, who
had brought it there from California. That ancestor of Pier
Giorgio had a peculiar personality: rebellious in temperament and liberal at heart, in 1848 he had enlisted voluntar-
ily in the army of La Marmora; in 1851 he left Italy to sail
for Peru. Tall and robust, Francesco Ametis became a gold
prospector, a merchant, a dock worker, and a sea captain.
But that was not enough; he also became the owner of a
brig, landed in California, and, after sympathizing with the
North during the American Civil War, returned to Pollone
a rich man. He brought with him as a souvenir of his adventures two sequoias and had them transplanted in front
of his spacious, stately residence, which can still be admired
today. He planned it back in 1865 and finished it ten years
later, contributing to the construction of it with his own
manual labor. He wanted it to be situated so as to have an
excellent panorama, from which the viewer can see Mount
Mucrone, Monviso [Monte Viso] and, beyond the plain,
the Giovi Pass.

The *Wellingtonia gigantea californiana* did not set down roots
in the soil, whereas the *Washingtonia glauca* took root perfectly: that appeared to be a good omen to Pier Giorgio's
grandfather, especially because the name of the surviving tree
recalled the first president of free America, George Wash-

ington. In the shade of that sequoia, he declared his love to his fiancée, Linda Copello (promising her a honeymoon trip to Peru, where they remained for eight years, returning even richer than before), watched his three daughters grow and play, mourned the premature death of his firstborn, Emilia, of a heart attack, and celebrated the wedding of her little sister Adelaide to the rich and famous Alfredo Frassati, who was expected to be even more successful. The tree, which had grown extremely tall with heavy braches, was also the companion, under the watchful eye of the grandfather, to the summer games of Pier Giorgio and Luciana.

Like indiscreet intruders, we now enter the Frassati household in Turin. A couple of domestic servants, a cook and a chauffeur: from 1902 on, they actually owned an automobile. The furniture is in the elegant Imperial style, other pieces in the austere Novecento style. There are expensive carpets on the floors and paintings by Mama Adelaide, but also by Falchetti, Faretto, Delleani, Michetti, and Segantini, on the walls; these are flanked by very valuable tapestries and paintings from the seventeenth and eighteenth centuries.

The table is set with silver cutlery and, after Alfredo's appointment as ambassador of the kingdom, with plates and ceramic items by Meissen, Nymphenburg, and Delft, precious objects that are brought out of the cupboards every day. Pier Giorgio is accustomed to this style of living; he got used to it as a child without questioning it; nor would he later renounce his father's riches and cast off his fine clothing as a young man had done in the city of Assisi six hundred years earlier: Francis, the son of Pietro di Bernardone. Sanctity is capricious; it is not static and does not duplicate itself. The son of the wealthy cloth merchant, who used to frequent the marketplaces of Champagne, radically changed his life.

Pietro di Bernardone's fortune enabled his son to live like an aristocrat and to be one of the city's well-to-do bachelors. The head of an association of merry revelers, Francis became more renowned among his friends the more willing he was to pay for them from his own pocket. Then he changed during the two years of his illness (1205–1206), which impeded his military career. For him that was the beginning of a period of restlessness and of "mental yearning".

Disappointed by the life he had led until then, he searched for a long time to find his way, gradually becoming aware of his vocation: to love—not some noblewoman, but Sister Poverty; to accomplish heroic deeds—not on battlefields, but in the service of Christ, whose face could be recognized in those of the least of his brethren. Thus he began to meet and care for the lepers. The victory that he won over himself is acknowledged in his testament: "What had seemed bitter to me was changed into sweetness for my soul and body. After waiting a while, I bade farewell to the world." After his conversion, he did not delay: he broke publicly and in a spectacular way with his father, who scolded him for ruining the family fortune by distributing to the poor money that did not belong to him. Giotto marvelously depicts the famous scene in which Francis removed his clothes and returned them to his father so as to walk away, naked, and place himself under the protection of Bishop Guido of Assisi.

Whenever someone tries to define it in abstract terms, the message of Francis gets reduced to a formula that may appear trivial. Saint Francis was neither a great theologian like Saint Augustine nor a profound thinker and philosopher like Saint Thomas Aquinas nor a theologian of the spiritual life like Saint Bernard or Ignatius of Loyola. The *Poverello*, the Little Poor Man, left essentially one testimony: that of a man who wanted to live out the letter of the Gospel and to be a witness to the love of God in the world.

The same definition could be given for Pier Giorgio Frassati, who was interested in the personality of Francis, so much so that in September 1919 he decided to visit Assisi, Foligno, and Loreto so as to become better acquainted with the lands of the *Poverello*. This rich young man of the 1900s basically dealt with the same experience as the Little Poor Man of Assisi, but with different methods. His refractory nature was manifested outside the domestic circle: he disliked receptions, official meals, and worldliness in general, but he never pointed a finger at his father. Pier Giorgio grafted onto an arid, sterile, middle-class way of life a profound Catholic spirituality and thus represented in an altogether original way the fusion of the *haute bourgeoisie* and the evangelical spirit, definitively proving that the rich can enter the kingdom of heaven.

Motivated by Gospel values rather than by profits, he, unlike his father, rejected as a matter of principle the primacy of economics and politics over morality and of self-interest over the common good. And yet Pier Giorgio's father was for him an example of honesty, seriousness, and consistency.

> Alfredo Frassati adhered to those humanitarian principles of solidarity of which the Catholic circles of Turin were the standard bearers. Indeed, Frassati had a strong inclination to works of charity. . . . It was an attitude akin to the ideals of socialism, too, which had long since been spread through the Piedmont region and throughout Italy by cultured men such as De Amicis and Arturo Graf, Cesare Lombroso and Giovanni Cena, Giuseppe Giocosa, Zino Zini, and Guglielmo Ferrero.[11]

[11] Staglieno, *Un santo borghese*, 26.

On July 3, 1923, he wrote in his journal:

> We who are not socialists cannot help but rejoice to see that
> the intellectual and moral direction of the socialist party is
> entrusted, not to forbidding, rigid sectarians, to inconclu-
> sive demagogues, but to strong intellects that are able to
> understand the present needs of Italian society. . . . We lib-
> erals have a great interest in following the socialists in this
> work of minute study and practical action.

It was not by accident that Frassati began to write what was
later a regular column, "Mirror of the Times", which started
as "Saturday Charity" and was published in the *Gazzetta
piemontese* from 1890 on with anonymous lists of donations
received during that week. And he never forgot to perform
acts of charity personally, a philanthropic and paternalistic
attitude that traditionally was deeply rooted in that Subalpine
region.

Pier Giorgio, as we have already had occasion to say, was
a tenacious lad, somewhat stubborn and proud. Some have
pointed a finger at him, accusing him of having continued
to eat at his father's table without making a drastic, decisive
choice consistent with his social and political ideals. Yet the
saintly youth Pier Giorgio did not spurn his father's house
but continued to live there, while spending time with priests,
laborers, the poor, and the disinherited; his very deep feelings for his family never diminished.

It is important to say this right now: In Pier Giorgio a
sort of contradiction was established with regard to his parents that nevertheless produced advantageous results: he was
extremely obedient as long as he considered it just and in
virtue of his immense love for them, and yet he was light-
years away from them in his thinking and in his view of life.
Hence a sort of rebellion. But his was a strange rebellion:

he would continue to share in the familial routine while immersing himself in ideological and economic realities that were quite different from those at home.

His father wrote in February 1922: "If I were always to act without reflection in matters that ought to be extremely important to you [for example, in this particular case, not forgetting the book that you were supposed to use for your next examination], I would become a man useless to others and to you yourself." Sometimes we cannot judge even our own children: we think that we know them like our own hands, yet in reality they do not belong to us but are destined for things quite different from what our shortsighted, petty opinions might expect. Misunderstood and scorned in his family, Pier Giorgio, the "useless man", carved out places in eternity, and today he is known on all five continents, and in his name Catholics kneel down and join in prayer.

Again in 1922, Pier Giorgio, who later became the beacon lighting up whatever was contradictory and artificial in his parents' life, had to read harsh parental criticism:

> You have to convince yourself, Giorgio, that it is necessary to take life seriously and that the way you are doing things will not work either for you or for your relatives, who wish you well and are much embittered by all these things that happen too often and are repeated monotonously and painfully. I have little hope that you will change, and yet, strictly speaking, it would be necessary to change immediately: to approach things methodically, always to think seriously about what you must do, to have a little perseverance. Not to live for the day, thoughtlessly, like some harebrained fellow. If you want to do your relatives a little favor, you must change. I am in a very, very bad mood.

For such a stubbornly pragmatic man of action as Alfredo Frassati, a son like his, devoted to prayer and transcendence, to a struggle for ideas of justice rooted in the Gospel, was incomprehensible. Two hectic lives, one absorbed by professional work and the management of power and property, the other devoted to laboring in the name of God and of his kingdom. Little inclined to study, but having a fervent, lively intellect, Pier Giorgio was able to take what was best from his own family and to draw out what was positive so as to make it fruitful in his own life. He traveled no road to Damascus, nor did he experience sudden changes of will and conscience. His was a spiritual journey that was kindled and grew constantly and continually year after year. His silent faith received the necessary impetus from the Jesuit Fathers. Let us see how.

After passing the entrance examination, Pier Giorgio and Luciana began in October 1910 to attend the first class in the famous secondary school named after Massimo d'Azeglio, which educated intellectuals and politicians such as Cesare Pavese, Leone Ginzburg, Massimo Mila, Giancarlo Pajetta, Vittorio Foa, Salvatore Luria, and Giulio Einaudi. There Mario Soldati was a classmate of Pier Giorgio for a short time and remembered his "dark but sparkling eyes and his lips always open in a beaming smile".[12]

The Frassati children attended first-year courses (in October 1910, Don Cojazzi began to tutor the two siblings privately) and the second year at the school, at the end of which Pier Giorgio, however, who was already very weak in written Italian, failed in Latin:

Dear Papa,

I am bewildered and sorry and do not even know how to write to you; I saw Mama's sorrow, and I thought of yours, so much that I do not know how to ask you for a word of

[12] Codi, *Pier Giorgio Frassati*, 293.

forgiveness. I regret it also because I am still behind and am embarrassed around my classmates and my sister, who have gone on ahead of me. I hope that you will still believe in the sincerity of my resolution to study this year and to try to do whatever remedial work is possible. You will see that I will try to demonstrate my affection for you in deeds. A kiss from your Pier Giorgio.

Pier Giorgio's mother asked her children to cooperate specifically with Don Cojazzi so that they might, as he puts it,

acquire the *sensus Christi*kern.75pt: I was authorized not to stay within the strict limits of the school subjects, so that there were rather frequent digressions and religious discussions. I noticed right away that Pier Giorgio (to use a nice Spanish expression) still had baptismal water dripping from his head. I understand better now the pleasant surprise that I had during our first lessons when, after finishing his schoolwork, he rose from his seat and, standing erect in his black pinafore, planted himself there with his arms folded and, staring at me with those two dark eyes, said to me: "And now tell me about something Jesus did." [13]

On June 11, 1911, Pier Giorgio received First Holy Communion together with Luciana in the chapel of the nuns of the Society of the Helpers of the Holy Souls at corso Re Umberto 26.

After he enrolled in the Social Institute of the Jesuits, he was promoted, and his parents enrolled him again at the D'Azeglio school along with his sister. So he attended the fourth and fifth grades of secondary school and the first year of the lyccum. But once again he had to repeat a year of Latin. He returned to the Social Institute in the school year 1917–1918 to attend fourth- and fifth-year secondary

[13] Cojazzi, *Pier Giorgio Frassati*, 28–29.

school courses and the first year of the lyceum. In that way he made up for the lost year and was able to complete the second and third years of the lyceum in one year, thanks to government arrangements that made it easier for students who were soon to be called up for military service.

As they reached the age of sixteen, Adelaide relaxed her control over her children: she now considered them responsible for their actions and therefore loosened the reins. At last their social life began and contact with others their own age.

He was seventeen years old, and his parents would have preferred to have a different sort of son: he was supposed to enter into society now, there were nice prospects for a young man from his family, but he lacked interest.

His mother and father thought he was in a bad way, but convinced as they were that Pier Giorgio's great obedience to them would win out in the end, they allowed him to continue attending the Social Institute of the Jesuit Fathers. In the meantime, Pier Giorgio spoke to no one at home about his parallel spiritual life. No one knew that he had enrolled in the conference of the Saint Vincent de Paul Society at the Social Institute. But there were those outside the walls of his home who became acquainted with that extraordinary young man, such as Ernesto Fassone, the janitor of the Social Institute, who experienced Pier Giorgio's great sensitivity. One day as Pier Giorgio arrived at school, he noticed the sadness on the janitor's face and asked him the reason for it. He learned that his only son had died at the age of fourteen. The following year, on the same day, he stopped in front of the man: "Today is the anniversary of your son's death . . . I will remember at Holy Communion." "Fassone wept when he recalled these words. He knew him better than his family, who had no idea he paid such attention to life's sufferings."[14]

Pier Giorgio went through the change of adolescence: from a child to a man. Like his classmates, he too started to be attracted by girls. One friend relates:

> He may have been fifteen or sixteen years old, and, if memory serves me, it was during the days when there were student demonstrations to get a vacation or to pass a course with a six [a near-failing grade, a "D"]; as we—Pier Giorgio, B., and I—were returning from one of these, we met two young girls, who were certainly impudent because, I remember, they were the first to speak up. One remark led to another, and we made a date. In order to have on hand the small change needed to make a good impression, we had sold a notebook or a textbook. So we went to wait for the girls. I remember as if it were yesterday that Pier Giorgio came with us, but he was not convinced of what we were doing; he was altogether in good humor and was joking with us two. In a closed carriage (it was very early in the spring) we went to our rendezvous. I cannot say where we ended up, because too much time has passed since then, but I think that it was at the Ristorante del Parco to get something to drink. After a short excursion, everything ended there. The memory of that prank fills my heart with sadness and regret, because I think that I was the one to urge him on.[15]

This was in February 1917, and Pier Giorgio had not yet turned sixteen. One day his mother found among her son's papers a note in his handwriting "which contained indecent

[14] L. Frassati, *A Man of the Beatitudes: Pier Giorgio Frassati*, trans. Dinah Livingstone, adapted and ed. Patricia O'Rourke (San Francisco: Ignatius Press, 2000), 45.

[15] Cojazzi, *Pier Giorgio Frassati: Testimonianze*, 50.

words addressed to one of those two friends". The time had arrived that Adelaide had perhaps feared the most, and she was not only afraid but also troubled; this was the reason why she preferred to bring up a girl rather than a boy. How to deal with this situation? She discovered that her son had not sold books in order to get money; instead, she recalled that Pier Giorgio had withdrawn a substantial sum from the savings account set up in his name. She called together the mothers of the other two friends, and they compelled the boys to confess. "However, while the other mothers pressed their weeping sons to their hearts and gave them a kiss of forgiveness, that kiss was denied Pier Giorgio."[16] Adelaide had not seen sincere repentance on his face. A few days later, he was in his room, and suddenly the door was thrown open, and Pier Giorgio walked over to her, begging: "Mama, please forgive me, please! I did not know what I was doing; I swear, I swear that I will never do it again!" Despite the fact that he was opposed to theatrical gestures, he fell on his knees and kissed her hand. Very probably he had gone to confession to the spiritual director at the Social Institute. That experience made him a better man, and later on, when someone praised him for practicing his faith, Pier Giorgio replied: "I was not always this way! I, too, had moments in my life that were not very edifying, while I was in the lyceum, and if the Lord had not touched my heart, who knows what would have become of me."[17]

Because he had been unsuccessful in his schoolwork and had failed courses, Pier Giorgio had the opportunity to spend time in a Catholic environment, the Jesuit school, the first of a long series. At that moment, his spiritual matu-

---

[16] Ibid., 51.
[17] Ibid., 53.

rity began, his ascent to things beyond this world, aware of the struggles and the victories. One surprising thing in the life of that extraordinary young man was the major choice that he made among the movements and organizations of the Catholic world; it was so important that to this day the associations to which young Frassati belonged proudly boast that they had Blessed Pier Giorgio among their members. The enemy of sophistry, like his father, he learned from him to look reality and men in the face and to measure them, not by their appearance, but by their substance. "Every admonition from his father, even the slightest and gentlest, left a profound impression on him. At every turn, he sensed that promises are nothing and that life is measured by deeds."[18] He was also an enemy of literary rhetoric, and, despite the fact that he left an enormous correspondence, Pier Giorgio did not like to write. Don Cojazzi tells us:

> I admit that, during his first years of secondary school, I tended to interpret this lack of literary effort as a sign of late intellectual development. And I used to tell his anxious mother: "He will mature! . . . he will mature!" Just as he did not lie with his life, so too he was unable to lie using a pen, not even in a classroom exercise. It is understandable, therefore, with what triumphant joy he abandoned the obligation to rack his brains over subjects that meant little to him, once he had earned his secondary school diploma. In his family he made such an uproar that the day was an unforgettable one; and he ended with the heroic proposal: "The professor who passed me in composition [writing] deserves a monument!" A remark that was often repeated later.[19]

[18] Ibid., 30.
[19] Ibid., 30–31.

It is clear, therefore, that at the Social Institute the youth was able to listen, learn, and be formed in the religious dimension to which he felt strongly attracted. There he had the opportunity to become acquainted with Father Pietro Lombardi, the Jesuit in charge of the spiritual formation of the young students and a diligent apostle of Eucharistic devotion. In him he found the ideal guide to help him follow the path that had matured within him as a self-taught Catholic layman. And from then on, the Blessed began the daily practice of receiving Holy Communion, for which he yearned ardently. Father Lombardi reports:

> I have a glowing memory of my student. I was his spiritual director at the Social Institute for one year, and even though I have seen many boys before and after him, I still have Pier Giorgio clearly in mind. But one fine morning Signora Adelaide Frassati came to call on me. I fought in vain against her unbending aversion to the practice of daily Communion, which she feared might become a habit for Pier Giorgio and not a true practice of faith. Obviously she did not know her son, and I limited myself to assuring her that I would tell him to receive Communion once a week.
>
> Four days later, I heard someone knocking at my door; it was Pier Giorgio, jumping for joy, who told me: "Father, I won." I replied, "And what ever did you win to be so happy? The lottery?" He immediately said: "Hey, Father . . . you know very well; I can receive Holy Communion every day. I insisted so much!"
>
> I will never forget the joy on his face that day. When he came into the room, it seemed to me as though the sun had entered.

An avalanche of sunlight, filled with color and warmth, swept over all who met his eyes and his smile, causing them to think of the presence of God among men. "Whatever happens, do not change": that was his father's advice in that letter from 1922. Only death would silence the course of that overwhelming, shattering life.

5

GREAT IDEALS

It was a real struggle for Pier Giorgio Frassati to study for school. For him, spending hour after hour poring over books and then repeating the lesson was a veritable torture. His father very often scolded him in this regard and used to humiliate him, repeatedly telling him that he was less intelligent than the brilliant, quick-minded Luciana, whom he favored; he made it clear how unhappy he was that she was not the son who would take over *La Stampa* someday. Luciana, for her part, understood very well her own social position and was proud of the newspaper's success. Not even their mother spared him harsh jabs: "At the age of forty Giorgio will have not even half the good sense that Luciana has." Nevertheless, while "branding him a simpleton, our father experienced the mysterious bafflement the man of the world feels when confronted with unworldliness. On the whole, in spite of his remarks, he respected his son even though he had to give up the hope that he would be like him."[1]

One day the senator told the editor Cassone: "Pier Giorgio leaves me in awe, as though I were dealing with someone older. I do not know what it is, but, I repeat, some-

[1] L. Frassati, *A Man of the Beatitudes: Pier Giorgio Frassati*, trans. Dinah Livingstone, adapted and ed. Patricia O'Rourke (San Francisco: Ignatius Press, 2000), 39.

times he inspires awe in me." And meanwhile his son upset his plans, his projects: without him, who was the thread of continuity, Alfredo knew that he would not attain complete success, that his vainglory would not be fully satisfied.

Although Pier Giorgio had no fear of his father, but rather respect and consideration for him, quite a different relationship had developed with his mother. His respect for her was the result of an unconditional submission, a strong psychological dependency that is very often typical of a son, resulting from the enormous power that a mother acquires over her children, especially if she is authoritarian, since she and she alone assures their survival in the first years of life. In reasoning this way, we do not mean to set ourselves up as psychoanalysts, but there is no doubt that in the Frassati household Pier Giorgio was always fearful of disturbing or saddening his sensitive mother, and he often restrained his exuberance so as not to have to deal with the negative reactions of an unhappy mother from whom he often received great love and tenderness.

One evening Alfredo discovered Pier Giorgio beside his bed with a rosary in his hand; he said nothing to him, but he went to the parish priest of Crocetta, Monsignor Alessandro Roccati, to express his disappointment: "What have you done to my son?" The priest replied, unruffled: "Perhaps, Senator, you would prefer him to fall asleep with some cheap novel on his night table?"[2]

In their early childhood, the religious education of Pier Giorgio and Luciana was their mother's prerogative, who used to observe precepts and rules to the letter; her adherence to rituals reached its high point at feast day Masses and in practical conversations with priests and nuns. In this

[2] Ibid., 40.

field of education, she allowed her sister Elena, who had a similar religious attitude, to have some sway, and also their pious mother, Linda Copello, the one truly religious person in the family, who had clung fervently to the faith after the death of her sister Rachele, who had been carried off by consumption and died in her arms. Alfredo Frassati let them be, limiting himself to correcting homework papers from time to time. He made few demands on his children: "Love each other! Do not play cards [since that is the most dreadful vice there is]. Study!" Otherwise they would not have a successful career. "He also told us to go back to our grandmother's house in Pollone as soon as possible."[3]

Their father, moreover, considered a religious education an indispensable part of a complete pedagogical program suited to the social decorum of the day. At home he never let himself say anything that might sound offensive to religion: sometimes it was Adelaide's hypercritical nature that created "a somewhat anticlerical atmosphere", as her daughter recalled in her books. From his father, Pier Giorgio learned "a heartfelt affection for all poor people, with a fervent desire to try to help them".[4] He loved his father's philanthropic works and the great good that he used to do for the poor and the unfortunate; when he donated an enormous sum to a charity in memory of the dear departed engineer Pietro, Pier Giorgio wrote these affectionate words to him (in a letter dated September 27, 1923): "Dearest Papa, tomorrow is your feast day, and I very much regret that I will not be able to express to you personally all the sentiments in my heart. However, tomorrow I will be close to you, and I will

[3] Ibid., 28.
[4] A. Cojazzi, *Pier Giorgio Frassati: Testimonianze* (Turin: SEI, 1928), 28.

pray that God may give you all possible consolations for the good that you have done and are doing."

Another hypercritical individual in the Frassati household, besides Adelaide, was always Luciana, particularly with regard to the mother, to whom she appears to attribute most of the responsibility for the lack of affection in the family. There are plenty of accusations, not even hidden between the lines but formulated explicitly and directly. Her preference for her father is likewise extremely clear. Unfortunately there is no testimony from Pier Giorgio; we know, however, that he was more inclined to take his mother's side. Let us pause to listen to this harsh, cutting examination:

> The memory of those far-off days still hurts because we lacked a mother's tenderness. Our childhood was painful: the days at Pollone . . . , or in the Turin house in, where we spent our winters, were days during which we were unable to get away from the same faces, the same rooms, and the monotonous streets. We were not allowed to walk about in the city, stand in front of windows, give way to little stirrings of curiosity. We had to walk briskly, without turning our heads.[5]

> [That] trained us to be quick and prompt. Alacrity, promptness: a harshly imposed system. . . . We lived in an ill-defined nightmare, where allegedly health-related reasons brought about true hunger: it was not permitted to take any food between meals; for us there were no drinks and no bar, and whenever, tired from climbing the interminable mountains from which I always descended with a high fever, I complained of thirst, Mama used to encourage me with the remark, "Bring up some saliva." Papa's great satisfaction with the mountain of pasta that regularly awaited us

[5] L. Frassati, *A Man of the Beatitudes*, 22–23.

when we returned with him from *La Stampa* was an oasis
that prolonged the joy of the time when he stopped once
in front of the shop windows and even under the marble
counter of the delicatessen.[6]

The remark "Bring up some saliva" sounds disagreeable
and jarring. Certainly the innate elegance of Alfredo Frassati
would have prevented her from saying such a thing; but it
sounds even harsher because it is the expression of a lack of
maternal sweetness, a trait that, regardless of the filial sympathies and antipathies of Pier Giorgio and Luciana, Adelaide
Ametis must not have known very well.

"The best proof of affection that you can give me is to
be hardworking and serious about life", the senator used
to say. These were traits that he did not manage to find
in Pier Giorgio. Alfredo's life was guided by faith in the
values of liberty and correctness, and he printed his newspaper in accordance with these principles. And the sharing
of these ideals was at the origin of his exceptional, strong
bond with Giovanni Giolitti. The two men were twenty-five
years apart in age, but this difference never jeopardized the
friendship between them. After all, they were not rabidly
anticlerical. Often the respect that some liberals have for
different professions of faith is improperly considered to be
irreligiousness—a judgment that seems to apply neither to
Frassati (in his newspaper not one word against the Church
and her ministers ever appeared) nor to Giolitti, who used
to make visits to isolated churches, far from the people and
the journalists.

When his beloved wife died, Giolitti retired, as he always
did, at ten o'clock in the evening, but shortly after midnight, through the deserted streets of Cavour, he went to

[6] Frassati, *Pier Giorgio Frassati: I giorni della sua vita*, 3rd ed. (Rome: Edizioni
Studium, 1990), 18–19, 22–23.

the church where the remains of his wife had been brought and remained there for about two hours for a private wake. A nun was the one who reported this, because the president had sent away his security guards. Although he was very reserved and introverted, we can find traces of his sorrow in an accounting book. Alongside the list of expenses for the burial and for works of charity, we read a comment that one might not have expected from him: "May 10, struck by the most atrocious misfortune: My beloved, holy wife died in Torre Pellice." It is not surprising, then, that a liberal agnostic like Giovanni Giolitti, although considered rabidly anticlerical by Don Sturzo, was nevertheless the dear friend of the pastor of the village church of San Dalmazzo and elicited sympathetic responses from the ecclesiastical world.

Alfredo never made his children sharers in his own intellectual or spiritual life: "He always kept them distant from displays that could have left indelible memories, such as his swearing-in ceremony at the Senate, of which they did not have the slightest inkling."[7]

Although he limited himself to teaching those few necessary pedagogical precepts, Alfredo loved his children also for the pleasure and relaxation they gave him. Back in 1905, Adelaide wrote to her sister: "Alfredo always has a great need for the children, given his moral depression, and he is becoming increasingly attached to them." Adelaide, who was often oppressed by her husband's ill humor, took refuge in her sister's consolation and confessed to her: "This sitting at table without saying a word to each other! Blessed are the children, and blessed are you when you are among us" (June 11, 1907). "I have a strange fixation," Alfredo had written in a letter to his fiancée in August 1897, "fed

[7] L. Frassati, *Un uomo, un giornale: Alfredo Frassati*, vol. 1 (Rome: Edizioni di Storia e Letteratura, 1978), 43.

by the most insignificant things: that in serious matters we are not in agreement. How different our opinions are in so many of them!''

Neither Giolitti nor Frassati could be accused of favoritism. Everyone knows that the prime minister never accepted gifts, not even modest ones. But few know that one day he ordered a magnificent piece of wild boar, a trophy of the king's hunt, to be refused. The two friends, punctilious in everything, distrusted anyone who rose late in the morning, and both were endowed with exceptionally good health. The people of Biella had the opportunity to see the ninety-year-old Frassati walking on the slopes of his mountains. He loved Pollone more than himself: the garden, the plants, the mountaintops that restored and refreshed him. From Germany, where he had been sent in 1920 as ambassador, his passion for trees prompted him to order his eighteen-year-old daughter to watch over their growth with binoculars.

Recalling Bismarck's saying, ''The forest is an indicator of the psychological depth of a people'', Alfredo Frassati was a staunch defender of the need for reforestation and wanted the mountain vegetation to multiply and plants to grow along the banks of the streams to reinforce and beautify them. His interest in and commitment to this cause would be rewarded with the gold medal of sylvan merit, conferred on him by the minister Amintore Fanfani on November 21, 1951, in the Palazza della Civiltà in the EUR,[8] in the presence of the authorities, many inhabitants of the city, and ten thousand Roman children and students from every grade level.

---

[8] A residential and business district in Rome, south of the city center. —Trans.

Another passion of his was horseback riding. A skilled horseman, he rode the indomitable Irish steed Parsifal (who allowed only Alfredo and Pier Giorgio to mount him) through broad tracts of the Serra or of the Stupinigi woods: the Irish horse accompanied him also to Berlin, where he galloped every afternoon in the Tiergarten, inspiring envy and admiration. On February 18, 1921, he let his daughter share in his own satisfaction: "Yesterday I took a magnificent excursion on horseback. Two round trips to the Wannsee. And I am not kidding you! The horses, except for Parsifal, were exhausted: the riders, except for your father, dead. Ruggeri,[9] the major, slept for four hours after lunch!"

Giolitti was very fond of hunting in the mountains and of fencing, a sport that trained him for the thrust and parry of political battle. Both men were shrewdly thrifty. In a letter dated January 1921 that he wrote home from Berlin, Frassati recommended: "Do not make so many purchases . . . there is no real need . . . I economize to spare a cent, but I would not save a hundred thousand lire if saving would cause me to make a bad impression." In fact, he was heedless of the expense needed to lend decorum and prestige to the embassy. "A master of restlessness and nostalgia, slowly and stubbornly he elaborated future successes, never allowing the competition to degenerate into social climbing."[10] A major industrialist once tried to entice him with easy profits that were not very transparent: he threatened to toss him down the stairs if he ever again dared to make proposals like that.

[9] The major in question was Paolino Ruggeri Laderchi, member of the Italian section of the Inter-Allied Armistice Commission and Commission of Control.

[10] L. Frassati, *Un uomo, un giornale*, 1:52.

Unlike Giolitti, who had a rather patient temperament, Frassati had little tolerance for the defects of others and was not very forbearing, even though he realized it: "I forgive everything", he wrote to his fiancée in a melancholy letter dated June 30, 1896, "because I need so much to be forgiven. God, who is great and good and who reads the depths of the soul, will help me."

The senator often sought in other women what he did not find in Adelaide, and since he loved the fair sex, he was extremely fastidious about his appearance and strove to be elegant; however, aware of his charm, he did not follow fashions much. He never went into a shop, but certainly he would never have done what Giolitti used to do: acquire a dozen identical ties. "Frassati's rejection of any form of mannerism was also generated by a hidden sense of superiority: accustomed to giving categorical orders, he nonetheless welcomed the humblest laborer or farmer with the same human warmth with which he would have had Giolitti sit down in front of him."[11]

Giolitti's greatest friend and admirer would have liked to see a more Frassatian Giolitti, without so much "Roman parliamentary protocol", not so attached to compromises and little electoral games, with a less provincial concept of foreign policy. Giolitti, for his part, used to watch what Frassati overlooked, namely, the South.

The senator always kept in mind, especially when he was speaking about foreign policy, the political model of the dukes of Savoy, who were "brave in battle, shrewd in their choice of ally" (*La Stampa*, December 1, 1908), besides being realistic and enterprising.

Both Frassati senior and Frassati junior had a real distaste

[11] Ibid., 1:60–61.

for so-called worldly life. Neither one knew how to dance, yet Alfredo demanded that Pier Giorgio learn that art. In order to have support in his refusal to participate in an activity for which he had no talent, Pier Giorgio asked for help from his pastor, Monsignor Roccati, who immediately asked him: "Does your father know how to dance?" "No", was the boy's reply. "You see, he himself managed to do without it!"

"True glory", the senator maintained, was to be found in books and not in honorific titles; that was why he initially refused the official award of the detested Knight's Cross (which he then accepted out of courtesy). In a letter from Senator Roux dated August 15, 1913, we read:

Dear Frassati,

I was very surprised by your telegram. As of last Friday I had had a promise from Giolitti to arrange for some decorations for you in 2 or 3 months, as was understood. What ever happened to change your mind? Are you retiring? Did someone else intervene? I am so preoccupied and irritated by the ongoing scandals and by the political hysterics of this place. God help us all. These are nasty times.

The title was awarded to him only several years later. Nor was he pleased by the commendation that he received in 1911, just as it pained him to wear the decorations and the uniform of an ambassador, a vexation that we find in a letter sent from Berlin to his mother on November 14, 1921: "Dear Mama, enclosed with this letter you will find a photograph of me dressed up a bit like a clown. In a few days I will send you a really nice one. It will serve to make you laugh when you are in a bad mood." A laugh would come, a sneering one, fifteen years later from Achille Starace, secretary of the Fascist Party.

It is interesting to read Adelaide's comments after she received a letter from Pier Giorgio that enclosed portraits of him and of his father in uniform (Turin, November 15, 1921):

Neither father nor son is at his best. . . . Alf[redo] with the plume over his eyes—in the photograph he has to hold the cap in his hand without the cape that looks like a cab driver's—and then he did not raise the right side—I make all these observations because I would be anxious to have a nice photo of him in uniform that was expressive and a good likeness—the best of the family is still P.G. with his little pipe and his mouth upturned on one side! Luciana is a living image of . . . something between Dadà (the governess) and Signora Ginzburg [Leone's sister] but without the beard! . . .

And if a tutelary Divinity protects me, the day will come when I will put an end to this meditation about clothing —and I will use what remains of the gray material for my paintings. Tomorrow is the 16th, and I think that on the 25th I will embrace Giorgio. I am very happy . . . and yet I so much miss Luciana! And when I see her again my thought will once again be with the one whom I leave behind. It is a sad life! To think that the world is so beautiful —that the sun rises and sets over so many marvels—that life is so short—energies slip away . . . and I will be at a tea or will change my outfit so as to go to a dinner!

There are major strikes at the Polytechnic School, as you will have read in the newspaper. And so P.G. is missing many lectures. Will he still have the good will and the energy to study without interruption? I am glad that you bought the raincoat for him—and the watch? Poor little lad! *He* has no need of it, is not asking for it, so it is a bit neglected.

Pier Giorgio never asked for anything for himself; he was content with the great ideals of the Gospel and charity, and since he never goaded the members of his family with requests, they neglected his needs, unfortunately the deepest and most intimate ones, too.

La Stampa was just starting when, in May 1900, the citizens of Biella offered to let Frassati run as an opposition candidate against the illiberal minister Pelloux. The journalist turned down the opportunity, explaining that "he had absolutely no ambitions and did not want to abandon his offices." The calls to draft him did not cease. Two years later, Frassati refused candidacy for the position of provincial councilor, and once again in 1913 he did not yield to the insistent invitations of the populace, who at all costs wanted him as their representative in their electoral college. He declared, without any false modesty, that as publisher of a major newspaper he considered his position superior to any participation in politics.

On the other hand, Alfredo Frassati proudly accepted his appointment as senator, which arrived on November 24, 1913, thus liberating him from the constant need to turn down requests from the people of his region. "As though to testify to the certainty of an earthly successor in his very handsome son, . . . the newly elected senator had a portrait photograph taken of himself alongside him", Luciana Frassati noted.[12]

During Giolitti's tenure, Italy emerged definitively from the long period of recession that had afflicted it, made a great leap forward along the path of industrialization, balanced the budget, won a military victory with the conquest

---

[12] Ibid., 1:63.

of Libya, and started to pass social legislation by planning a bold, courageous reform: universal suffrage.

Giovanni Giolitti did not govern Italy uninterruptedly until the First World War. He was too prudent and crafty to give those who accused him of "parliamentary dictatorship" such a pretext to blame him; nevertheless, Cavour and Depretis were accused of the same thing. Twice he handed on power, now to his friend, now to his enemy, while always remaining the majority party leader. He had a clear political plan in mind, in which power proved to be only a means: integrating the masses of the people into the structures of the liberal State, which until then had excluded them.

"The sole criticism that hits the target is that of the misconduct on which Giolittism was founded. Giolitti did nothing to eliminate the patronage that tainted Italian political life with its long trail of corruption, intimidation, and blackmail. Indeed, he even made use of it",[13] and whenever someone accused him of it, he replied that "when a tailor makes a suit for a hunchback, he has to make sure that the suit has a hump, too."

Giolitti understood that it was no longer possible to marginalize the power of the working people, an electoral prize that was benefiting socialism hand over fist. Since 1901, there had been violent waves of industrial and agricultural strikes, and, in 1904, Italy witnessed the first major general strike in its history. Two years later, the General Labor Confederation was formed in Milan, which subsumed all the previously existing national trade organizations and the local labor exchanges. This marked the transition toward a central management of the labor movement, in which the reformist socialists prevailed against a revolutionary union

[13] I. Montanelli and M. Cervi, *Storia d'Italia: L'Italia del Novecento* (Milan: RCS, 2001), 18–19.

movement that aimed at direct action against the State.

Giolitti's power began to wear thin because of the increasingly aggressive attacks of the socialists, especially after the entrance of Benito Mussolini among their ranks and the appearance of "long-winded nationalism", as Indro Montanelli incisively describes it, which was ennobled by the intellectual Gabriele D'Annunzio. The so-called "Gentiloni Pact" was no help; this agreement was reached in 1913 between Catholics and the moderate candidates in the individual electoral colleges and modified by the president of the Catholic Electoral Union, Count Vincenzo Ottorino Gentiloni, to resist an advance by the leftists in the general elections in October. In a circular letter addressed to the leaders of Catholic associations, the only ones capable of counteracting the socialists' efforts among laborers with an adequate organizational network, Gentiloni listed seven points that ministerial candidates had to accept in order to obtain the support of the Electoral Union. These points revolved mainly around questions of a "confessional" sort, such as protection for private schools, religious instruction in the public schools as well, opposition to divorce, and non-discriminatory treatment of Catholic economic and social organizations by the State. The final note explained that, in politically more delicate situations, it was not indispensable for those who were elected to make public their adherence to the conditions set by the Church.

Giolitti, in his memoirs, says very little about himself; moreover, he completely overlooks the existence of Alfredo Frassati; but this should not appear so odd, since the senator himself used to declare that "With his friends Giolitti had the delicacy of a young unmarried woman." This was not out of modesty, but rather because he was a man of few, very few

words: "One word is not much, and two are too many."
The senator, too, was reluctant to leave footprints. His existence, he thought, was already contained entirely in his newspaper. Long before, in November 1896, he confessed to his fiancée:

> I already told you in person the things that are troubling me: our affection itself, for example, my boundless desire to do something for my country, and not seeing how; the sorrow of seeing it day by day losing its position among the nations, and more than its position, their esteem and confidence; a splendid ideal of purity, unchecked ambition that is nevertheless strong, healthy, and decent, intolerant of any baseness and averse to any compromise; the fear that, by leaving this post open, I might completely betray the mission that has smiled at me since the day my intellect opened up to the true light; the fear of betraying my heart by being faithful to the ideal: I disdain the world and feel the fatal need to live within it; I have a desire to do, to act, to accomplish, to do good, and I fear that I may lack the strength and the means, now that my past is essentially consistent with the present: it is the past of every young man who has placed work above all else, who has had only one passion, to distinguish himself soundly and honestly, and for this purpose has sacrificed almost all his strength.

Adelaide replied wisely to this appeal, inciting her future husband to follow the ideals to which he felt called (November 5, 1896):

> My poor Freddy, I wish you, Alfredo, from the depths of my heart, success in attaining your ideal of doing good for our country—which is a noble and great ideal—not a desire to climb higher to satisfy a wretched vanity to shine and to stand above the others—but the holy ambition to make yourself useful to your country, although still ob-

scure and not understood: continue to work and study, and by being a decent, respected citizen, you will have already paid a tribute of affection and thanksgiving to the country. I understand that, sensing your intelligence and energy, you are looking higher . . . and you do well . . . —to work to attain it but without apprehension—with calm serenity— if you attain it, it will be the crowning of your whole life —but what if by chance you should fall along the way? If would be no less glory for you, dearest, because you would fall having done your duty.

Obstinate dedication to right choices, a total, unconditional patriotic love devoted to liberty and justice, to industriousness and righteousness: these were his ideals; therefore, he had to fight every day, constantly, for them. His attitude toward reflection was not nourished spiritually, and unfortunately he did not allow himself to be stimulated by the teachings that might have come from Pier Giorgio: there was no exchange of intellects or of profound thought by the two men in the Frassati household. Who knows whether the son knew what his father had said in his youth? He would have been rather happy about it:

> Remember me, pray for me, and tell everyone that without a lot of poetry it is impossible to endure such great struggles, one cannot ascend (we say it without irreverence) so many Calvaries. Christ's was much more bitter, but he was God, and I am nothing but a miserable creature.[14]

In contrast to Luciana Frassati, who wrote: "For this end [realizing his own ideals] Frassati fought and won",[15] we believe that Alfredo Frassati really won and realized his great ideals, but not only by spending himself completely in his

[14] L. Frassati, *Un uomo, un giornale*, 1:65.
[15] Ibid.

immense passion for his work. His desire "to do, to act, to accomplish, to do good" was expressed later on, at the death of his beloved son, on whom he had counted and who, apparently, disappointed him, not bringing him the desired results on a gold platter: he would have liked to model that son on himself, to make him in his own image and likeness, and only later, when he had slipped from his hands, did he understand that God, who had taken, stolen, snatched him away, was the one who shaped him: the misunderstood treasure of his sojourn on earth was the real "splendid ideal of purity" that he had glimpsed in his youth. But when he understood that, the game was over, and you cannot compete with God.

6

LIKE A CASTAWAY

The atmosphere in the family continued to be harsh and chilly; the secret war between the Ametis and Frassati continued along its path of hatred and rancor. Luciana was convinced that everything was due to the determination of the Ametis sisters to set themselves against her father. Adelaide and Elena used to repeat, as though in a litany, that the house in Pollone belonged to the Ametis, the vegetable garden and the greenhouses belonged to the Ametis, the gardener was in their employ, and therefore Alfredo could not give orders directly. Moreover, he did not have the right to offer guests a bottle of aged red Barolo wine, coming from his mother-in-law's wine cellar, and then he must not use the postcards of Pollone on which had been added, alongside the caption Villa Ametis, the name Frassati, considering that that clarification was an inopportune intrusion. Luciana disobeyed that order and continued to send postcards on which the two names were printed side by side. Luciana, who regarded her father as a myth in which to glory and looked at her mother with a great deal of commiseration, admits: "Father's nearness at table gave me security, but being opposite Mama made me uncomfortable. Now, though, the old fear of her weeping, which for years accompanied my every evening, has given way to an infinite sense of pity."[1]

The saddest time in the day for Adelaide Ametis was the one spent at table. Here the familial drama unfolded in its entirety. During meals the father, who first made sure that the cutlet was perfect and that the salad came from Pollone (and if not, a veil of sadness descended over his eyes at the thought of the unproductive vegetable garden he visited every Saturday), used to speak about wine, about the stables in Pollone and the land, but never about his work. The mother waited until she heard the sound of a chair moving upstairs. Pier Giorgio would announce that Aunt Elena had finished eating, glad to be able to offer his Mama the opportunity to go up and see her beloved sister. Adelaide's exit was apparently an escape, and as a pretext she attributed it to a migraine. In reality she went to visit Elena, and, sitting side by side, they got to talking while Adelaide smoked a Tuscan cigar.

In that setting of paltriness and pettiness, deprived of goodwill and a sense of life, Pier Giorgio finished secondary school. From the start, studying had been for him an immense, sorrowful burden. An obsession that stayed with him until the end of his brief days. But duty first, before all else; therefore, aware that he could not be exempted from university studies, in November 1918 he enrolled (as student no. 509) in the Faculty of Mechanical Industrial Engineering with a specialization in mining. He seems to have had no second thoughts about his decision. He was not interested in a career, but he imagined his life in the midst of one of the most disadvantaged social classes: the miners. The

[1] L. Frassati, *A Man of the Beatitudes: Pier Giorgio Frassati*, trans. Dinah Livingstone, adapted and ed. Patricia O'Rourke (San Francisco: Ignatius Press, 2000), 63.

work was hard, punishing, with very few rewards, always in the darkness and humidity and in constant danger of being buried by collapses. His Uncle Pietro,[2] the uncle to whom Pier Giorgio was very attached, was an engineer, too, but had followed his brother's aspirations and joined the staff of *La Stampa*.

Endowed with his father's dynamism and strong will, Pier Giorgio applied these gifts in carrying out the eight beatitudes. If we were to list everything that Pier Giorgio did over the few years of his transition from adolescence to young adulthood, that is, his years at the lyceum and the university, from 1910 to 1925, it seems that Blessed Frassati lived three times as long. "Do, act, accomplish, do good", his father used to say, and he put that rule into practice.

University examinations were a nightmare for Pier Giorgio. He went so far as to compare himself to a shipwrecked castaway fighting desperately in a stormy sea of textbooks, lecture outlines, and notes. "My mind, steeped in that arid science, every so often finds peace and refreshment and spiritual enjoyment in reading Saint Paul . . . it is marvelous and my soul is uplifted."

In the library of the Faculty of Mathematics, students and

[2] The engineer Pietro Frassati was tragically scarred by the murder of his sister Emma, so much so that of the brilliant official's genius only the memory remained. For the rest of his life, he was timid and irritable; his mood turned to sulkiness when he was with his mother. Humble and without any ambition whatsoever, unlike his brother Alfredo, Pietro was appointed, by a ministerial decree dated August 7, 1896, General Director of the Post and Telegraph Offices of Turin; the position disappointed Alfredo, though, who commented as follows to the Ametis sisters in a letter from that time: "The post office is very undistinguished for now and not what I would have wanted, but it is a means of making a career later on. If you knew how painful it is to think that Pietro has not started a good career! To me it is just like a thorn, a large thorn in my heart."

librarians often saw Pier Giorgio arrive panting and over-
heated. From his pockets and briefcase emerged one after
the other pieces of paper on which were written the names
and addresses of poor persons to help and visit. It was not
uncommon then to see him pensive and saddened because
he had not managed to accomplish all the daily visits he had
planned.

One day his mother, who perpetually supervised his studies, told him, for the umpteenth time, that he did not know
how to organize, that he wasted his time, and she held up for
him the example of an acquaintance: "You see, he takes exams, and yet he finds time to row every day on the Po River,
to ride a motorcycle, and to go about in society. You, on
the other hand, find time for nothing. If I ask you to come
with me to Venice for a few days, you say no." Pier Giorgio
looked at his mother and told her: "But, you know, he is
intelligent and I am not." That time Adelaide kept quiet.
But she did not give up: "Studying when you're half-asleep
the way you do is useless and harmful to your health. You
will be a good boy, but you are so stubborn."

Adelaide lamented the situation with her sister. "You
know, talking with Pier Giorgio is a little like talking to
the wind." Or else she wrote to her when they were apart:
"You did well to give Pier Giorgio a sermon: I already gave
him one, but he is always right . . . now there is nothing
to do but to look forward to the end of these exams and
to hope meanwhile . . . that he will mature." This boy of
hers, whom she scolded for his bristly beard, who did not
straighten the knot of his tie (the cook Maria Miletto, who
had been in the service of the family for fifty years, used to
do it for him), made her think so much, too much . . .

Often in Pollone he used to study sitting beneath the
trees and especially under the tall sequoia: "First he greets

the Lord, and then he studies his lesson, and that pine tree is also his studio because, you see, there, on the place where the branches cross, there is a sort of writing desk."[3] Toward the end of his university studies, he was truly weary of taking exams, and only the thought of the mountains, organizing trips and then thinking about them afterward, brought a breath of fresh air to those boring hours spent over his books. Sometimes all his efforts ended in disaster, and in the middle of an examination he had to quit. Sustaining and accompanying him in his burdensome task was his very keen memory.

In the new century, universities in Italy had organized so as to be at the level of the other European nations. Italian science, characterized by strong experimentation, went through a profound crisis: after the death of Galileo Ferraris, the greatest of all the technical scientists, there were almost no results at the theoretical level, and applied research was entrusted entirely to the engineers. Turin and Milan had the leading schools in Italy, which were the first to set up an "adequate industrial formation for engineers, thereby beginning, amid delays and contradictions, a process of modernization of institutions of scientific learning in Italy".[4]

In the twenties, Turin was like a big laboratory in which many people found opportunities for new experiments, receiving strong incentives from the development of industrial and aeronautic technologies. The policies of the Fascist regime showed a remarkable attention to the undertakings of architecture and urban planning in major projects of

[3] L. Frassati, *Mio fratello Pier Giorgio: La fede* (Rome: Edizioni Paoline, 1954), 164.

[4] See N. Tranfaglia, ed., *Storia di Torino: Gli anni della Repubblica*, vol. 9 (Turin: Einaudi, 1999), 675.

social redevelopment: "In the press, in the newsreels, on the radio, every blow struck by the stonemason's hammer to the urban fabric was wrapped in an aura of redevelopment and progress."[5]

The Polytechnic, inaugurated on November 5, 1906, with its main offices on the via Ospedale, had as its objective teaching "technology" to three different categories of professionals: civil engineers, industrial engineers, and architects.[6] Compared with the humanities faculties, the Polytechnic was better protected and defended against the sickening propaganda activities of Fascism; this was demonstrated in 1923 by the appointment of Gustavo Colonnetti (1886–1967) as director. He was an instructor and a scientist, an organizer of scientific research, president of the National Research Council (CNR), a staunch anti-Fascist, a Catholic, a member of the management and of the National Council of the Popular Party of Don Luigi Sturzo, as well as president of the Diocesan Council.[7]

In the first years after the war, besides his political activity, Colonnetti intensified his efforts in the academic field. In the

[5] Ibid., 679.

[6] In 1808, in the Castello del Valentino in Turin, the first industrial exposition was held. On that occasion, Prospero Richelmy, Quintino Sella, and Bartolomeo Gastaldi founded the School of Applied Engineering, which in 1906 merged with the Museo Industriale, the one institute of its kind in Italy (created in 1862 for the purpose of higher learning in technology), thus giving rise to the Politecnico.

[7] On December 26, 1925, Professor Gustavo Colonnetti, in the name of the Diocesan Council, sent a letter to the Office of the Prefect of Turin, requesting the introduction of a "ban on blasphemy" into the rules of the city police, as had already happened in other cities. In addition to providing for sanctions, the ordinance would have allowed "No blasphemy" signs to be posted in streetcars and public places. A similar request was presented to the leaders of the Industrial Union so that a ban on blasphemy and coarse language might be introduced in their establishments.

turbulent postwar atmosphere, the general situation in the schools had deteriorated, and, in order to resolve the many problems, Professor Colonnetti carried out a radical educational and administrative reorganization. In those years, the number of university students had grown progressively, creating a worrisome phenomenon of intellectual unemployment. The solution to the problem was found in stricter criteria for admitting students; to that end, effective tools were provided by the Gentile reform, which Colonnetti applied vigorously. The number of periodic progress tests was increased, and the so-called group examination was introduced. Pier Giorgio therefore faced the difficult tests introduced by the director. These were written and oral tests that the student had to take in all the subjects covered in the first two-year curriculum, which was mainly dedicated to the study of topics in physics and mathematics; the second two-year curriculum, in contrast, dealt in greater depth with scientific and technical subjects. For Colonnetti, the group examination had the purpose of stimulating the ability to synthesize, fostering a personal, creative sort of learning rather than rote memorization. "In reality the group examination amounted to an increase in the workload and of the school's selectivity, against which the students reacted with massive demonstrations",[8] in which Pier Giorgio Frassati never participated.

Alongside the educational reorganization, an administrative restructuring took place. In the years 1915–1918, the State subsidy to the school of engineering had remained essentially unchanged, while the monetary devaluation had rapidly eroded its value. Colonnetti's prescription, based on strict economy and drastic dismissals, yielded its initial

[8] B. Gariglio, *Cattolici democratici e clerico-fascisti: Il mondo cattolico torinese alla prova del fascismo (1922–1927)* (Bologna: Il Mulino, 1976), 228.

results. But his relations with the Fascists were difficult, and he often came into conflict with them; they started a nasty press campaign against him, openly calling for his dismissal. Now considered a bitter enemy of the Fascist government, Colonnetti, after accomplishing the most unpopular part of his reform of the Polytechnic, was removed from his position of authority. Since its annual budget had now surpassed five million lire, the institute occupied a central role among the academic institutions of the city, and it was also connected to the interests of large-scale industry and the political world. On December 2, 1925, Colonnetti submitted his resignation, and the same thing would happen with his leadership post within the diocesan Catholic Action.[9]

[9] The critical, polemical letter sent on January 21, 1924, by Professor Gustavo Colonnetti to the founder of the Popular Party, Don Luigi Sturzo, is significant: "Dear Sturzo, I am very sorry that I absolutely cannot get away these days during which the negotiations for the contracts for the Polytechnic are being brought to a conclusion; I ask you and the friends of the administration to excuse my absence and to keep in mind that if I had given a speech, I would have lamented the slow but constant trend toward the opposition, of which *Il Popolo* gives a clear impression daily. Indeed, I would not like us to join the opposition by imperceptible steps, without some deliberation to that effect being taken by the responsible groups: as far as I am concerned, I intend to stand firm in the position of independence and free criticism but not of opposition, the stance that we agreed on when we accepted the formula: neither collaboration nor opposition. But what is happening now? *Il Popolo* gives the impression of taking sides against the government, multiplying reasons for criticism of governmental measures, and often finding absolutely baseless ones, as it did recently with regard to Gentile. . . . I find all this excessive criticism very inopportune . . . and utterly useless. Turning then from the general problem to a more particular one, I note the continuous journalistic gossip in which the Turin edition is indulging, not to mention the prose about the Church that we read every day. . . . As it is, the Turin edition does us more harm than good; it discredits us in the view of all balanced persons, alienates the clergy, which was all for us, and plays the same game as *Il Momento*. As president of the Diocesan Council I have reached the point where I must acknowledge that the Turin edition of *Il Popolo* is as deplorable as *Il Momento*. I think that I will come to Rome next week: on that occasion

In a conference that he gave on campus at the University of Losanna on April 25, 1944, Colonnetti explained his thinking and proclaimed:

> You young men, whom insane propaganda may have lured with illusory, false promises of dominion and power; you, whom today's unleashing of the worst instincts of human nature may have led to think that every problem can and must be resolved by the use of violence and force; you must find the courage to practice three major forms of renunciation that are, in my opinion, the indispensable prerequisite for reconstruction: renunciation of nationalistic ideologies, renunciation of class selfishness, renunciation of the spirit of violence.[10]

Although very severe and intransigent as an instructor of building science, Professor Colonnetti was appreciated and highly esteemed by Pier Giorgio Frassati: Pier Giorgio was not a model student, and his reputation for lightheartedness was proverbial, but that did not compromise his idea of study, a reality that he took extremely seriously.

A born fighter, Pier Giorgio brought his wave of truth, healthy protest, and righteousness to every group to which he belonged. He wrote in a letter dated April 8, 1922:

> Here in Turin at the Polytechnic, we must fight energetically against the anticlerical elements that, by giving themselves over to acts of vandalism, such as the destruction of our circle's glass display case twice now, compel us to isolate ourselves so as not to compromise our dignity. . . .

---

we will speak about all this again: but I felt obliged to mention it right now so as to make up in some way for my forced absence from tomorrow's meeting. With constant affection and the most cordial greetings, Ever yours affectionately, Gustavo Colonnetti."

[10] Tranfaglia, *Storia di Torino*, 674.

Luckily at the Polytechnic we have many Catholic professors; among them the most active is Prof. Colonnetti, who is always ready to defend us on every occasion.[11]

Acts of aggression against Catholics in Turin became increasingly frequent. In order to cope with the dangers, Pier Giorgio prudently and shrewdly went back to practicing at the national shooting range, where he had been enrolled since 1920. After a violent break-in by the Fascists into his own house, Alfredo Frassati advised his son to start carrying a weapon to defend himself.

On the glass-covered bulletin boards of the university, alongside a thousand manifestos of every sort, the Catholic students had posted a notice and a spiritual warning. A group of vandals lunged at the notices; Pier Giorgio, fearless and heedless of his own welfare, resisted until he was overpowered: the glass case was shattered, and the notice destroyed.

Let us read the remembrance of his student that Professor Colonnetti has left us:

> Pier Giorgio truly had all the virtues and all the graces that contrast with the bad characteristics of our time: he was pure in a world contaminated with vices; he was just in a world in which injustice triumphs; he was meek in a world in which the spirit of violence rages; he was generous in a world dominated by cupidity; he was kind and loving in a world torn by selfishness and hatred; he practiced fortitude in a world where consciences so easily yield to wicked deeds, small and great; he was rich in happiness and joy in a pleasure-seeking world that has lost the sense of true joy.[12]

[11] P. G. Frassati, *Lettere*, ed. L. Frassati, preface by Luigi Sturzo (Rome: Studium, 1950), 277.

[12] M. Codi, *Pier Giorgio Frassati: Una valanga di vita* (Casale Monferrato [AL]: Portalupi, 2001), 255.

"What are you, a bigot?" they asked him one day at the university, because that was the insulting name for Catholics used by the Masonic liberals, the Socialist-Communists, and the Fascists. Pier Giorgio's response was simple and trenchant: "No. I am still a Christian."

In January 1925, when he saw some manifestos with calumnies aimed at Colonnetti posted in the courtyard of the Polytechnic, Pier Giorgio started to tear them down, but immediately several students came up, threatened him, and demanded reparation for the damage and in particular for the offense against freedom of thought. But he, with calm assurance, replied that "error and calumny have no right to any freedom. And if I find others, I will tear them all down, too!"[13] His adversaries went off crestfallen, and Pier Giorgio himself was amazed, since he had been prepared for the worst.

His relationship with Colonnetti was personal as well, as some documents demonstrate. His friend Antonio Villani from Emilia, who had already earned an engineering degree and wished to return to Turin as an assistant professor at the Polytechnic, asked Pier Giorgio to intercede for him with Professor Colonnetti, and on June 27, 1923, Pier Giorgio responded as follows:

Dearest Villani,

[Y]esterday I took the electro-technical exam and passed with a 90 percent. Today, finally, I was able to speak to Colonnetti on your behalf . . . he told me that now they are reviewing some of the assistants currently on staff, and for now he does not know what the decision will be about new assistants. So for now you need to have patience and wait until after July 15, at which time Colonnetti will give

[13] A. Cojazzi, *Pier Giorgio Frassati: Testimonianze* (Turin: SEI, 1928), 105.

me a full explanation and clarification about the assistants who will have to be hired for the coming year.

Many people sought help with private questions from Pier Giorgio, who was often the privileged channel by which to reach his powerful father. This was the case for Isidoro Bonini, also, who wanted to start a farm in America and asked his friend, of all people, to intercede with his father for advice and assistance: "You do well to dedicate yourself to agriculture; I will submit your plan to my father, but certainly you will meet with approval, because he is very happy when the conversation is about agriculture, and he always says that Italy's future and fortune are in agriculture."[14]

With his stubborn determination, Pier Giorgio was approaching the coveted finish line in the spring of 1925. "As of May 1, I intend to begin my thesis so as to be able to liberate myself, with the help of God, by July and thus to spend this last summer free, completely free."[15] In July he did in fact attain full freedom, but from earthly life.

His plan was to start his thesis and, meanwhile, to prepare for the "sleep-inducing" examination on mineral technology; in order to carry out his plan, he wrote from Pollone to Isidoro Bonini (April 15, 1925): "Once I have arrived in Turin, I will be dead to everyone except the Saint Vincent de Paul conference, and I will study from morning until evening." Charity above all else. Two more exams and then the degree in October, as proof of the effort spent to arrive at the goal; as early as 1923 he imagined how he would celebrate the final victory: "I was very glad to have been in Monviso, inasmuch as some other year, if I am still alive, I would like to stay in those regions for two weeks to

[14] See P. G. Frassati, *Lettere*, 198.
[15] Ibid., 199–200.

train so as then to be able to climb Mount Cervino on the day I receive my degree." That is how he would have celebrated the longed-for degree, by hiking to the summit and singing God's praise: to reach the summit of the mountain for victory and freedom, the conclusion of the long ascent in his studies that had cost him so dearly. It is impressive to read again and again in his letters the phrase "if I am still alive"; death arrived very swiftly and unexpectedly, preventing him from enjoying the success for which he had struggled so much and so obstinately; and yet it did not take him by surprise, because his lamp had already been lit for a long time on his journey of truth.

"Believe me, we are getting older day by day, and every day that passes there is less will to study . . . but the thought of soon being able to take a degree gives me the strength to continue", he said to his friend Antonio Severi in a letter from Pollone dated April 17, 1924. On January 10, 1923, he wrote to another friend, Tonino Villani, after visiting the miners of the Ruhr Valley in Germany, where he was staying with his ambassador father: "In two years I, too, if God grants me life, will be working in the Ruhr." In another letter to a priest, he declared: "I will be a mining engineer so as to be able to keep devoting myself to Christ through the miners. I will not be able to do that as a priest, but as an exemplary and truly Catholic layman, I can."

Never one to do something superficially, he was not content to visit the miners in the Ruhr Valley; he deepened his knowledge in several other locations: Cogne, Silesia, Herzgebirge, Carrara, Oneta, and Katowitz (Katowice), where the young Karol Wojtyła would later work, too. It was during his stay in Germany that Pier Giorgio stopped thinking of a future as a priest and chose to specialize in mineral engineering: "In mining I want to help my people, and I can do that better as a layman than as a priest, because in our country the priests are not in contact with the people", he explained to Louise Rahner, mother of the famous theologian Karl, in whose house he stayed for a time. His aspiration was to become "a miner among miners".

Thus, according to his plans, the choice that he had made might have one enormous and altogether personal advantage: it would hide very well from his family's eyes his missionary vocation. We know for certain that he would have liked to travel to South America, not just to live and to share the risks and toils of the Indios who were being exploited in the mines in Chile, Bolivia, and Argentina, but also to be a missionary, in other words, to proclaim the Good News and to bring the Gospel to the poor. To serve God in man was his great ideal, and it is significant that some of his companions changed the course of their studies because of Pier Giorgio, after visiting the mines and observing firsthand the life that the laborers were leading.

Spurred on by this motive and imagining a future among "the pariahs of the working classes", as he described the miners, he pursued his university studies with an extraordinary determination. His repeated sojourns on German soil caused Pier Giorgio's plan for his life to mature, giving him the opportunity to observe the mining world close up. Moreover, he would have liked to complete his engineering studies in Berlin, where the mining business was especially appreciated.

His final degree was a mirage that Pier Giorgio wanted to reach at all costs and with all his strength, despite the fact that the Polytechnic was "becoming increasingly treacherous". In his letters, particularly to his friends, he recorded step by step his successes and failures, with all his anxiety about finishing in time and all the toil of someone who is better suited for activity than for theory, called to work projects rather than to books.

In order to win his battle, he spent entire nights over his books. He outlined and learned formulas and rules by memory; he repeated aloud what he would have to know for his examinations. He went so far as to tie himself to his chair like Vittorio Alfieri in order to study: "To think that I am so stupid that I am ruining my summer so as to hasten the day on which I receive my degree, and I want to shorten these few remaining days of my life as a student which is, alas, too beautiful." He liked being a student, and we can tell this very clearly from his letters; the thought of the future filled him with "sadness" (letter sent from Forte dei Marmi to Marco Beltramo in August 1924).

> Nevertheless, I need to hurry, because the years are passing very quickly, and I still have to serve our country, but afterward, when I return home, then it will be ugly, and I will mourn over my student life, whereas now I am looking forward to the end of it. But man is always an animal that can never be satisfied, and therefore it is not surprising. (Pollone, October 23, 1924)

These were the years when Franz Kafka was working on his stories about existential malaise and anguish, in which the characters experience situations that are distressing and incomprehensible to them. Often his fictional works reflect biographical features and are based on the uncertainty of individual existence, in absolute dependence on anonymous, inscrutable authorities. Pier Giorgio Frassati diligently commended his uncertainties, weaknesses, and fears to Jesus Christ. He knew, though, how to "take a stand" when needed, as he himself says: "*Ruit hora* [Latin: The hour is hastening], and therefore it is necessary to study", he used to say, and "with great strides the day is coming when we will have to reap what we have sown."[16]

On April 6, 2001, a hundred years after his birth, the Polytechnic in Turin conferred on him a *post mortem* degree in engineering. The subjects and the examinations that he took eighty years ago are for the most part the same ones with which those who are enrolled today in the Polytechnic still have to deal, but the degree in mineral engineering, the course of studies that Pier Giorgio followed, is no longer granted by the institute. The instructor of mathematical analysis, Marco Codegone, who gave the eulogy in the presence of Severino Cardinal Poletto, then archbishop of Turin, and of the rector, Rodolfo Zich, declared:

> Pier Giorgio wanted to go into mining so as to be close to the laborers and to improve their working conditions as much as possible. But there is another aspect, too, that makes this figure especially "dear" to us: Frassati was able to combine academic life and social commitment, for example in the FUCI or in the Popular Party. While intensely involved in university life, he was able to correlate it with social concerns.

[16] Ibid., 212.

7

PLURALISM IN ONE CREED

Before joining various Catholic movements, groups, circles, and associations, Pier Giorgio completed a journey of very balanced spiritual formation. His was not some mere youthful infatuation with Christ, but a deliberate and well-meditated religious maturation. Before launching into social action, in which he became totally absorbed, he learned the foundations of spirituality with the Apostleship of Prayer and the Company of the Most Blessed Sacrament. Only in a second phase, after he had finished his secondary school studies, did he decide to join the ranks of Catholic Action. At the time of that decision, the movement was organized according to the guidelines given by Pius X in 1905. Benedict XV gave full recognition to the movement, making it "an instrument of Christian judgment on history and of Christian action in the world to change it".[1]

Pier Giorgio, who breathed life deeply, thirsted for spiritual experiences and sought the instruments, methods, principles, and rules for living, not just in one group, but in several movements, so as to make himself as well attuned with God as possible. He entered into a relationship with the Lord, seeking to encounter him wherever he thought he could find him.

---

[1] D. Veneruso, "Pier Giorgio Frassati e l'azione cattolica", in *Sociologia: Rivista di Scienze Sociale* (Rome: Istituto Luigi Sturzo, 1990), 179.

Pier Giorgio had a heart that was born and formed to love; he looked at everything in the light of the faith at a time when political and antireligious passions were unleashed and being Catholic was often considered synonymous with stupidity.

A modern young man, with his sights set on the future rather than turned to the past, he participated in the activities and initiatives of the Church of his day, a Church that was in ferment, intent on renewing herself and becoming fully involved in the social and political fabric of the nation after years and years of silence (especially because of the Roman question). Pier Giorgio enthusiastically joined a number of projects and spiritual activities: the Apostleship of Prayer, the Eucharistic League, an association of university students devoted to adoration of the Blessed Sacrament, the Marian Sodality of the Third Order of Saint Dominic . . . Through these channels he was educated above all in prayer: not a mere recitation of prefabricated prayers, because Pier Giorgio made his life a constant prayer with his mind, with his heart, in every daily activity, even in the simplest gestures and acts, placing God, Christ, and Mary at the center of everything; anything else came to be at the service of the kingdom.

In 1919, when he was already a student at the Polytechnic, Pier Giorgio enrolled in the Cesare Balbo circle of FUCI (Association of Italian Catholic University Students) in Turin. Since he was still a minor, he had to obtain permission from his parents. To count on his father for that was unthinkable, so he turned to his mother, who was very distrustful of the members of Catholic Action; being "a good artist", as her daughter Luciana describes her, she considered them dreary and awkward. We have no way of telling whether Adelaide's reaction to Pier Giorgio's request was calm or stormy, but we know that she went to Don Antonio Cojazzi at the Salesian Istituto Valsalice for advice and that she emerged from that consultation with permission for her son, but without enthusiasm. Her sister relates:

> No one realized that the Cesare Balbo increased Pier Giorgio's detachment from the family. Now, away from home, his joy, purity, humility, simplicity, and faith led him to the apostolate. In the club, he was often surrounded by mediocre people. However, their very mediocrity made them ready to follow, and he ended up a leader. Those luminous eyes could look any man or woman in the face without his having to lower his eyes. He shook hands with new and old comrades, without reserve or visiting cards. No one realized, no one if you had asked then would have said, that he was everything to the club and totally committed to the club.[2]

In that environment, the young man observed the somewhat snobbish attitude of some members toward the common pedigree of Catholic Action, and therefore, without hesitation, he reacted by enrolling in other groups, such as the branch of the Milites Mariae in his parish; moreover, he periodically contacted other local and national circles and applied to the Catholic Youth Federation in Guastalla when he learned that it was being particularly persecuted by the Fascists, whom he called "Hottentots" (savages).

Pier Giorgio frequently participated in processions, and often he was called on to keep order, in a period in which subversive groups opposed public manifestations of faith with whistles, shouts, insults, and threats.

---

[2] L. Frassati, *A Man of the Beatitudes: Pier Giorgio Frassati*, trans. Dinah Livingstone, adapted and ed. Patricia O'Rourke (San Francisco: Ignatius Press, 2000), 52.

Belonging to one group does not mean excluding other possibilities; Pier Giorgio was able to seize opportunities without pitting one against another; he took the best from each one and profited from it. By this "multiple attendance", he meant, on the one hand, to emphasize the social diversity in membership to which Catholic associations ought to tend and, on the other hand, to oppose the ecclesiastical and bourgeois haughtiness of some in the Cesare Balbo circle. We read in a flyer for the election of officers in the same circle: "Students! Do you want to rejuvenate and reinvigorate the circle? Do you want it to live a healthy, boldly Christian life, above and beyond all that stale, reactionary 1848 stuff? Then cast your votes for the following colleagues: Borghezio, Olivero, Bertini, Collo, Negroni, Frassati, Scotti, Tealdi, Villani, Bonini, Caligaris."

In Pollone, too, he did not fail to attend the rural youth group, which for years had been sluggish and sleepy, while actively and directly striving for its religious reawakening. It is clear that as a matter of principle Pier Giorgio rejected exclusivity and ceremoniousness in volunteer groups, but he did not deny that Catholic Action transmitted positive, strong values, at least the circles that still followed the guidelines of Pius X, a pope whom he highly esteemed also for having promoted Eucharistic devotion. What he thoroughly approved about this system was that it had given full rights of citizenship, within the militant laity, to students, laborers, farmers, sailors, clerical workers, and athletes.

He looked for all sorts of pluralism: of groups, of voices, of faces; yet it all had to be consistent with one creed, belief in Christ; anything else was banished from the start. His "intolerance" was derived directly from his love for that creed, for which he would have given his life; therefore, as a soldier of Christ, he defended it everywhere, and he automatically felt the urgent need to defend the weakest. He was a "fundamentalist" because he was firm in his faith, because he was a herald of the civilization of love.

Pier Giorgio was present practically everywhere in the Catholic world. He diligently attended youth group meetings and conventions; his was a lively, vivifying presence that manifested his staunch faith and deep rootedness in the fabric of Church life. When he traveled to Ravenna to participate in the tenth congress of the FUCI and to Rome in September 1921 for the National Congress of Italian Catholic Youth on the fiftieth anniversary of its foundation, he behaved more like an associate of the Catholic Youth itself than like a member of the Cesare Balbo circle. Pier Giorgio had a personality of his own and never let himself be influenced. A personality always ready to expand, always keen and bold: on that same occasion, he proposed the merger of FUCI with Catholic Youth so that the students might join with the laborers, farmers, and clerical workers. The idea was voted down.

When the congress was over, he traveled to Rome with thousands of other young Catholics. The Sunday Mass was to be celebrated in the Colosseum, where the crowds of young people from all over Italy converged, each group with its banner. But the liberal-Masonic Roman police department marshaled the mounted guards to prevent the celebration, and around fifty thousand young people were compelled to pour onto Saint Peter's Square, where the Mass was celebrated on the plaza in front of the basilica, followed then by an audience with Benedict XV in the Vatican gardens. When the young people decided to walk from the Vatican to the Altar of the Fatherland, while singing "Brothers of Italy" and "We Want God", the police department intervened again, ordering the policemen to disperse them and to take away their banners. After a cavalry charge in which the butt ends of muskets flew freely, the banners were torn up and young men and priests were mistreated, with torn clothing and bloody cheeks. Pier Giorgio and his friends were led to the courtyard of the Palazzo Altieri under arrest. He, the son of the liberal senator and Italian ambassador Alfredo Frassati, was mixed in with the others. Many were wounded, but they courageously defended the banners of the various associations tooth and nail. One young man from Sardinia who did not want to give up the flag was threatened with a bayonet, and then Pier Giorgio intervened, revealing his own identity. The official quickly changed his attitude and immediately offered him his freedom. But Pier Giorgio used his father's name and prestige to help that young man. And with the banner of the Cesare Balbo circle reduced to tatters but still proudly clenched in his fist, he remained with his fellow members without requesting or wanting any privileges.

The following day, the young Catholics went again to Saint Peter's Square, and Pier Giorgio walked with them through the city carrying in triumph the remains of the banner, to which he had appended a sign saying: "Tricolor defaced by order of the Government". In the following hours, there was a lot of talk about Frassati being ready to defend the banner of Christ with his own life, but he proved reluctant to accept congratulations: it was a simple duty; in those circumstances, a young Catholic man could not behave in any other way. He would again find himself confronting violent, dangerous situations, but he continued to declare: "Your violence cannot overcome the strength of our faith, because Christ does not die."

His defense of the flag gave Pier Giorgio a moment of notoriety; the news was reported by several journalists. His

cousin Olga Battistella Torello exemplifies very well the reactions to that adventure in a letter sent to Adelaide Ametis
on September 13, 1921, in which she praises Pier Giorgio's
mother:

> I was so greatly edified by the courageous demeanor of your
> son, who was able to uphold the name of Christian and
> Catholic in front of everybody, without any human respect,
> that I am prompted to write to you about my admiration.
> When good example and the courage of one's own opin-
> ions come from above, the good that results for the masses
> who are fearful of inward convictions is immense. Honor
> to you, who were able to impart an education to your chil-
> dren. The good fruit that you are already gathering now is
> only a reward given to you by God for the good that you
> were able to lavish silently all around you. The remem-
> brance of all your holy work of helping my poor grand-
> mother will remain in my heart eternally. If it had not been
> for you with your very fine tact and foresight, how could
> that poor martyred creature have reached the end of her
> Calvary?

The testimony of Salesian Father Ercole Provera is illu-
minating:

> To judge an angel, a man is not enough, it takes an angel,
> and therefore I limit myself to recalling certain conversa-
> tions that have remained impressed on my memory forever.
>   Several times I happened to confide in him the difficul-
> ties that I was encountering in my life. He would stop and
> say to me: "Don Provera, what about the Lord who left
> heaven for earth?"
>   He was genial, angelic, and evangelical in the expressions
> he used. Often I would say to him, "Pier Giorgio, you
> are fortunate and rich; your father is ready to do anything
> for you, you have a dear sister who is fond of you", and I

would list all his earthly advantages; and then he would reply: "Don Provera, what is that compared with eternity?"

Once, probably in 1914–1915, I told him: "Pier Giorgio, how will you be able to make a life for yourself independent of your father so as to follow your noble ideals? . . ." "I have Jesus with me," he replied, "and I fear nothing."

I met him again in 1919–1920 and asked him what he thought about the war that we had just been through: "God is guiding humanity, and everything cannot help but go well", was his response.

He had an adamantine faith, even in the last things. "God permitting", "God willing."

I found him well instructed, and I lamented that I had had to cut short all my studies for the war: "But Don Provera, if one has done God's will, then everything goes well. Whatever happens, God has his reasons." Even when I told him that I did not trust Mussolini and that I hoped for nothing from Fascism, Pier Giorgio replied: "God wills it and permits it to be so", which was disarming.

He was God's, and it is not possible to describe him better than that. He was not a sentimental believer; he was a reasoning man guided by faith, obeying the will of God even unto death.[3]

His friendship with university student Antonio Villani opened up for him the doors to the Dominican friary. This was in 1922, the year in which he witnessed with horror in Rome the march of the Black Shirts and was infuriated whenever Catholics yielded to the dictatorship. That same year, celebrations were held for the seventh centenary of the death of Saint Dominic, and he decided to enter the Order. It was not a decision reached in euphoria, but rather one

[3] L. Frassati, *Mio fratello Pier Giorgio: La fede* (Rome: Edizioni Paoline, 1954), 339–40.

that matured over the course of four years, from his first contact with Dominican spirituality (1918) to his desire to become acquainted with it (1920) and then to his entrance.

His fresh, youthful, impetuous, energetic enthusiasm was not immature and certainly not superficial. "In him one can note the ability to reconcile and combine seemingly opposite traits. Indeed, being a Dominican also means being able to keep together such different elements of Christian life as contemplation and action, the life of intense prayer and the apostolate, serious, constant study and generous, cheerful availability."[4]

But what does it mean to enter into the Third Order of Saint Dominic? This decision is made in order to pursue one's own personal growth, to seek perfection, to change one's "clothing" in a sort of conversion; for this reason, the candidate changes his name, and Pier Giorgio became Brother Girolamo (Jerome), as he often signed his letters later on: it was a new life signaled by a new name. And the moment arrived for him to make a more radical choice: ideals follow one another when one lives by the Spirit. The closer he came to the finish line of his life, the more he elaborated his philosophy and spirituality. Thus he wrote on January 15, 1925, to his friend Isidoro Bonini:

Dear friend,

I should have waited for a letter from you before writing to you, but this is the Holy Year, and since the Vicar of Christ has opened the gates of justice, gates through which we all should fortify ourselves in grace so as to obtain our Eternal Reward, it would be an unworthy thing to bear a grudge. I offer you the olive branch, a symbol of that peace which I

---

[4] *Pier Giorgio Frassati Terziario Domenicano: ricordi, testimonianze e studi . . .* (Bologna: Edizioni Studio Domenicano, 1985), 25.

am insistently seeking. Ah, dear Isidoro, with every passing day I am more convinced that the world is ugly; how much misery there is! Unfortunately good people suffer while we who have been endowed by God with many graces have, alas, corresponded poorly with them. This is a terrible observation that torments my brain when I study. Every so often I ask myself: Will I continue to seek to follow the good life? Will I have the good fortune to persevere to the end? In this tremendous clash of doubts, the faith given to me in Baptism reminds me in a voice of assurance: "By yourself you will do nothing, but if you have God as your center, then every action you attempt will arrive at its goal." That is precisely what I would like to be able to do, taking as my motto Saint Augustine's remark: "Lord, our hearts are restless until they rest in Thee."

Unfortunately, one by one, worldly friendships produce sorrows in our heart through the departure of those whom we love, but I would like us to promise to abide by an agreement that knows no earthly confines or temporal limits: union in prayer. . . . When I come to the city where we spent so many beautiful, happy hours (which perhaps will not return) at a time when we were free from all worries and laughed thoughtlessly; alas, hours like that will not return again for me. I will always be happy externally . . . being Catholic means happy young people; but internally when I am alone I will give vent to my sadness. . . .

Pier Giorgio felt the arrival of adulthood weighing over him and suffered terribly to see the friends with whom he had studied and gone on excursions in the mountains dispersing, each one following his own path—not out of childish sentimentality, but out of an awareness of human existence, the "complications" of what would have to come afterward:

The struggle is difficult, but it is necessary to try to win and to rediscover our little road to Damascus so as to be able to walk along it toward the goal at which we must all arrive. A little more effort, and I too will have earned the much-desired diploma, but then there is a whole problem that is much more difficult, which is an altogether weighty responsibility. Will I be able to solve this serious problem? Will I have the strength to persevere? Certainly it is necessary to hold fast to the one faith, the anchor of salvation: without it what would our whole life be? Nothing! Or rather, it would be spent uselessly, because in this world there is only sorrow, and sorrow without faith is unbearable, whereas sorrow nourished by the little torch of faith becomes so beautiful because it strengthens the mind for its battles. Today in this battle I can only thank God that in his infinite mercy he willed to grant my heart this grief so that through these painful sorrows I might return to a more interior, more spiritual life. Until now I had lived too materially, and now I need to reinvigorate my spirit for the future struggles, so that from now on every day, every hour will be a new battle to fight and a new victory to win. (Letter to Isidoro Bonini, Turin, January 29, 1925)

As a man of action, he put into practice the motto of Saint Catherine of Siena: "Working always helps." In his studies, as in every other activity, including his charitable works, he invested himself entirely, just as he did in sports, as a member of the Alpine Club and of the Giovane montagna (a mountaineering association).

In the associations to which he belonged, Pier Giorgio gave; in religious life, as an affiliate of the Third Order of Saint Dominic, he received. In order to attain the perfection of Christian life, Pier Giorgio, together with many other young men, received the habit on May 28, 1922, in the

presbytery of the Church of Saint Dominic in Turin from
the hands of Father Arrighini. Present, among others, was
Father Martino Gilet, Master General of the Order, Father
Reginaldo Giuliani, Father Enrico Ibertis, and two friends of
Pier Giorgio, the brothers Filippo and Francesco Robotti.
Father Ibertis has left a testimony:

> For all of us it was a real surprise and genuine cause for
> astonishment to see him included in the gathering for the
> investiture ceremony. For anyone who was used to seeing
> him continually burst into his inimitable good humor, it
> was as though being unexpectedly plunged from daylight
> into the thick darkness of night: it was more than a sur-
> prise, it was a reversal that gave us a glimpse of a secret,
> very tenacious new character.[5]

Other Dominicans were quite impressed: the guy with
the pipe or the cigar in his mouth now resembled a mystic. Religious, friends, instructors, poor people, including
the domestic servants of his household (but not his family members) were fascinated by Pier Giorgio: in him they
saw that a Christian does not need to camouflage his own
spirituality, except as required during worship in church,
and that being outwardly religious does not mean speaking
in an unctuous voice or presenting oneself to others in a
hypocritical, bigoted way. His sanctity was vital, vigorous,
virile, without any sugarcoating and full of energy.

Father Mario Desiderio recalls: "I was struck by the
composure, seriousness, and devotion of a tall, robust, ele-
gantly dressed, handsome young man who took the name of
Brother Girolamo. I also remember that young man's happiness and joy, . . . the noise that he made in the sacristy with
his companions once the ceremonies were over: it seemed

[5] Ibid., 30.

like they were about to ruin the church and the sacristy and the friary."[6] The chambermaid in the Frassati household, Ester Pignata, testified: "His mother scolded him so much, maybe because she was very nervous. I remember, for example, that before entering the dining room the little master used to make the sign of the cross and say his prayers, while his mother kept calling to him: 'What are you doing, Pier Giorgio? Are you still not coming?' and he used to finish his prayer." He did not want anyone to see him, probably because they would have found fault with him or else simply because the others at table would not have understood.

Brother Girolamo was the convert absorbed in the marvelous pages of Saint Thomas Aquinas: "Every thought of the world will be dead, and I will live joyful days because they [those pages] alone give the heart that joy which has no end because it is not human, it is true joy."

His profession took place in the chapel of Our Lady of Grace, in Saint Dominic Church; this time Father Francesco Robotti was present. Pier Giorgio's face was streaked with tears.

Saint Thomas, Saint Augustine, Saint Bernard, Saint Paul, Saint Catherine of Siena, and Dante were his favorite authors. Brother Girolamo thought, prayed, and hoped like a brother.[7] He knew the Rule of the Third Order thoroughly, was diligent about attending the monthly meeting, and, besides the rosary, recited every day the Little Office of the Blessed Virgin, which he always carried in his pocket. But where did he find the time to pray? Some witnesses tell of having seen him praying intently even on the streetcar or while walking on the street.

[6] Ibid., 31.
[7] Ibid., 32.

He loved and admired Saint Thomas, the teacher of wisdom, who in the innocence of his heart had succeeded at contemplating the immensity of God. Despite his many commitments, he would have liked to study the Thomistic works in greater depth. He did not do so in time.

Although his family members considered him not that gifted intellectually, this young man, without realizing it, showed Catholics who were often lost and confused, because of their weak faith, the path marked out by the Fathers and Doctors of the Church to rediscover the unity of the Church, which is often threatened and undermined. From Christ in the Eucharist he drew energy and strength, and he urged the young men of Pollone with these words, which he pronounced on June 29, 1923, at the dedication of the banner of the circle of the Catholic Youth of Pollone:

> I exhort you with all the strength of my soul to approach the Eucharistic Table as often as possible; feed on this Bread of angels and from it draw the strength to fight the interior battles, the battles against your passions and against all adversities, because Jesus Christ promised, to those who feed on the Most Holy Eucharist, eternal life and the graces necessary to obtain it. And when you are totally consumed by this Eucharistic fire, then you will be able more conscientiously to thank God, who has called you to be in these ranks, and you will enjoy the peace that those who are happy according the world's standards have never experienced, because true happiness, O young men, consists, not in the pleasures of the world or in earthly things, but in peace of conscience, which we have only if we are pure of heart and mind.

Then, after fortifying the spirit, Pier Giorgio says, the Catholic layman turns to action in three forms of apostolate: "The first is the apostolate of example; the second is the apostolate of charity, and finally we have the apostolate of persuasion." His teachings are sure:

> In all things and by all means we must sacrifice our ambitions, our whole selves to the cause of the faith. In order for it to be Christian, our life must be a continual renunciation, a continual sacrifice, which, however, is not burdensome if only we think what these few years spent in sorrow are in comparison with eternal happiness, where there will be no measure or end to our joy, where we will enjoy a peace that is unimaginable. . . . The times that we are going through are difficult because the persecution against the Church is raging as cruelly as can be, but you good, bold young men are not frightened by this small obstacle; rather, you keep in mind that the Church is a divine institution that cannot end but will last until the end of the world, and "the gates of hell shall not prevail against it." Therefore, keep this white banner spotless, and if tomorrow the occasion presents itself, defend it, because from now on it is sacred; it represents not only your circle but also the finest heritage of our Italy and of the civic world.

Aware of the persecution of the Church, Pier Giorgio shouts his truth, sure that the gates of hell will not prevail over the spouse of Christ; here are the concluding words of his speech: "Allow me to shout with you: 'Long live Jesus, long live the pope!'"

Several times he went to the friary of San Domenico di Chieri to pray in front of a relic that was very dear to him: the cincture of Saint Thomas Aquinas, which is preserved in the church itself. There, in silence and peace, he relived the events that had occurred in the saint's life and, perhaps, identified with them: Saint Thomas, as a young man from a noble, well-to-do family, decided to abandon luxuries, riches, the secure career desired by his parents, and any ambitions to power in order to embrace the Gospel and follow the Savior. Unable to make him change his mind, his brothers resorted to force and trickery: they brought into his room a beautiful woman to seduce him and dissuade him from his religious vocation. Thomas drove the woman back with a burning firebrand and then traced a cross on the ground with it. That night two angels girded his loins with a fiery cord. In front of the relic, Pier Giorgio, who was also from a rich and powerful family, with a father and a mother who wanted their son to have a splendid future, heard his call to be a layman in the midst of the people of God.

Pier Giorgio was a staunch, faithful tertiary, and therefore he did not forget that, in order truly to be one, it is necessary "to work, to win, and to save many souls in Christ's name". Either he spoke with God or he spoke about God. That was Brother Girolamo, just like Saint Dominic of Guzmán. Following his example, many of his friends became tertiaries; in some cases they, too, took the name Brother "Jerome".

From Pollone on August 31, 1923, he wrote to Antonio Villani:

> Dearest friend . . .
>
> I am very glad that you want to join the great family of Saint Dominic, where, as Dante says, "ben s'impingua se non si vaneggia" (one is well fattened if one does not go astray). The obligations are minimal; otherwise, you would certainly understand that I could not belong to an Order that made many demands.
>
> When the saint instituted the Third Order, he designed it as a militia to fight against the heretics, and then they had very severe rules; it almost followed the ancient Rule of the First Order; but now it has been revised, and not a trace remains of the severe obligations. It would be necessary to recite daily the Dominican Office of Our Lady or else the rosary, but without committing a mortal sin

if you deliberately failed to recite it one day or for a few days.

I hope that you can be invested in the magnificent church in Turin, and then I will be near you to give you the fraternal embrace; since you are already bound to me by the ties of brotherhood through the Blood of O.L.J.C., you will be so doubly by having Saint Dominic in common with me as a father. I would be pleased if you took the name Brother Girolamo, not because it is the name that I have as a son of Saint Dominic, but because it reminds me of someone who is dear to me and certainly to you also, who like me has the same feelings against corrupt customs, the figure of Girolamo Savonarola, whose name I bear very unworthily. As a fervent admirer of that friar who died a saintly death on the gallows, in becoming a Tertiary I decided to take him as my model, but unfortunately I am very far from imitating him. . . .

He drank deeply of the *Dialogue* [*A Treatise of Divine Providence*] and of the *Letters* and the *Life* of Saint Catherine; these readings accompanied him in the days immediately before his death: on his nightstand, besides the Little Office of Our Lady, they found, open, Jørgensen's volume on the life of the Dominican saint and a volume about Catherine of Siena. Pier Giorgio gave it to Luciana, on the day he took his degree, "that it might be for you in the ascetical life a guide to spiritual perfection".

He adopted the motto of the Dominican Third Order, "Contemplata aliis tradere" (Hand on to others the things that you have contemplated), but why did he choose the name Brother Girolamo? The figure of Savonarola fascinated him. The Friar from Ferrara attracted him by the courage, ardor, and determination with which he berated the immorality of the social classes of his time. Surprised by his egalitarianism and the fact that he was burned at the stake for the spiritual welfare of the citizens of Florence, it seemed to him that the fiery preacher should be better known and imitated.

He was excited by Savonarola's fight for the purity of the faith against mediocrity, injustice, hypocrisy, and superficiality. He admired the way in which the intrepid preacher had defended his own ideals and the intensity with which he had combated the tyranny of the Medici family. He attentively read *De ruina mundi, Gloria al Re*, the work dedicated to Christ the Redeemer, and the commentary on the penitential psalm *Miserere*, savoring the feelings of profound humility and repentant humanity expressed by the Dominican friar.

"[Pier Giorgio] was logical and needed certainty, and Savonarola, a bold reformer whose sermons reawakened souls and left their mark on his times, gave him the conviction that the ideas for which he was spending his own youth were just and sound."[8] In him he saw not only the moral reformer and the Christian Democrat, but also his personal model of sanctity; he represented the militant friar, with no illusions or hypocrisy, fearless, not diplomatic, uncompromising, and consistent even to death.

The troublesome Savonarola, about whom the Church began to speak only during the pontificate of Leo XIII ("Savonarola is ours"),[9] is a Servant of God today, and in 1997

[8] Ibid., 35.

[9] Saint Pius X declared: "If only there were many Savonarolas", while Pius XI said: "His hour, too, will come." But the pope who said the most about him was Pius XII, who described him as "an ascetic and an apostle": "Savonarola shows us the strong conscience of an ascetic and an apostle who has a lively sense of things divine and eternal, who takes a stand against rampant paganism, who remains faithful to the evangelical and Pauline ideal of integral Christianity, put into action in public life as well and animating all institutions. This is why he started preaching, prompted by an interior voice and inspired by God."

the archbishop of Florence, Silvano Cardinal Piovanelli, introduced the cause for his beatification, for which the diocesan process has already been concluded.

Many people sought to dissuade him from taking that name: the tradition was to choose one from among the saints and blesseds of the Order, and Savonarola was neither a saint nor a blessed. Not yet for the Church, at least, but Pier Giorgio was sure of it, and when someone greeted him with his religious name, Pier Giorgio smiled and replied: "May I be able to imitate his fight and his virtue."

So many organizations but one faith, and precisely for this reason he managed not to scatter his efforts: he always had the truth in front of him; he referred to it alone, and in order to attain it, he used the lay and religious instruments that he had at his disposal. Pier Giorgio's final spiritual commitment was unique: his entrance into the Dominican Third Order.

He was looking for a fraternal organization, governed by a precise Rule but by rules that were not too rigid: with his free spirit, which was the enemy of routine and uniformity, he would not have succeeded in subjecting himself to regulations that were too pedantic or repetitive.

It is said that Saint Dominic was "hard as a diamond but tender as a mother". Pier Giorgio was like that. As he gradually matured, one could see in him a Christian entirely mobilized for Christ, a fearless, completely unrestrained conqueror who was ready to proclaim the Word everywhere and to bring the Good News.

In his prayers, nocturnal vigils, and hours of Eucharistic adoration, he nourished his faith and his immense charity. We could not understand the apostolic quality of Pier Giorgio's life without considering his prayer. Dominican Father Filippo Robotti recalls:

I met Frassati for the first time in the offices of the Cesare Balbo circle, where I went every so often for conferences or to stay with the students. He attended functions there regularly, and so I met him quite a few times.

He was usually not very outgoing, but when there was talk about the circle and its development, not only his eyes but also his speech, which was usually sober and rather cold, became animated and caught fire, as it were, as though he were speaking about his most passionate interest. He was not one of those who were content with the exterior life, participating only in public demonstrations, but he enthusiastically participated also in the cultural meetings and never missed the religious practices; not only those announced by the members of FUCI, but, insofar as his studies permitted, also those announced by various Catholic associations, particularly the youth groups, in which he was intensely interested. Every time a Catholic gathering of some importance was held to which young people were invited, you could be almost certain of seeing there his manly, tanned figure, which distinguished itself from the others, not because of his liveliness or loquacity, but because of the seriousness with which he followed the talks by the speakers or the animated discussions.

The beaming, jovial lad joked and laughed on excursions in the mountains or when he was with his friends, but when studying, praying, or at social or political meetings, he was serious, extremely serious. Father Robotti continues:

Sometimes Pier Giorgio came to see me at the Friary of San Domenico; it was on one of those occasions that I spoke to him about the Dominican Third Order, but without inviting him to join. He told me that he had thought about it, and then I gave him a copy of the Rule. He pondered his decision for more than a year, which proves that he took such things very seriously.

Everyone can imagine the joy I experienced when such a beautiful soul chose to enter the Dominican Third Order.

It was a decision that sprang up spontaneously in his heart when he realized that the ideal of the religious apostolate that burned ardently in his heart was in harmony with the purposes of our Third Order.

I had grown extremely fond of him, and therefore it was very painful for me when my superiors ordered me to leave Turin to perform my humble ministry in other fields. In his candid, youthful naïveté, he feared that Catholic Action would suffer badly because of my absence, just because I had been intensely involved in it. But when I explained to him that, in this world, we could all be useful but no one was necessary and that God arranged everything for the better in human matters, even when they appear to run contrary to our plans, he calmed down and was immediately resigned to it. This was because, even though he had an enthusiastic character, he was very gentle toward those whom he considered to be his superiors in any way.

After my departure from Turin, I saw him now and then at a religious or youth meeting; for instance, during the Catholic Youth Congress in Rome in September 1921; then at the Dominican Conference in April 1922 in Turin; afterward at the National Eucharistic Congress in Genoa in 1923, and finally at the Young Convention in Novara that same year. However, before leaving for America in January 1924, I wanted to say goodbye to him; nor would I ever have imagined, seeing him so young and jovial, that I would never see him again here below.

On that occasion, knowing that because of the fluid political situation a bit of a crisis was lurking and that one could observe some disbanding in our Catholic organizations, I took the liberty of asking him whether he would always be faithful to them at any cost. Without hesitation he replied with his tone of manly determination: "Father, only death will be able to make me stop working for a cause that is now so much identified with my spirit!"[10]

Only death stopped him.

[10] *Pier Giorgio Frassati Terziario Domenicano*, 100–103.

8

HIS HYMN TO CHARITY

Tending to and helping the poor was for Pier Giorgio the number-one priority of his hyperactive days. To serve Christ in man was the purpose of his life.

"Fracassati",[1] as his friends sometimes called him because of the vehemence with which he displayed his irrepressible personality to others, made no sound in his loving aid to the poor. "True good", he used to say, "should be done unnoticeably, little by little, daily, confidentially", and his left hand never knew what his right hand was doing.

His desire to immerse himself totally in charity found good soil in Turin. The city now had more than five hundred thousand inhabitants, and the automobile industry, with Fiat in the lead, had become somewhat stronger, along with the small and mid-sized businesses and the shops of artisans and merchants. The capital of the Piedmont region appeared as a discontinuous urban environment; it had grown up with pronounced separations between the small towns that it absorbed, and, given the industrial development that had concentrated in the city the workmen coming from the countryside, the perennial problem of the housing short- age remained. The workers' mutual aid societies had the

---

[1] A play on his last name and fracasso, meaning "racket" or "uproar". —TRANS.

highest numbers enrolled in Borgo San Paolo, Borgo Vittoria, Barriera Milano, Barriera Nizza, and Valdocco—all places that witnessed the industrious charitable activities of Pier Giorgio.

Let us listen to an account by one of his companions, Ettore Moccia:

> Since the days when he attended the D'Azeglio [his secondary school], Pier Giorgio knew where the true poverty was hidden and especially the poor old people who lived in attics, as was the custom then. Those dwellings beneath the roofs, alas, were rather cold, and those poor creatures suffered. Under his guidance, we supplied ourselves with burlap sacks that we filled with wood and coal. We hauled it all on a wheelbarrow that had been parked in a dark corner of the courtyard of a house on via San Secondo.
>
> One day I asked Pier Giorgio who was the owner of the wheelbarrow and why he had allowed him to use it. His answer was: "I don't know; a lady who had seen me with a sack on my shoulder pointed out this means of transport, and so I use it."
>
> At the time I did not dwell on the fact, also because it seemed such a natural thing. Today, though, I realize that the presence of that vehicle in that courtyard was not fortuitous.

Pier Giorgio was a young man of few words but many deeds. The school on via Melchiorre Gioia adjacent to the D'Azeglio was temporarily housing several Venetian children who had been sent away from their homes because of the war. And so Pier Giorgio, during recreation periods in the courtyard, never failed to approach the little refugees, distributing to them the small change he had in his pocket.

Pier Giorgio created a veritable network of volunteer

workers, not only among his friends but also among the doorkeepers of many apartment blocks, who pointed out to him the needy households and delivered the packages of provisions when the recipients were absent. He also involved motorists and taxi drivers in this charitable activity. He used to ask the servants in his house whether they had clothing to donate, but "good items, because you should not give them rags", and he brought the clothing to female friends in the FUCI to mend so as to deliver them in good condition to the poor.

Through the Saint Vincent de Paul conferences, Pier Giorgio met the abandoned, orphans, the unemployed, elderly people who lived alone, the homeless, the sick: inconvenient human beings who had been forgotten and hidden away. Specifically through the Saint Vincent de Paul Society, he laid the foundations for a much broader mission that also included his serious political activity, which was aimed, not at allotting power, of course, but rather at building up the kingdom of God among his peers.

But where did Pier Giorgio get the money to help the recipients of his charity? His father, like any other head of a middle-class household at that time, did not fill Pier Giorgio's pockets with money (as parents often do today for their children), but what the young man had he did not spend (his excursions in the mountains cost little: train ticket, bag lunch, and he was on his way) but, rather, saved it for the poor. No theater, no restaurant, no cinema, no pretenses of elegance; he had other pastimes, first and foremost the company of his friends and mountain climbing. Occasionally he even borrowed money from friends for emergencies.

Saint Paul's hymn to charity (1 Cor 13:1–13) was for him the flash of inspiration that opened up his spirit to eternal horizons. He was so enthusiastic about this discovery that he read the epistle aloud to a friend on a streetcar.

Pier Giorgio often repeated: "What would the faith be if we did not clothe it in charity?" and one day he said to the chambermaid Ester Pignata: "Someday when I am old and can give orders, I will do as Cottolengo did. I will try to help all the poor people and the children who are in need."

Senator Frassati remarked to Don Antonio Cojazzi: "If I had come home one day and told him, 'Giorgetto, we have become very poor; take a suitcase and we will go live in an attic', I am quite sure he would neither have rolled his eyes nor asked for an explanation; he would have said in his usual tone, which was manly and at the same time sweet: 'Ready! Let's go, Papa!' "[2]

His spirit of poverty was indisputable. Goods, money, and lands did not interest him except as part of a conversation about a charitable project. Sometimes his father would describe the beauty of a farm that he had bought for his son, the work that had been done and the improvements made. But Pier Giorgio was distracted and bored. He, who used to thank people for trifles he had received, scarcely said "Thanks, Papa", after being prompted by signals from his mother and sister.

His friends and the poor knew about the many acts of charity that he performed in silence, but not his family. No one would have understood. One day the German governess Frieda Villa learned that Senator Frassati's son, as a member of the Saint Vincent de Paul conference, constantly visited

[2] A. Cojazzi, *Pier Giorgio Frassati: Testimonianze* (Turin: SEI, 1928), 181.

poor families in the slums where vice and violence were also lodged; in amazement she asked the leader of these expeditions his reason for planning them. She heard him reply that "Jesus pays me a visit in Communion every morning, and I repay him in the miserable way I can: by visiting his poor."[3]

Charity, therefore, that was understood not merely as volunteer work, but as a meaningful, deliberate practice rooted in his astonishing faith. This was the self-taught man of God who, filled with grace and aspiring to be poor in spirit according to the beatitude, expressed his thanks by helping his neighbor. Since he loved Christ intensely, with all his strength, he loved the least and weakest of his children; whenever he entered their miserable dwellings and attics he would uncover his head in a very humble act of respect.

His days were an eloquent practical treatise on charity, poured out in his love for his neighbor, for the unfortunates who did not know God, for those afflicted by any sort of poverty, physical or moral.

He considered the poor his superiors and served them, going so far as to carry cumbersome burdens for them, with the demeanor of someone convinced that he is enjoying a privilege; in their sufferings he honored the Passion of the Savior. "Around the invalid, the miserable wretch, around the unfortunate I see a light that we do not have. . . ." For him, visiting the sick and the poor was like visiting Jesus Christ. And heedless of the consequences, between 1918 and 1919 he went to care for them and perform the humblest services, even those related to hygiene, among people afflicted by the epidemic of Spanish influenza.

---

[3] L. Frassati, *Mio fratello Pier Giorgio: La Carità* (Turin: SEI, 1957), 5.

The son of one needy mother could not go to the Salesian oratory because his mother did not dare to send him barefoot. As soon as Pier Giorgio heard the story, he provided shoes for the boy so as to grant his wish.

The biography by Don Cojazzi relates a very significant episode. A few days before his death he was at a concert.[4] Two female friends[5] stole his wallet to play a joke on him. They emptied it and among other things found two tickets from a pawnshop; the girls exclaimed, "Our fine friend pawns his mother's gold jewelry, and then who knows what he does with the money!" In reality, they were pawn tickets that he himself was about to redeem. He greatly admired the women affiliated with the Saint Vincent de Paul Society (Laura Hidalgo, too, was one of the ladies) for their humble charitable activity: cleaning, making beds, dressing the little ones, preparing food for the sick . . .

On a weekday, a little before noon, the maid at the Frassati house, Matilde Eiche, heard the doorbell and went to open the door: it was a poor man. Before he said a word, the maid ran to the kitchen to bring him something to eat; but when she returned, he said: "Thank you, Signorina, but I did not come to beg for a piece of bread. I would like to speak with Signor Frassati about getting a job."

At first, Matilde Eiche did not know what to say; then, hesitantly, she had him step into the vestibule. Pier Giorgio returned home from school just at that moment and immediately asked about the presence of the stranger in the house: "He wants to talk to your father; he is out of work", the

---

[4] Cojazzi adds that it was a "benefit" concert, but in her copy Laura Hidalgo crosses out that detail.

[5] "They were ladies", Laura notes in the margin in pencil, in other words, ladies of the Saint Vincent de Paul Society.

maid explained to him. Very promptly, Alfredo Frassati arrived for the midday meal and rang the doorbell in his customary way. The senator was furious with the unexpected guest, opened the door again, and drily, forcefully, told the man to leave, pointing out to him that he ought to have appeared at *La Stampa* and not at his house. Seeing that Pier Giorgio was very sad about the incident and moved by his words: "Maybe Jesus came by, and we chased him away", he gave him a lira to give to the poor man. Pier Giorgio rushed out to catch up to him; then, at table, his father assured him that he intended to inquire about the man and would find him a job.

At the end of every month, Pier Giorgio arrived at the lowly residence of the Sisters of the Immaculata, asking for Sister Ida Bertolazzi. While standing in the hallway, without even going into the parlor, he would pay the room and board for the little girls who were sheltered in the sisters' house. It was enough for him to know the total, without information about the particular expenses; but he did not forget to say: "Mother Superior, take in as many of them as you can, do not leave them on the street exposed to dangers!" Moreover, he did not allow his name to appear; he would say only: "I am a brother in the Saint Vincent de Paul conference."

Once he asked a beggar why he did not work instead of asking for alms; he learned that the man no longer had utensils with which to cook and sell chestnuts. He obtained them for him, thus giving him the opportunity to work again. For another man he acquired all the equipment needed to be a tinsmith; in short, nothing went unnoticed as he worked eagerly in his intense mission of charity. A seamstress in Vercelli had been forced to sell her sewing machine in order to be treated for a serious illness. She was cured but desperate, until a new machine arrived. Pier Giorgio, as usual, had provided it.

One day in 1923 he was walking with his dear friend Marco Beltramo: in front of the Rossini Theater, they met a drunk who struck Pier Giorgio. Being hot-tempered and agile, Beltramo punched him twice and threw him down on the ground. Pier Giorgio bluntly scolded Marco and decided to carry the drunk to a pharmacy to revive him with a cordial. He did not forget to take his name and address.

Charity, the *Catechism of the Catholic Church* explains, is the theological virtue by which we love God above all things for his own sake and our neighbor as ourselves for love of God. Jesus himself makes charity the new commandment, the fruit of the Spirit. Charity, we read, is "over all these [virtues]", and the practice of all the virtues is animated and inspired by charity, "which binds everything together in perfect harmony" (Col 3:14), which guarantees and purifies the human ability to love, elevating it to the supernatural perfection of divine love. Blessed Pier Giorgio experienced all this, embodying principles that he did not discuss theoretically but systematically put into action. It seems to us that there is a perfect parallel between his activity, which was always "in haste", and the teaching of Saint Augustine: "The perfection of all our works is love. Here is our end; this is why we run, toward this goal we run; when we arrive, we will find rest."[6]

Most of the confreres of the Saint Vincent de Paul conference at the Social Institute named after Saint Giuseppe Cottolengo limited themselves to offering material assistance only to needy families: donations of clothing, food, money

---

[6] Saint Augustine, *In Epistulam Johannis ad Parthos tractatus*, 10, 4.

. . . but that was not enough for Pier Giorgio; he wanted a warm, human, evangelical relationship with the poor people. Charity was love, not public assistance agreed on at a council meeting. "I would abolish some conferences of the Saint Vincent de Paul Society", he wrote to his friend Carlo Bellingeri on December 14, 1922: "When they are made up of men from another era that was so full of Christian zeal, who are not even capable of warning parents about the presumed conduct of their daughters and of trying to do a good deed, but instead prefer to abandon the family, it is better for the conference not to exist; not because the persons are acting in bad faith, but because it is not adapted to modern times." Uncompromising and straightforward, he did not tolerate well-wishers who then, when confronted with real needs, turned their backs. At a meeting of his conference, he proposed to those in attendance the Zanatta family, in which he was particularly interested because of the serious situation they were in. But the proposal was abruptly voted down because one of the four daughters, who lived in Rome, was notorious for her immoral conduct. This was a revolting decision for a just man like Pier Giorgio, who considered the decision unfounded: precisely for that reason the family needed help more. Despite the obstacles, with his intervention the Zanatta family was put on sounder financial and moral footing, thus regaining their peace of mind. For that reason he decided to quit that group and to join, on January 23, 1923, the university conference (of which he also became secretary) of the Cesare Balbo circle of the Saint Vincent de Paul Society that operated from the parish of Our Lady of Peace.

Pier Giorgio always thought for himself and did not conform mindlessly to the groups he joined, and so by leaving the Saint Vincent de Paul conference he demonstrated that it did not correspond to the demands of Christian justice; in the new conference, he argued against the principle of not giving poor people money beyond the amount determined at the council meetings. Therefore he did not observe that regulation, and when he considered it appropriate, he left in the attics and hovels that he visited an additional envelope of money—his own, of course.

This was not mere philanthropy; this was solidarity across the board, full understanding and full consideration for those who were less fortunate. He directed many jobless men to his father, who duly found them employment.

Some witnesses happened to see him return home wearing slippers, which he had kindly and selflessly exchanged for his own shoes. No one in his family noticed it, not even his mother; who knows what she would have said about her "dear blockhead" (*buon stupidone*) and "real madman", as she used to call him.

In an article published in *L'Osservatore Romano* (May 20, 1990), Giovanni Cardinal Saldarini, already archbishop of Turin then, explained very well the charity of the Blessed:

> Pier Giorgio chose the poor, but he did not reject or condemn his rich family, nor was he ever harsh or rude to them. He did not visit the poor as a reaction to the liberal culture of his environment or for merely sociological reasons, but out of his passion for evangelical charity, which among other things prompted him to change his Saint Vincent de Paul Society conference so as to go to one where charity was not reduced to mere administrative calculation. Above all, in going to the poor, he did not remain outside of their poverty: rich at home but personally poor, he was not ashamed to become a beggar for the sake of his beggars. Love for the poor and for poverty, as well as sobriety,

temperance, and the use of goods without wasting them, are things that go together, and the one kind of love is never found without the other.

Ida Marconi is a living eyewitness of Pier Giorgio's charity: "My father died of tetanus a week after contracting a terrible infection at his workplace. My mother therefore had to go to work in order to earn money and support us, and she began to wash the clothes and clean the houses of well-to-do people."[7] Ida was three years old when the assistant pastor of Mary, Queen of Peace parish, Father Solero, sent Pier Giorgio to that needy family. "Even though I was very little, I have a very vivid memory of that kind, happy young man who for almost three years looked after us." The Blessed went to take the little girl to kindergarten and encouraged her to play and sing. Every Friday her "big brother" brought her the *Corrierino* [a children's publication] and on other days never forgot to bring her little gifts that were always very welcome. Coal and wood arrived punctually. Pier Giorgio even donated the First Communion dress for the little girl and the Confirmation suit for her brother.

When Pier Giorgio died, Ida went with her mother to the funeral. On Christmas Day of 1925, a package arrived at the Marconi house with a note: "Pier Giorgio Frassati continues his work." They found in it food items and clothing. For many more years, the parents and friends of Pier Giorgio provided assistance for this and other needy families who had had a friend and a brother in Pier Giorgio.

He had a habit of involving other young men in his expeditions and often made an appointment to meet with his

---

[7] P. Nicolussi, "Quel giovane buono e allegro", *La Voce del Popolo*, June 24, 1990.

friends beneath the bell tower of the Shrine of Our Lady of Consolation so as to begin the work of Sister Charity in that way.

The Salesian priest Don Pierino Scotti tells the story: "I remember one evening when he, along with other companions, left from the Cesare Balbo circle with a wheelbarrow to go transport the furniture of a poor family. Several companions marveled at him. He went through the streets in the center of the city acting like a porter."[8]

Pier Giorgio's reputation as porter for the evicted spread, and so his friends invented a title for his business: FIT, meaning *Frassati impresa trasporti* (Frassati Moving Company). Often in the morning, before going to lectures at the Polytechnic, he had already performed his service with FIT. People saw that handsome young man dressed in a dignified way, with his hair well combed and his tie adjusted, and said: "But that is the son of the famous Senator Frassati!" The remark could have several possible meanings: admiration, disappointment, scandal, scorn, and derision.

Aid to the poor came before any other duty, even his studies. An administrative assistant at the Polytechnic, Teresa Bertino Albenga, gives us invaluable testimony in this regard: "I was strict with the university students and granted extensions for their written assignments only for serious reasons. The reason that Pier Giorgio gave me to obtain one was that he urgently had to move one of the many evicted families that he cared for by providing a cart and a new residence. I could not refuse his request."[9]

It often happened that Pier Giorgio asked to borrow money from his friends, either to take the streetcar—since

[8] M. Codi, *Pier Giorgio Frassati: Una valanga di vita* (Casale Monferrato [AL]: Portalupi, 2001), 211.

[9] Ibid., 212.

he was left without any small change in his pocket because he had given it away to some poor person—or to telephone so as to ask them to donate to some unfortunate persons such-and-such a sum when he was prevented from going to see them directly.

He knew an eleven-year-old boy named Alessio who was crippled in one leg. He was an errand boy and pedaled his bicycle with his one sound leg in order to provide for himself, his mother, and his little brother. Pier Giorgio went with him to meet them—it was time for the midday meal—but on their table he saw nothing, and there was no fire in the stove. He bought them some food and ordered a quintal of wood from the charcoal dealer. From then on, that family appeared in his papers, the diary of his charity. Only after Pier Giorgio's death did the mother of the two boys learn that their young benefactor was the son of Alfredo Frassati, and she happened to discover this when she saw his photograph in a newspaper: he was the one who had redeemed two gold earrings for her from the pawnshop, bringing them to her in a little box, and who had given her younger child a new suit for his First Communion and the traditional medal on a ribbon for his Confirmation.

When entering into the households of the poor, Pier Giorgio was very courteous: he used to remove his hat and shake hands respectfully with the people. He immediately took an interest in the state of their health and their problems, and then he spoke about faith and hope and God.

He was detached from wealth and indifferent to its claims. His father, when questioned about his son's sanctity for the informative process, had to admit: "As for his detachment from everything that could be considered wealth, I can declare that it was complete and that he had nothing to do with it at all."

He was concerned also about schooling, and several times he enrolled little boys in private institutes; but he also paid great attention to the sick. He used to say:

Someone who tends the sick is almost always blessed, since it is difficult to endure the illnesses of others, with their thousand needs and the thousand annoyances that they bring with them. We ought to be mindful of them; we ought to do our duty toward persons like these who cannot get medicine or doctors for themselves. We should recall at every moment that there are in the world beings more unfortunate than we, with sufferings and sorrows greater than ours, who have no joy, no smiles at all, and toward whom we have very serious obligations and duties.

With his sick people he behaved like a nurse and sometimes like a physician. He periodically visited the San Lazzaro Leprosarium and the Cottolengo Hospital for the Incurable. He walked through the wards with vigilant, reliable charity. He would console and patients who, when they recognized him, were happy to see him. He used to bring them sweets, money, and clothing. He fed children who were deaf, blind, or mute and approached them with the utmost care, radiating love in every gesture of humility. And he used to travel in third class—"because there is no fourth", he said —and the money that he saved went into the pockets of the poor, like a thousand other little savings. Pier Giorgio used the five thousand lire given to him by his father for his twenty-fourth birthday to start a conference of the Saint Vincent de Paul Society at his parish, La Crocetta. He also accumulated debts for the sake of his poor people, as his sister assures us: "Considering our education and our manner of living, Pier Giorgio, acting as he did, showed a rare courage: he went against a principle considered as sacred, the danger of debt which in our father's moral reckoning smacked, if not of dishonesty, at least of the height of irresponsibility. And then, what about family dignity?"[10]

To commemorate the fiftieth anniversary of Pier Giorgio's birth, Giuseppe Lazzati wrote as follows:

> People, starting with his family, would look with bewilderment at that young man who seemed to have everything it takes to be a champion of worldliness . . . dragging through the streets of Turin carts filled with the furniture of poor people in search of housing, sweaty, walking beneath the burden of large, ill-made bundles, entering the most squalid households, where misery and vice often went hand in hand, beneath the hypocritically scandalized gaze of a world that does nothing to help them to escape from their lot, with surprising humility . . . , begging for his poor people, and by them reduced to pennilessness, so that he would return home late because he did not even have the few cents that he needed for the streetcar.

He knew very well that charity was first of all a matter of social justice, and therefore he gave joyfully, but even more than that he wanted to enable the poor to work so as to make them independent.

His charity resulted from the practice of his religion. He acted on concrete situations, for the material needs of persons and families, but also on souls, as it happened for many people. Italia Nebbia, owner of a tobacco shop on the corso Vercelli, who several times witnessed Pier Giorgio and his friend distributing packages to the poor, gives this testimony:

> I became curious and started to watch, and I noticed that one of those young men, when he climbed down off the

[10] L. Frassati, *A Man of the Beatitudes: Pier Giorgio Frassati*, trans. Dinah Livingstone, adapted and ed. Patricia O'Rourke (San Francisco: Ignatius Press, 2000), 93–94.

open cart, took with him two packages under his arms and two in his hands and carried them somewhere. Every so often he returned, loaded himself with other packages, and disappeared. When he returned with one package, he came into my shop and asked me to make the delivery to the absent family. He told me that he would have preferred to deliver it himself so as to encourage them and try to give them hope that something would change, suggesting that meanwhile they should offer their suffering to God and go to Mass. I explained to him that I could not invite others to go to Mass because I myself did not attend and never thought about God. We spoke about these things. He convinced me by telling me that if I did not go to Mass for myself, I at least had to go for my baby's sake.

The next Sunday I went to Mass and was struck by the explanation of the Gospel. I, too, started to say good things to the families to whom I brought the packages. I learned from my husband that that young man was the son of the publisher of *La Stampa* and that in Pollone the poor people for whom he did so much good used to look forward to his visits.[11]

Even in his own family he worked diligently in the apostolate, without preaching but by his example. "He was the first to do what he taught others", and therefore he did not say, "You need to do this", but rather, "We need to do this."[12] Then, when it was a question of winning back a soul, he deployed all his powers of persuasion, as was the case with his Uncle Pietro, the engineer,[13] who had always

[11] L. Frassati, *Mio fratello Pier Giorgio*, 16–18.

[12] See Cojazzi, *Pier Giorgio Frassati*, 240.

[13] Pietro Frassati left as a bequest to his niece Luciana and his nephew Pier Giorgio the considerable sum of a million lire. It appears that Alfredo did not consult his children but decided to give the money to charities, making use in particular of the column "Saturday charity" in *La Stampa*. They say that Pier Giorgio commented: "Papa gave me nothing for my conference and for my

been indifferent to the faith. In August 1923 the engineer, with whom Pier Giorgio had started a dialogue that was short on words but full of affection, was at the point of death but conscious. His nephew convinced him to take part in all the religious rites, and when he succeeded in having him receive Holy Communion, Pier Giorgio could not restrain his emotion and wept:

> God, certainly in his infinite mercy, was not mindful of my countless sins, but heard my prayers and those of my family and gave my uncle the great grace of having him receive the last rites while fully conscious; . . . this life should be a continual preparation for the next, because we never know the day and the hour of our departure.[14]

Pietro Frassati's position, which was temporarily held by Colli, was improbably intended for Pier Giorgio. A document dated May 18, 1925, and addressed to Giovanni Agnelli and Riccardo Gualino, reports that his father intended to appoint as his successor in managing the firm A. Frassati e Compagnia, which was less and less his own because of the Fascist regime, "my son Pier Giorgio Frassati, in my absence from Turin or in the case of my death".

---

circle" (cf. C. Casalegno, *Una vita di carità: Pier Giorgio Frassati* [Casale Monferrato: Piemme, 1990], 115). Furthermore, with that money the senator endowed the Società interna di mutuo soccorso [Domestic mutual aid society], founded in 1904, and renamed it Cassa mutua pensioni comm. Ingegnere Pietro Frassati [P. F. memorial mutual pension fund] and also endowed the school and the orphanage in Pollone in memory of his brother and sister (cf. L. Frassati, *Un uomo, un giornale: Alfredo Frassati*, vol. 3 [Rome: Edizioni di Storia e Letteratura, 1978], 187). Giolitti greatly appreciated his friend's gesture: "I have faith in the immortality of the soul and in the continuity of the relations of the deceased with the living, and I am certain that your generosity was the greatest joy that your brother could have."

[14] Letter to a friend from the Cesare Balbo circle dated August 20, 1923.

9

POLITICO-SOCIAL COMMITMENT

Political involvement was something self-evident for Pier Giorgio. But his real commitment was more social than political, strictly speaking. Exerting pressure on the centers of power was necessary in order to improve the social, workplace, and economic conditions of the poor. For him, politics was part of an evangelical plan of charity and humanitarian activity.

Opposed to war but not to the battle of ideas, intelligent, open-minded, determined to act directly for the sake of the people and in particular for the weakest, Pier Giorgio found himself many times on a public square side by side with those who were extolling liberty, justice, the cross of Christ, and the ransom of the poor. Turning to the other young men, he said: "The times that we live in are difficult because persecution against the Church is raging more cruelly than ever, but you bold, good young men are not afraid of that: keep in mind that the Church is a divine institution that cannot end but will last until the end of the world, and the gates of hell will not prevail against her."

Since he was opposed to Fascism, Marxism, and positivist liberalism, there was no other choice left for the Blessed but to choose the path taken by Don Luigi Sturzo. Proud to be an Italian, he was against the restoration of a Papal State: in his opinion, spiritual authority should not be mixed with temporal power. As he saw it, the urgent need was outreach to the disappointed masses, not only to fight against political adversaries, but also to try to heal the situation. For the furious populace that waved the red flag and advanced with clenched fists, he wanted to present specific social reforms so that there would be no oppression and no outrages in the factories.

The biographer Staglieno explains:

The opposition of Catholicism against liberalism, Catholicism against Marxism, appears in him in a richly nuanced form. His father's liberal values . . . (his sense of loyalty and honor, his spirit of sacrifice, dedication to work, and charitable impulse) and the "bourgeois" idea of ordered social stability, the legacy of the Giolitti "decade", prompted him also to consider the nascent industrial *Lumpenproletariat*— which in Turin, too, was taking shape as a political "class" —from the now uncommon charitable perspective shared by the old liberal "notables" and the most conservative part of the Church. Namely, in terms of Manzoni's "world of the humble", a collective of "poor people" and not of "proletarians".[1]

In order to do something about the social question, in Pier Giorgio's opinion, it was no longer enough to employ *caritas*; *justitia* was necessary, the justice pursued both by socialism and by Catholic social teaching. Some were fighting against Marxist labor unions without giving much consideration to the emergence of "national syndicalism", as understood by Benito Mussolini, which would have far-reaching consequences.

[1] M. Staglieno, *Un santo borghese: Pier Giorgio Frassati* (Milan: Bompiani, 1988), 102.

Having emerged prostrate from her experiences in the war and weakened at the parliamentary and governmental levels, Italy welcomed the return of Giovanni Giolitti to the political scene. The liberal from the Piedmont region committed himself to a drastic plan of economic reform in order to counteract the recession in progress, allowing the price of bread to float freely so as to reduce the domestic deficit. But the crisis in institutional politics was obvious: the central lines of the debate had shifted to the party secretariats, the labor union movements, and the protests in the streets.

The judgment of Indro Montanelli has always been rather positive with regard to the Italian statesman:

> With his disconsolate "rational pessimism", Giolitti never undertook projects that were beyond his means and those of the State. This is one of the two reasons why I admire him. The other is that this great "notable"—which he was by wealth, class, and tradition—instead of strengthening or at least perpetuating the prerogatives and privileges of his caste by continuing to exclude the masses of the people from civil rights (the right to vote extended to one-tenth of the population) and to deny them the one weapon with which they could fight for economic and social betterment—the strike—granted both, contrary to the interests of his caste and of his own family and friends, as facts demonstrate, because the parties of the masses—Catholics and Marxists—were the ones that made his Giolittian majority difficult and sometimes impossible. Confronted with what was necessary (and nothing was more necessary than those two reforms in order to start integrating the so-called proletariat, which until then had been bomb-throwing extremists, into the democratic game), the man of the possible did not turn back. And the reward that he won was this: that when once again there was need of him to cross the aisle to those who were marching on Rome, it was the

popular Catholic and Socialist parties that prevented him from forming a majority. And then naturally—and fairly enough—they paid the penalty.[2]

The violent agitation of the metalworkers convulsed the summer of 1920, leading to the occupation of many, many factories scattered throughout the country. Thus, while the liberals lamented a government that was on the road to extinction, the popular movements rejected the subordinate role foreseen for them by Giolitti himself, entrenching themselves with the opposition to the bitter end. Meanwhile, the Left was experiencing a drastic break-up. From the time of the Soviet Revolution, the socialist reformers of Turin had engaged in a fierce battle to seize control of the party from the maximalist majority from Milan. The socialist executive board was divided between the reformists and the maximalists, headed by Turati and Serrati respectively, and in the extraordinary congress in Livorno in 1921, the grass-roots workers dissociated themselves from the leaders. The left wing, headed by Gramsci, Terracini, and Bordiga, left the hall disappointed, singing the "International" [socialist anthem], starting a division that made inevitable the birth of the Italian Communist Party with a Leninist political program. The right-wing movements, in that chaos, would more easily make headway.

"Sociologically speaking, the strongest, most battle-hardened sector consisted of the former combatants of the urban *petite bourgeoisie*: it had paid most dearly in blood during the war and now was paying more seriously for its consequences with inflation and unemployment. In that class, moods prevailed over ideas, and these moods were revolutionary,

---

[2] L. Montanelli, "Giolitti, l'uomo del possibile", *Corriere della Sera*, May 23, 2001, 41.

even destructive."[3] The "brutalized" petty bourgeoisie, as Trotsky contemptuously called them, was somewhat furious with everyone: against the socialists who had attacked them on their return from the trenches, but also against the "sharks" (the capitalists), the monarchy, the Church, the parties, in short, against the establishment, thus becoming easy prey for the Fascists.

In November 1919, with the implementation of universal male suffrage and the introduction of proportional representation, which enabled people to express their own preference, the Socialist Party and the Catholic party won the majority of votes, routing the liberal interest groups.

Pier Giorgio was fighting for a better world in the light of the kingdom of God, in which the rich would abdicate their own privileges for the sake of a livelier, intense moral praxis. Unaware of the persecutions against the Church then going on in the name of Marx, Lenin, and Stalin, he went so far as to say in a letter to his friend Antonio Villani dated July 18, 1922:

> We hope that finally our country could have an administration capable of commanding respect; and that such a crude scandal as the one presented by the Fascist movement might finally come to an end. I would hope for a Popular-Socialist administration. I still justify the violent acts that the Communists have unfortunately committed in some countries; at least they were for a great ideal: to raise up the working classes that for so many years had been exploited by unscrupulous people. But what ideal do the Fascists have? Filthy lucre, paid by the industrialists and also, unfortunately and shamefully, by our government; they act only under the impulse of money and dishonesty.

[3] I. Montanelli and M. Cervi, *Storia d'Italia: L'Italia del Novecento* (Milan: Fabbri, 2001), 62.

This ideological justification has to be read in the historical context of the time, during the handful of years in which he argued politics: like the liberals, he saw the Fascists as a bunch of thugs, whereas he saw in Communism the intention to improve the condition of the proletariat, totally unaware of how that principle would then be implemented in Communist regimes, with violence and the abuse of power, using coercive measures and persecution even against the Church of Christ that Pier Giorgio loved so much. With Monsignor Giovanni Battista Montini, he could have incited others forcefully: "We cannot fail to have a brain, ideals, and an intellectual light. We must train ourselves to think as Catholics."[4]

His disdain for those whose sole ambition was to make money is obvious. Several times he said, even in public, that when he inherited his father's goods one day, he would share them with the poor. His sister Luciana states:

> It may seem strange or at least bombastic that he, who had been born and was living in a well-to-do bourgeois family, should oppose so vehemently the industrialists and a government that clearly relied on the magnates of the world of finance. But we must remember that he, besides making no claims whatsoever for himself to our father's property . . . was obviously uninterested in his present and future rights.[5]

Pier Giorgio was not only an anti-Fascist, but also an anti-Communist, or, as they said then, an anti-socialist or anti-Bolshevik. The disastrous Marxist doctrine spread like an oil spill, making inroads particularly into the proletarian masses at a moment when industry had just got off the ground and

[4] G. Marcucci Fanello, *Storia della Fuci* (Rome: Studium, 1971), 149.

[5] P. G. Frassati, *Lettere*, ed. L. Frassati, preface by Luigi Sturzo (Rome: Studium, 1950), 130n1.

there were still no clear legal relations and duties between capitalists and workers. The wave of the Russian revolution made itself felt everywhere. Having missed the opportunity to start down a path of modernization and reforms, the empire of the tsars collapsed during the ferocious, bloody October Revolution. The First World War had displayed the weakness of the tsarist regime: the military failures of the Russian army, an imperial court that for a long time had been under the influence of the sinister mystic Rasputin, and, finally, the crisis in supplying the cities with food had provoked a series of rebellions.

Peace for all peoples, land for the farmers, power to the soviet: by dint of these propagandistic slogans, the coup d'état on November 7 (October 25, on the Russian calendar) met with vast popular acclaim. Lenin was the victor who had seen in the Bolshevik Party the only reliable basis for revolution.

Pier Giorgio paid attention to Russian current events and, even though much was well concealed by Soviet censorship, he understood the dangers of that unsound materialist ideology which also fought against religion and the Church. Proof of this is his great friendship with the Dominican Father Filippo Robotti.

Father Robotti had been born in Frugarolo, in the province of Alessandria, on September 29, 1885. Ordained a priest in 1908, during the First World War he was appointed a military chaplain and merited the silver medal. Upon his return to Turin, he was elected prior of the Friary of San Domenico, which was the destination of hundreds of veterans, soldiers, and comrades-in-arms, to whom Father Robotti had been a friend, a father, and a confrere during the war years. He dedicated himself to social works, organizing Christian labor unions and youth groups as part of Catholic Action, eliciting the hostility of the Communists.[6] It was right during that period, between the end of the 1910s and the beginning of the 1920s, that Pier Giorgio consulted and associated with him. We have this invaluable testimony about Pier Giorgio from Father Robotti:

> He never failed to be present when there was some danger from the subversive or Masonic mob; and even then he was remarkable for his imperturbable calm in facing threats and dangers. Sometimes, in the turbulent years 1919 and 1920, I happened to be called on to speak in the evening to young workingmen, in the suburbs of Turin, such as Borgo San Paolo, Borgo San Donato, Campidoglio, and so on, where, if we were attacked, we could not have counted on police protection. Generally I traveled in the company of a small group of young men, more as moral protection than physical, because we were few and unarmed. Pier Giorgio accompanied me several times on those dangerous missions to propagate the faith, and when the Bolsheviks surrounded us, shouting and threatening, I never saw him become frightened. He used to stand close beside me, ready

[6] In 1923, Father Robotti, who was already known throughout Italy for his brilliance as an excellent, indefatigable preacher, was sent to North America to propagate the faith among the colonies of his emigrant fellow Italians. Already the recipient of a military medal of honor for bravery, he was nominated president of the flourishing Blue Ribbon district of New York. In 1933, he participated in the triumphal welcome ceremonies for the trans-Atlantic pilot Italo Balbo and his flight companions. Father Robotti, of all people, who was afterward accused of cozying up to Fascism, was the one to greet the flight crew during the religious ceremony conducted in the cathedral in New York City. In 1936, he was called back to Italy and continued his preaching mission. In the summer of 1948, he returned to the United States to participate as a "definitor" in the General Chapter of his Order. On that occasion, President Truman received at the White House the officers of that religious assembly. In 1949, he traveled to California for a series of conferences and radio broadcasts aimed at the Italian-Americans who were living and working on the Pacific Coast, then to return at last to Italy. He was also a profound writer and popularizer: his enthusiasm and the depth of his thought shine through his works. He died in Turin on May 5, 1965.

to defend me with his life, if someone had dared to do me physical violence. To Turin's credit, I must say that even in those times of such violent political passions, I never had the occasion to witness truly bloody acts, even when the hecklers reduced the sessions to a chaotic uproar. At most, a few punches were thrown, because no one carried arms, not even clubs.

In Turin, however, we had our victim, we could say our martyr: Pierino Del Piano. It is well known that his murder took place, not on the occasion of a Catholic demonstration, but rather in a conflict between Bolsheviks and the police. That brave young man of ours, who was hit by a bullet for having shouted "Viva l'Italia!", was a close friend of Pier Giorgio.

One day, a few weeks before Pierino fell, the two young men came to visit me at San Domenico and discussed with me at length their desire to work for a holy cause, and they listened with docility to my counsels. When they left, I noted that they both stopped in the church to pray before the Most Blessed Sacrament.[7]

Pier Giorgio was very attentive, too, to the problems of the veterans: many had returned from the war expecting to resume their life as civilians or to continue the studies they had interrupted when they were called to arms. Several of his companions were veterans, and he decided to found a group for them, the Bianchetta, where they met to spend their free time and, above all, to discuss and resolve their problems, which were often of an economic sort: lack of funds with which to obtain books, to pay the rent for their rooms, or for university fees. Frassati would then intervene, became their guarantor, lent them his books, or gave them money to buy their own, and occasionally someone took advantage of his boundless generosity.

[7] A. Cojazzi, *Pier Giorgio Frassati: Testimonianze* (Turin: SEI, 1928), 100–101.

Pier Giorgio associated with the most active workers' groups, such as the one named after Girolamo Savonarola in Barriera di Nizza, which was made up of machinists from Fiat and well positioned against one of the most militant Communist groups, the Laborers' Union, where students used to meet with the workingmen. Yet he was interested in all the associations for youth. Every time a Catholic gathering was held to which young people were invited, you could be almost certain of seeing him there.[8] As his classmate Gigi Olivero recalls: "We went almost every day to meetings of religious, cultural, political, social, and labor associations. You might say he was present everywhere; he cooperated with and participated in every initiative. And he knew how to adapt to each setting marvelously, making himself at ease and yet always remaining himself."

Giacinto Zaccheo, another companion at those meetings, who expressed his convictions very energetically and, like Pier Giorgio, rejected compromises, had this to say: "Injustice made Pier Giorgio shudder, and anyone who experienced the days of our workingmen's movement knows that there was no conference or convention organized to affirm and defend the rights of workers at which the fraternal and loving words of Pier Giorgio did not make themselves heard with the passion of an apostle."

The workers' group at Fiat, the "Savonarola", had been founded in 1914 by Father Filippo Robotti with the collaboration of Professor Serafino Dezani, an instructor at the University of Turin. The members of the group were workmen who opposed both the Socialist-Communist ideology and the nationalistic reaction of the postwar period.

Some workmen started saying: "Ma l'è 'na masnà" [dialect for "But he is a child"], and "How does he ever think of

---

[8] Testimony of Father Filippo Robotti, O.P., in M. Codi, *Pier Giorgio Frassati: Una valanga di vita* (Casale Monferrato [AL]: Portalupi, 2001), 120.

all these things?" They also said: "We workmen liked him a lot because we sensed that he had something different going for him." He courageously confronted Bolsheviks and Fascists, and whenever someone told him to be cautious, he would say: "We have to go [to these meetings] and we do; those who commit injustice should fear, not those who suffer it."

Pier Giorgio loved the workers and loved the farmers to whom he would have liked to give land; this was a key point in his social thought, and if he had been the owner, instead of his father, he would have signed over the land.

The Italian Socialists, some of them warmongers, who then became Fascists only to go back to being Socialists, predicted revolution, declaring that the liberal, bourgeois state was finished and that for this reason they refused to take part in the government. The atmosphere in 1919 was highly charged and suffocating. Strikers paralyzed national life, and to understand specifically what was in the air it is enough to cite two facts: if someone at the station shouted "There is a priest on this train!", the train did not depart. Or at the alarm, "Someone with clean fingernails is here!" the work of the engineers would stop, because it was unthinkable to transport a bourgeois. Alfredo Frassati, who was resolutely against general strikes and in favor of holiday rest for laborers, understood the workmen's demands for improved conditions but suggested purely economic action: "Then public opinion will force business owners to recognize your unions, and the owners will have no alternative but to grant the improvements that advanced civilization requires. If instead you give yourselves up into the hands of the politicians, you will surely go to your defeat: your movement will no longer appear to be an economic tool, but a political one."[9]

Turin was considered the moral capital of Italy because it was the modern industrial capital, and it was generally made up of two classes: the capitalist bourgeoisie and the proletariat. According to Gobetti, in 1919 only Turin was capable of welcoming the more active and spiritually interesting social movement in the nation: the organization of factory councils by metal workers on strike. On September 7, 1920, Piero Gobetti wrote to his future wife, Ada Prospero: "Here we are in the middle of a full-fledged revolution. I follow with sympathy the efforts of the workers who really are building a new world." Pier Giorgio was the same age as Gobetti; moreover, he saw where the thought and the plans of Antonio Gramsci were formed and developed. He never had personal contacts with them, but the political atmosphere was the same, despite the enormous, irreconcilable ideological differences between his way of thinking and theirs.

Gramsci went to Turin in 1911 to study literature, joined the Italian Socialist Party [ISP] in 1913, and collaborated with *Avanti!*, the same newspaper of which the socialist Benito Mussolini later became publisher. During World War I, Gramsci remained loyal to the uncompromising faction, insisting that it was necessary to prepare revolutionary solutions to the crisis of war.

In February 1919, the metal workers won their "eight hours", and by April Gramsci, Tasca, Togliatti, and Terracini decided to found the magazine *Ordine nuovo* [New order], a weekly review of socialist culture. The first issue came out on May 1. The offices were located in the same building as

---

[9] A. Frassati, "Sconfitte dolorose", *La Stampa*, April 8, 1902.

the editorial offices of *Avanti!*, on the via Arcivescovado 3, and Gramsci was the office manager. In 1922 he went to Moscow to represent the ISP at the Third International. In 1924, after a long rivalry with the extremist positions of Secretary Bordiga, he replaced him at the head of the party and was elected a deputy. Gramsci's theses, which then became a rallying point for the future group of party leaders, were approved at the 1926 congress in Lione, and they signaled the final defeat of Bordiga's followers and the full Bolshevization of the ISP.

Gramsci and Gobetti were relentless opponents of the Fascist regime; the first died after years of imprisonment beginning in 1926 with other Communist leaders, and the second perished in exile from the effects of a Fascist attack.

That period witnessed an intensified and renewed commitment on the part of Catholics, thanks also to the stimulating presence of industrialization in the North and a consolidated, combative workmen's proletariat.

The rise and then the rule of Fascism provoked a diversification of positions within the Catholic movement.

> The very presence on the scene of a massive workmen's movement in Turin seemed to affect not only the choices of the ecclesiastical hierarchy: in a Catholic context in which "faith" and "ideology" appeared closely intertwined, these choices seem to have had an immediate effect on the political level, even before being translated into a coherent plan for renewal on the religious and pastoral level. The process that led to the alliance of the Catholic world with Fascism went through various phases in Turin, moments of considerable tension and internal conflicts that should not be underestimated . . . the winning groups produced massive support for the regime, but it appears to us not insignificant for the purposes of understanding subsequent events

that they tried not to lose autonomous control of the popular classes present in the Catholic movement: on the one hand, that predetermined the scope and explained the limits of Catholic anti-Fascism, within or rather in the shadow of the institutional Church; on the other hand, it allows us to understand better the birth of Christian Democracy on a massive basis in the period after World War II.[10]

Pier Giorgio, after World War I, came into contact with a Popular Party, which in his city was politically a minority force that had to deal with a firmly rooted liberal bourgeoisie and a robust workers' movement that was a tributary to the Socialist Party. At the polls in November 1919, the Popular Party won 8,842 votes (11.2 percent), as opposed to the 18,873 that went to various liberal groups and the 47,589 won by the Socialists.

The Popular Party, which had come into being that same year, 1919, acted within the social fabric, making use of a solid Catholic background and leveraging several advantages: an ecclesiastical structure that by way of the hierarchy was allied to an international institution and through its parochial organization branched out through the cities in the diocese. There was also the Catholic press, which included one daily newspaper, *Il Momento*, which Pier Giorgio often visited and which was more to his way of thinking than his father's *La Stampa*, a few weeklies, and a myriad of parish leaflets and newsletters; moreover, it even had a system of local banks and a trade union that was adequately united and militant.

Pier Giorgio's political involvement and membership in the Popular Party took on a very clear significance: it was the historical victory of the Christian judgment on history and

[10] B. Gariglio, *Cattolici democratici e clerico-fascisti: Il mondo cattolico torinese alla prova del fascismo (1922–1927)* (Bologna: Il Mulino, 1976), 15–16.

of its action in the world to change injustices and negative elements. In this sense, the Popular Party had every right to be counted among the branches of Catholic Action. Logically enough, Pier Giorgio did not think there was any division between life and faith. For him, everything was part of that existential plan called the kingdom of God: "It is unthinkable that a Christian should adopt, in politics, economics, and social relations, any other parameters than those of the Gospel."[11]

Pier Giorgio was proud to belong to Catholic Action, just as he was proud to be registered with the Popular Party. Just as he did not view the party as being detached from the spiritual wellsprings that animated Catholic Action, so too he took it for granted that the practical results of the Catholic movement would be no different from the democratic results suggested by the Gospel message. Therefore his judgments about the two organizations ended up becoming one. Don Luigi Sturzo was his teacher in both areas, and he was now certain that true democracy resides in the Gospel and that "Christianity, in order to last, always needs the complementarity of heaven and earth."[12]

His love for the Church and the Catholic cause were demonstrated tangibly when he became a promoter of the Catholic newspaper *Il Momento*, an evident competitor with his father's newspaper. The latter must not have been very happy seeing his own son supporting a newspaper that was not his own; and we can also understand the change in Alfredo Frassati's attitude toward his son, who was fed by *La Stampa* and then went about publicizing *Il Momento*:

---

[11] D. Veneruso, "Pier Giorgio Frassati e l'azione cattolica", in *Sociologia: Rivista di Scienze Sociale* (Rome: Istituto Luigi Sturzo, 1990), 179.

[12] Ibid., 180.

"That means when you're hungry you'll go and eat at *Il Momento*."[13]

The reorganization of the ecclesiastical world following the suppression of the Work of the Congresses in 1904 was accompanied by an important process of strengthening the Catholic press. This consolidation had begun in 1907 with the merger of two newspapers in Milan: *L'Osservatore cattolico*, which followed a Christian Democratic line, and *La Lega lombarda*, which was moderate in its orientation, resulting in *L'Unione*, published by Filippo Meda. In 1908, thanks to the interest of the last president of the Work of the Congresses, the Roman Publishing Society came about, an editorial organization financed by the Bank of Rome and the Italian Banking Federation, the latter made up of the rural banks and the Catholic people's banks, for the purpose of improving news services so as to confront the competition of secular newspapers.

The group also acquired *Il Corriere d'Italia* in Rome, *L'Avvenire d'Italia* in Bologna, *Il Messaggero toscano* in Pisa and *Il Corriere di Sicilia* in Palermo. In 1912, with its acquisition of the daily newspapers *L'Unione* in Milan, which changed its masthead to *L'Italia* (the future *Avvenire*), and *Il Momento* in Turin, the business "trust" of the Catholic press was further strengthened. For this reason, as you might guess, the new chain of newspapers played a decisive role in supporting Catholic candidates in the 1909 elections and especially in those of 1913.

No doubt, in dealing with these issues Pier Giorgio assumed responsibilities beyond his chronological age. Car-

---

[13] L. Frassati, *A Man of the Beatitudes: Pier Giorgio Frassati*, trans. Dinah Livingstone, adapted and ed. Patricia O'Rourke (San Francisco: Ignatius Press, 2000), 47.

dinal Ruini wrote about him: "A man of God, endowed with great ingenuity and exceptional initiative . . . completely faithful to the priestly charism, always obedient to the Church and the Supreme Pontiff, was able to instill in Italian Catholics the sense of their right and duty to participate in public affairs . . . through the application of the principles of the social doctrine of the Church."

Pier Giorgio "placed morality before the economy, common interests before individual ones, preferred poverty to wealth, and the good of others to his own."[14] In the name of the poor, he was ready for anything, even to sacrifice his own life, and therefore, believing that the Communists were acting on their behalf, he went so far as to justify their acts of violence, while he vehemently castigated the Fascist political class that was ready to resort to violence and corruption merely to win political and economic power. He knew perfectly well that his father disagreed with him and that his mother did not understand him, but he never lost his respect for them and used to say: "In me they carried out the will of God."

The antipathy between the liberal party, which had anticlerical origins, and the Catholic party was insuperable and irremediable. There could be neither dialogue nor agreement between them. For Catholics, liberalism was the sin of the new century and therefore had to be fought, because it was direct, satanic opposition to the Catholic faith. And the two men of the Frassati household became proponents of these two camps. But coarse words were never exchanged. Alfredo, who was exceedingly sure of himself and of his own prestige, limited himself to being annoyed by his son's political choices. There was mutual respect between them,

---

[14] Codi, *Pier Giorgio Frassati: Una valanga di vita*, 91.

and, on the other hand, Alfredo considered Pier Giorgio pure of heart: "What is Giorgio doing? With his beautiful, honest soul, what did he think about the intrigue that culminated in Sturzo's order to make the spiritual exercises at Monte Cassino? Of course even there some were of the opinion that Mussolini ought to perform his experiment undisturbed, and some preferred to destroy a party rather than to allow it to be consistent and to honor its own commitments."[15] "On the other hand, for my brother, taking this position against the political ideas of our house meant setting himself against a society, a class, a mentality, crossing the Rubicon."[16]

"His beautiful, honest soul" crossed the Rubicon, but at home no one spoke about it. There was no debate or discussion: each of the two men was quite sure of his own truths, and both of them were too intelligent to quarrel.

The first attempt by the Catholics to enter into politics was the Work of the Congresses, founded in Venice in 1874 and rigorously subjected to papal authority, and that was the same year of the pope's *non expedit* decision that forbade Catholics to participate in political elections. At the national level, this was the chief organizational instrument of Catholic opposition to the liberal State, but it ceased to exist in 1904.

The founding of workingmen's mutual aid associations and agricultural cooperatives received a major boost from the publication of the encyclical *Rerum novarum* by Leo XIII, for whom the liberal Alfredo Frassati must have had great esteem if he wrote so touchingly about his memory in *La Stampa* in 1903 on the occasion of his death:

---

[15] L. Frassati, *Un uomo, un giornale: Alfredo Frassati*, vol. 3, pt. 2 (Rome: Edizioni di Storia e Letteratura, 1978).

[16] L. Frassati, *A Man of the Beatitudes*, 47.

With Leo XIII one of the greatest outstanding figures of the
nineteenth century, and of the one that is now dawning, has
passed away. We will not sing his praises. They are spontaneously on the lips of everyone, from the humble farmer of
the mountainous Abruzzi region to the powerful monarch.
All remember and will remember that man who, vested
with an almost divine authority, was for that reason great,
and great because of the wisdom with which he was able
to uphold it. In times of general revolution—of workmen,
of constitutions, of the king, of classes and of ideas—he always stood like a rock visible amid the turbulent seething
of the foamy waves. Several times they seemed to be trying
to suppress the idea of the great Catholic Church; but still
she rose up, more powerful and luminous, under the saga-
cious guidance of her wise helmsman . . . several times his
pastoral ministry, performed amid tumultuous furies, held
back the bloody work of armies . . . his encyclicals aroused
the admiration of experts, while his prayers and Latin compositions delighted with glad amazement the minds of the
learned. Leo XIII was great: though small in stature, he personally and valiantly harvested so great a quantity of the life
of the mind and of achievements as to enrich with the splin-
ters thereof [*sic*] the soul of a generation.

Before his tomb, which is now closing, is not the place to
speak about his polity. Whether friendly or hostile to us, it
was a triumph for Italy. Because his almost thirty-year pontificate, which was so courageous and distinguished, was
the most dazzling test of our completed political education
in this regard, it was the indisputable proof that we have
the greatest freedom of thought and action here. . . .

With his famous encyclical *Rerum novarum*, dated May
15, 1891, Leo XIII took a position on the labor question
and more generally on social problems, in order to increase
the Church's influence among laborers and to set her rela-

tions with States on new foundations, accomplishing a sort of "Catholic *riconquista* [re-conquest]", as some historians have described it.

This document expresses strong opposition both to socialism and to the excesses of capitalism, along with an explicit invitation to Catholics to join a mixed form of labor unions and artisans' guilds in order to bring about reconciliation between the classes; it also shows interest in associations of individual workers. It asked the State to promote the ownership of small and middle-sized farms, an important factor for social well-being and stability, and furthermore to respect Sundays and holydays as days of rest, while limiting the hours in the workweek and protecting women and minors. The practical result of these exhortations was the creation and fervent activity of Christian Democratic and Christian social movements and the formation of labor unions inspired by Catholic social doctrine.

Once the war was over, Don Luigi Sturzo's request to establish a party made up of Catholics but independent from the Vatican and with a nondenominational platform was publicly approved by Benedict XV, who from 1914 on had shown a willingness to create a new climate of trust in Church-State relations and in the Catholic world, putting an end to the polemics of the groups that were most intransigently opposed to the modernist threat.

Besides the traditional demands of the Catholic movement with regard to religious liberty, the freedom to teach, and the right to form associations, the platform of Don Sturzo's party also included among its essential points the reform of the electoral system to make it proportional and the reform of the administrative structure of the State. In addition to women's suffrage, it demanded tax reform, social legislation that would guarantee the right to work and regulate "hours, wages, and hygienic workplace conditions", the development of cooperatives, and the increase and defense of small-scale rural land ownership. The Popular Party organized rapidly, and, as early as the elections in November 1919, it asserted itself as the main voice in the government.

Pier Giorgio asked to register with the party, but the members feared that, being the son of an acclaimed liberal, he might act as a fifth column. And they made him wait until witnesses had testified to his religious faith and political views; his request was accepted on December 4, 1920, and then confirmed in 1925 by Alcide De Gasperi himself.

He did not tolerate what he considered hypocrisy on Mussolini's part: persecuting the Catholic associations, but then having crucifixes returned to the schools in 1923 (the anticlerical authorities had abolished them with the applause of the Socialists twenty-seven years before). Again thanks to Mussolini, Catholic schools had some financial assistance, and catechism was introduced in the elementary grades.

Soon after his march on Rome, Mussolini, an atheist[17] par excellence, concluded the programmatic speech of his first government with an invocation: "May God help us

---

[17] On March 25, 1904, the Socialist Benito Mussolini, then a little more than twenty years old, spoke publicly to the Maison du peuple in Losanna: "If God exists, I give him five minutes to make this enemy of his die." And for five minutes, detaching his watch from the chain connected to his waistcoat, he waited with his arms at his sides, in his characteristic imperial pose. After that encounter, in which he was heckling the Protestant pastor Alfredo Tagliatela, Mussolini, who had grown up in Romagna, a province full of revolutionary anarchists, wrote a short work in which he included a series of atheistic slogans: "God does not exist. The chubby friars invented him. The egg from which religion hatches is fear. Religion is a sickness because it is contrary to experience: with my hands I can touch a bolt, but not God. Priests are parasites who make a living by exploiting morality. In comparison to Buddha, the preaching of Jesus is rather shabby, because he converted only twelve vagabonds."

to persevere in our proposals." And even Cardinal Gasparri had words of praise for that final note, observing that for more than half a century no head of the Italian State had invoked the name of God in Parliament. So began Mussolini's policy of the carrot and the stick. He reserved the stick for the Popular Party, sending De Gasperi to prison and Sturzo, Ferrari, and Donati into exile or condemning others to silence, such as the father of the future Paul VI, Giorgio Montini, the publisher of the *Giornale di Brescia*, the main offices of which were destroyed. The carrot was offered to the Church, which he asked (albeit implicitly) to reject the Popular Party. Mussolini justified this sacrifice in terms of defending religion:

> The Popular Party came into the world to check the irreligion of the liberals and to thrash atheistic socialism. Well, then, the Fascist government puts the crucifix back in the schools and hospitals, increases the stipend of the clergy, dissolves the Masonic lodges, takes part in the anti-blasphemy campaign, defends the priests against the Red threat, and finally is willing to address the perennial Roman question. And therefore we are the best interpreters of the Popular Party in safeguarding religious liberty against Bolshevik oppression and against the tired anticlericalism of the liberals.

These words won for the leader of the Fascists the sympathy of many Catholics and elicited from Pope Pius XI himself the famous remark: "Providence caused the man to meet with favor, and we needed him, too"; or from Cardinal Schuster, in his sermons in the Cathedral in Milan: "Benito means Blessed." And this is not all that surprising, given that, before the advent of *Il Duce*, utter social chaos reigned and the Church correctly feared that Red sympathizers might seize power. At that moment in history, horrific atrocities and brutal crimes were being committed by Russia, the price in blood offered on the altar of the Bolshevik Revolution, not to mention news about the bloody antireligious war in Mexico. In 1917 Achille Ratti was apostolic nuncio in Poland and saw with his own eyes the armed bands of Bolsheviks who were martyring priests and nuns and burning down churches. For this reason also and above all, Mussolini, by posing the alternative "Either Rome or Moscow", proved to be victorious.

Besides the Popular Party, which gradually wore itself out because of its internal division (between the clerical moderates, supported by Pius XI, and those who, like Pier Giorgio, would have wanted an alliance with the Left, the only real weapon with which to counteract Mussolini seriously), and a liberal government in its death throes, the political landscape offered only two opposed fronts, the extreme Left and the extreme Right.

Pier Giorgio was one of the pure of heart, and naturally he applauded the uncompromising Sicilian priest Don Sturzo, who, in a speech given in Turin in December 1922, denounced the fact that the national convention of the Popular Party was digging a political grave for itself and for the entire party by throwing stones at the relations between Fascism and the Church: "Let no one think of monopolizing the Church for political and economic purposes, in defense of class interests or partisan advantage. Now and then the Popular Party has been reprimanded for speaking in the name of religion and the Vatican. But we are the ones who have taken care not to confuse these levels. And if the Popular Party must not monopolize religion, this must be true for the others, too." This was an explicit plea to the Church in Rome not to let herself be exploited. In these words we hear the early Sturzo, more precisely the priest of

1905, when he was fighting for the autonomy of the party, with Rosmini as his inspiration.

He concluded his speech as follows: "We are and remain Popular with our autonomous program. Our motto is *libertas*. Parliamentary activity is not the main thing; we are not a party with a specific clientele; we are a party of the masses." The speech displeased the leftists within the party, who were looking forward to a clear denunciation of the Popular Party members close to the government; it annoyed those on the right who supported collaboration with the government; it offended the Fascists because it defended proportional representation, and it also irritated the liberals, who felt that they were being accused of catering to special interests. Therefore the convention took place in a very tense atmosphere with heated polemics.

In 1922, Mussolini had about forty deputies in Parliament. No sooner was he elected than he declared that he did not support Giolitti, the one politician whom he truly feared, and Giolitti resigned. In the next year and a half, there was a merry-go-round of governments: first with Bonomi, then with Facta, while the nation was wallowing in blood: in the early months of 1922, there were more than two hundred deaths and hundreds were injured.

While encouragement from the Vatican for the moderate members of the Popular Party continued, in December 1922 the reform of Catholic Action was implemented; it was depoliticized, and only religious duties were entrusted to it. That could only be rather pleasing to Mussolini, who wanted no more political obstacles in front of him while he sought hegemony.

L'Osservatore Romano commented as follows on the slaughter in Turin in December 1922, in which Brandimarte's squadrons had killed twenty-two anti-Fascists, especially

Communists, in revenge for the killing of two Fascists: "The country is facing, on the one hand, people who are not disarming, for whom certain truces are only a chance to wait for the right moments in which to strike and betray them; on the other hand, organizations that are unable to restrain the violence." The daily newspaper looked forward to "prompt action to punish the stupid barbarity of the political attacks to make an example of them". But no one was arrested, and the subsequent amnesty for the crimes committed "for national purposes" erased every trace of those dismal deeds: the slaughter in Turin was condemned also by Monsignor Giovanni Battista Pinardi, who from the pulpit called for respect and freedom.

Mussolini was a wizardly power broker, and to stay in power he was willing to deny what he had supported at first. This was why he went from socialism to anti-socialism; he negotiated with the Mason Palermi on the eve of the march on Rome and then strangled Masonry; he fought against the monarchy and then made use of it; he aligned himself with anti-Catholic positions and then came to agreements with the Catholics. His compromise with the Church was not difficult:

> There are essentially four factors that help us to understand the rapprochement between the aspergillum of blessing and the cudgel of punishment: (1) the pope's anti-socialist complex; (2) the principle of order; (3) the Lateran Agreements, that masterpiece of Mussolini's cynical, Machiavellian cunning; (4) the pastoral mentality of the papacy, which, in order to salvage religious liberty, was willing to negotiate with any type of government whatsoever.[18]

---

[18] F. Molinari and V. Neri, *Olio santo e olio di ricino: Rapporto su Chiesa e fascismo*, 2nd ed. (Turin: Marietti, 1976), 53–54.

In January 1923, a secret meeting took place between Mussolini and Cardinal Gasparri in the palace of Count Cantucci, who was also a senator, one of the eight "Pipis" (a disparaging nickname given to members of the Popular Party) on the Right who in September had maneuvered to avoid an alliance between the Popular and Socialist Parties.

The count's palace was located between the via della Pigna and the piazza del Gesù, in the old papal district of Rome. The meeting took place early in the morning, with the utmost reserve. Both Mussolini and Cardinal Gasparri arrived in limousines with the curtains drawn. The two heads of State, who six months later would sign and seal their entente with the Lateran Agreements, "testified to their mutual good will".[19]

Mussolini took steps to have his children Edda, Vittorio, and Bruno baptized, and in 1925 he married his wife, Rachele, in church. Meanwhile, Fascism persecuted in haughty tones the "disturbed, cowardly Sicilian priest" who dealt with politics. The Fascist attacks multiplied: several popular mayors in the Trentino were violently defenestrated, and in the night of August 23, 1923, in the province of Ravenna, the archpriest of Argenta, Don Giovanni Minzoni, was slain by blows of an iron club.

Pier Giorgio, immune from any fascination with a reestablished order, stood aloof both from those who were quite willing to live with an authoritarian regime as long as it could maintain a governmental balance and from those who lay down and did nothing in the shadow of oppression. No, he admired heroic men like Matteotti, Don Sturzo, or Don Minzoni. Basically, he had courage and valor: Are the saints not heroes, after all? Apart from the heroicity of their

[19] Ibid., 81.

virtues, they fight for their faith with the exalting strength that only a bold knight can possess. As a knight of Christ, Pier Giorgio was ready for death, if only he could defend the Gospel and the truths contained in it.

Although he was willing to fight for his ideas and especially in the name of Christ, Pier Giorgio was also a man of peace. One morning in 1919, wearing his student's cap, he stood up on the plaza shouting: "Viva Wilson!", referring to the American statesman who was counting, in vain, on a lasting peace and cherished the illusion of uniting peoples in the League of Nations. Pier Giorgio shouted until evening, and when he returned home his voice was hoarse. He had worn out his vocal cords to manifest his convictions; yet he looked at reality with a knowing eye: "In the world there are so many evil people and even many calling themselves Christian, but in name only, not in spirit. I think peace will be a long time coming. But our faith teaches us that we must always keep on hoping we shall enjoy it one day. Modern society is wracked with the sorrows of human passions and is moving away from any ideal of love and peace."[20]

A critical person who was also critical of himself, Pier Giorgio did not let himself be completely influenced and believed solely in the Gospel. And this is why, with the correct standard of measurement, he succeeded in weighing and evaluating various institutions; so it happened with the Popular Party, too. He wrote from Freiburg im Breisgau on October 23, 1921: "I am very sorry that the P.P.I. [Populist Party of Italy] is merely taking votes and so the people are abandoning it; let us hope that at the next convention it will decide something specific, because Italy expects a lot of this party. I read the agenda for the day and found one big

[20] Frassati, *A Man of the Beatitudes*, 56.

mistake: forgetting agriculture, by means of which Italy will be rebuilt." Pier Giorgio was not entirely wrong, since *Il Duce* later staked a great deal on the revival of agriculture. In February 1923, he wrote to Antonio Villani: "After Easter, the P.P.I. will hold its convention; where finally, we hope, it will delineate a certain path to follow." It was one of the last free conventions of the Popular Party, during which it decided to leave the governing coalition. He suffered greatly when he began to discover the weakness of the party in which he had placed so much hope and trust.

With infinite sadness he saw Catholic institutions all around aligning themselves with Fascist policies for the sake of convenience. He wrote to his friend Tonino Villani on November 16, 1923: "What do you think about all the weather vanes who sell out to Fascism every day, as *Il Momento* did? I am more nauseated with each passing day; if I did not have the certainty that my faith is divine, I would surely give myself over to some insane act."

Pier Giorgio had a strong, impetuous personality, and, as we have seen, he was willing to take kicks and blows and to give some when the occasion arose:

> But what drives those thoughts away from me is the certainty of a better life in the next world if we work at doing good; therefore, let us stay united in our work and encourage each other and incite one another to lead a good life. Ahead of me I have a retreat with that wonderful minister of God, Don Luigi Sturzo, and in hours of discouragement I look to him, since I get the strength to go on not only from religion but also from him.

He lived in opposition. He did not accept half-truths, squalid, unctuous compromises, half-measures; when he said yes or no, he meant it decisively. Diplomacy, although useful in some circumstances, was not for him.

He would have liked to apply the Gospel literally, and sometimes he was a little harsh in his reactions. Clemente Ferraris di Celle, who testified in his cause, explains this quite well:

> He . . . [was] always on the opposition. Pier Giorgio did not understand half-truths, bland, diplomatic measures, although they were sometimes necessary to run a ship with such a large and difficult crew as a university group. He was a maximalist; he would have liked to apply the Gospel literally, and sometimes he was a bit rude and forbidding. He did not accept deviations; making allowances was contrary to his character, and he certainly was not the malleable sort.

But then what was Pier Giorgio in reality? A reactionary? A fundamentalist? A progressive? Pier Giorgio surely did not like labels, except that of soldier of Christ. Many have exploited him as a Catholic figure, using him for their own purposes and causes, without considering how radically different the historical times were in which he lived as an active participant. Pier Giorgio was a free man, completely free, both from stereotypes and from ideologies, subservient to no one except to God. His ideas, founded on one truth—that of the Gospel—did not allow him to make any compromise. He was with Christ, and that was the path he wanted to follow, under the banner of charity, making use of politics as well when the occasion arose; for this reason, he joined the Popular Party, because he found in Don Luigi Sturzo a political leader who was finally speaking and writing about Jesus Christ.

With the utmost forcefulness and confidence, he asserted his own point of view and defended it in depth. In a letter written to Antonio Villani dated November 19, 1922, he declared:

I took a look at Mussolini's speech, and it curdled all the blood in my veins: you can believe that I am quite disappointed by the stance of the Popular Party. Where is the fine platform, where is the faith that animates our men? Unfortunately, when it is a question of climbing for the honors of this world, men trample on their own conscience.

On April 6, 1924, in a very intimidating atmosphere, elections were held, which concluded with the victory of the "national big list" (Fascists, Nationalists, many liberals, and some Catholics) over the opposition (Popular Party, Socialist Party, and Communist Party). The constitutional parties limited themselves to being the ethical conscience of the nation, which now fought only in the newspapers. But that 9 percent won by the Popular Party was still quite disturbing. In the night of April 7–8, three hundred Black Shirts invaded the rectory in Sandrigo, in the province of Vicenza, and the pastor was ill-treated. The Ordinary of Vicenza, Bishop Rodolfi, wrote a telegram to Mussolini, then went to the parish and "excommunicated" the men responsible.

Alfredo Frassati wrote in *La Stampa* (October 30, 1920): "Fascism and Bolshevism are now correlative terms. The one generated the other, and together the two of them have produced and are producing the ruin of our country. Today the Fascists pose as saviors from Bolshevism. But one form of madness is not cured with another. We need to eradicate Fascism, the first cause, if we want to be spared Bolshevism." And again: "Nothing is more repulsive to us than violence cloaked with law" (*La Stampa*, January 12, 1923).

In 1924, Giacomo Matteotti denounced in parliament the violent incidents and intrigues perpetrated by the Fascists during the elections. He was abducted by some Fascists on June 10 on the banks of the Tiber (on the lungotevere Arnaldo da Brescia); his body was found on August 16 in the woods of Quartarella, near the via Flaminia, around twelve miles from Rome. Those responsible for the assassination were the Fascist squad members Amerigo Dumini, Albino Volpi, Giuseppe Viola, Amleto Poveromo, Augusto Malacria, all of them members of associations of Royal Italian Army storm troops ("Arditi") in Milan, whereas the automobile with which the abduction was carried out belonged to Filippo Filippelli, publisher of the *Corriere italiano*.

On the day after the abduction of the Socialist reformist deputy, the anti-Fascist opposition members walked out of the parliamentary sessions in protest (in an event remembered as "the secession of Aventino") and called for the disbanding of the Voluntary Militia for national security and the reestablishment of the authority of the law. Their intention was to weaken the Fascist government by preventing its parliamentary activity, thus compelling it to resign. But not all the anti-Fascists participated in the secession of Aventino: the Communists, for example, dissociated themselves from the initiative, considering it an abandonment of their struggle. Despite a fierce campaign by the opposition press and Mussolini's difficulties after the discovery of Matteotti's body, the weakness of the Aventines and the improvement of the country's economy enabled the government to get a grip on the situation again, and it eliminated any type of opposition in a short time.

Let us read what Pier Giorgio set down in writing eleven days after the abduction of Giacomo Matteotti (from a letter to Antonio Villani, Turin, June 21, 1924):

> In these moments, when evil manifests itself in its most nauseating aspects, I go back in thought to the days we spent together; I recall the first elections of the postwar period, the coming of Fascism, and now I remember with joy the fact that never in our past lives, not for a single instant,

were we in favor of Fascism, but have always fought against that scourge of Italy; and now, as this party is sinking into ruin, we can thank God that he willed to employ poor honorable Matteotti to unmask before the whole world the infamy and filth that are concealed beneath the sheaf [*fascio*, the symbol of Fascism]. . . .

Unyielding and stern, he courageously confronted his enemies, but also his friends who did not share his honesty and ideological correctness. So it happened in the Cesare Balbo circle, when it decided to display the circle's own banner in 1923 to pay homage to Benito Mussolini during his visit to Turin. To the head of the FUCI and of Catholic Action, who was in charge of the Guardia Riva circle, he submitted his own resignation and expressed all of his fierce disapproval (October 24, 1923):

I am really indignant because you displayed from the balcony the banner (which I, though unworthy, carried so many times in religious processions) to pay homage to the man who is demolishing pious works, who does not restrain the Fascists, lets them kill ministers of God like Don Minzoni, etc., and allows them to commit other foul deeds, and then seeks to cover up those misdeeds by putting the crucifixes back in the schools, etc.

I took the whole responsibility upon myself and removed that banner, unfortunately late in the day, and now I inform you of my irrevocable resignation. With God's help I will continue even outside the circle, although this causes me great displeasure, and I will do what little I can for the Christian cause and for the peace of Christ.

I want this letter, which is written in haste but dictated by the depths of my soul, to be read at the next assembly. With deep respect. Pier Giorgio Frassati.

After the incident with the banner, Pier Giorgio, together with Giovanni Maria Bertini, went to Bishop Giovanni

Battista Pinardi, an anti-Fascist, to ask his opinion: the auxiliary bishop spoke disapprovingly about the involvement
of Catholic associations in Mussolini's reception. We have
already had the opportunity to meet Bishop Pinardi in the
preceding pages, but it is worthwhile to become better acquainted with this auxiliary bishop who had plenty of contacts with Blessed Frassati. He had been made a pastor on
December 15, 1912, and four years later, on January 24,
notwithstanding his reluctance because of his great humility, he was appointed titular bishop of Eudoxias and auxiliary bishop to Agostino Cardinal Richelmy, archbishop of
Turin. In 1917 he founded an association to promote honest journalism.

Years later, Pius XI would say to Cardinal Fossati, the
new archbishop of Turin, who succeeded Cardinal Gamba:
"In Turin you have a holy bishop, but it is necessary to
leave him in the shadows so as not to have problems with
the regime."

Bishop Pinardi was one of the first to respond to the appeal made by Don Luigi Sturzo "to all men who are free and
strong" and became his friend and supporter until the Sicilian priest was exiled. He actively promoted the formation
of company unions that would rally around the Catholic Labor Union so as to oppose the spread of anti-Christian socialism, against which Pier Giorgio, too, was fighting. The
bishop wanted to live in his beloved parish and with his
parishioners until his death, and his ministry in the years of
the early postwar period led to his constant involvement in
support of Christian social action.

In 1919 the Labor Union started, by means of its company unions, a campaign to reduce the daily work of dressmakers to eight hours. They planned to begin with this
category and then to extend the right to include all work-

ers; this was achieved thanks also to the staunch presence of Bishop Pinardi. During those same years, in keeping with his wishes, the San Secondo Cooperative opened, with headquarters on the via San Secondo at the corner of the corso Stati Uniti, for the purpose of providing poor people with low-cost groceries and necessary commodities; but after a time the cooperative had to close because of the imposition of the Fascist regime. Through Pinardi's initiative, the Casa del popolo [people's house] opened at via Parini 7, and at corso Oporto 11 (today named corso Matteotti) a building was dedicated that combined most of the diocesan services.

From May 10 to 17, 1922, the diocesan Eucharistic Congress was celebrated in Turin to commemorate the threefold jubilee of Cardinal Richelmy: fifty years of priesthood, twenty-five years as a bishop in Turin, and twenty-five years as a cardinal. Pinardi was president of the planning committee, and photographs in which we can see the Blessed beside the archbishop testify that Pier Giorgio was present. On May 14, Pier Giorgio reacted vehemently against a group of Fascist squad members who were insulting the FUCI demonstration. He was present both amid the altercations in defense of the Gospel and its apostles and also in the national prisons, where he was interned because of the faith that he declared publicly; moreover, he was often noticed during the open conflicts with the police and the royal guards. During those few hours of respite, Pier Giorgio surely did not waste time but recited his rosary, until his last name was discovered and he was brought into the presence of the constable.

On August 10, 1923, Cardinal Agostino Richelmy died, with his auxiliary bishop beside him: it was the end of one of the longest episcopates in Turin. It had begun in 1897 and lasted more than a quarter of a century, and its most significant pastoral accomplishment was staunch support for Canon Giuseppe Allamano in the foundation of the Missionaries of Our Lady of Consolation, both a men's community (1901) and one for women (1910). He was succeeded by Monsignor Giuseppe Gamba, the first archbishop of Turin to come from peasant origins. On October 25, 1924, at San Secondo, Bishop Pinardi welcomed Don Luigi Sturzo, who was about to depart for London, the first stage of his exile without any hope of returning, and celebrated his last Mass in Italy in that parish, of all places.

But let us return to Pier Giorgio. With his typical decisiveness and determination, he turned in his membership card and badge to the Cesare Balbo circle, because "legally they do not belong to me any more." In order to fulfill a duty in conscience, he wrote a letter to the circle informing them that he would continue to participate in Catholic Action as a member of the Italian Catholic Youth, and he admonished them: "Jesus Christ said: The children of darkness are more shrewd than the children of light; but he also said: Beware of false prophets and wolves that come to you in the form of lambs" (October 26, 1923).

Even though he was against compromises, he let the incident rest, so as not to create tensions among the members of the circle and in order to keep in touch with the few anti-Fascists who remained in the group, but he did not forget; this shows quite clearly that he was not one to bear a grudge or retaliate. "So that there might be no misunderstandings, and so that my action might not be interpreted as opposition to a particular person or as having other motives, while protesting ever more vehemently the display of the banner, for the good of the circle I withdraw my resignation" (November 14).

In the group Milites Mariae (Soldiers of Mary), Pier Giorgio presented in October 1922 the objectives of the young Catholic men, who are called not to squander "the best years of our life, as unfortunately so many unhappy young men do who are preoccupied with enjoying those goods which do not bear good fruit but produce the immorality of our modern society." It is necessary to be temperate, he proclaimed, in order to be ready to keep up the battle that must be fought for the implementation of "our program and thus to give our fatherland in some distant future happier days and a morally sound society". The means for achieving these ambitious goals were: continuous prayer so as to obtain God's grace, without which every effort is in vain; organization and discipline so as to be ready for action; and the sacrifice of one's passions and "of our very selves".

Always up to date and well informed about every event, he subscribed to almost all the Catholic periodicals and newspapers in Italy. "It is incredible, the number of pamphlets, magazines, leaflets, and parish newsletters that circulate everywhere, seek to infiltrate even the most refractory families, and deal with so many things other than religion", Antonio Gramsci wrote in one of his first articles.[21] In order to counteract the widespread anticlericalism of the liberals and the diffusion of the atheistic ideas of Marxism, the Church had carved out for herself a conspicuous place within the local and national press, multiplying her own sources of information at the grass-roots level, thus lending substance and weight to a popular Catholic culture.

As of March 1915, Benedict XV, with the establishment of the National Association for Good Journalism (l'Opera nazionale per la buona stampa), not only acknowledged that the syndicate of Catholic journalists was licit, but assured

---

[21] A. Gramsci, *Sotto la Mole: 1916–1920* (Turin, 1960), 40.

it of an extensive, powerful organizational structure. In the Piedmont region, the daily newspaper *Il Momento* had been setting forth and spreading Catholic hopes for more than twenty years. Its masthead stated that the newspaper was to be "Catholic, well done, independent, and lively" in a well-matched competition with the liberal and socialist press. But the crisis of the Popular Party, which especially affected the former capital, which had now become a laboratory of ideas and plans, had important repercussions also in the political management of the press. Until then, men with various political convictions had been involved in the editing of *Il Momento*, but as the national situation developed, the crisis in the Popular Party led to the dismissal of those within the newspaper who were opposed to a clerical-Fascist policy, thus ratifying the transfer of ownership of the publication to the Catholic right wing. Members of the Popular Party in Turin in vain bid their 750,000 lire against the two million belonging to Baron Gianotti, who in September 1923 came into possession of *Il Momento*. Crispolti, Grosoli, and Gianotti had left the Popular Party after its convention in Turin; this was one of the main reasons for the battle over the financial management of the publication, which for the most part had already become a mouthpiece of the pro-Fascist forces.

Giuseppe Cardinal Gamba, together with Auxiliary Bishop Giovanni Battista Pinardi, was a strong advocate of a daily newspaper independent from any influence except that of the ecclesiastical authorities and of Catholic Action. Therefore, on December 31, 1924, a new daily paper appeared, *Il Corriere*, tangible proof that lay Catholic activists were not resigned to the Fascist attempt to get a monopoly on the news but intended to maintain direct, formative contact with the population. The publication became one of the best Catholic newspapers in the period following World

War I, one of the very few, together with Donati's *Il Popolo* and *Il Corriere del mattino* in Verona, that continued to take democratic positions in the years 1925–1926. Harsh attacks were aimed by the Fascist authorities both at Bishop Pinardi and at Gustavo Colonnetti (who went so far as to submit his resignation from the Popular Party),[22] the most fervent promoters and supporters of *Il Corriere*. "The political and ideological orientation of *Il Corriere*, which was suppressed by Fascism in 1926, and the appointment of Prof. Gustavo Colonnetti, an anti-Fascist member of the Popular Party, as president of the Diocesan Catholic Action Council, along with the activity of Auxiliary Bishop Pinardi, show the critical or at least very reserved attitude of the archbishop toward the Fascist regime."[23] When the editor-in-chief of *Il Popolo*, Giuseppe Donati, was compelled to go into exile, the only one at the border to greet him and shake his hand, challenging the watchful eyes of the Fascist police, was Pier Giorgio Frassati. Donati later wrote: "I saw him as the last friend of the fatherland that I was leaving."

There are some who maintain[24] that Pier Giorgio Frassati, in addition to wearing a badge showing a shield with a cross whenever he appeared among the workingmen, who were easy prey to the illusory materialistic ideologies of atheistic Marxism, wished that he could get to the Communists of

[22] See M. Reineri, *Cattolici e fascismo a Torino 1925/1943* (Milan: Feltrinelli, 1978). At the meeting of the Popular Party group in Turin at which the resignation of Professor Colonnetti was announced, it was declared that "from now on the Party will no longer accept resignations but will proceed to expel members who resign because of political unworthiness."

[23] G. Tuninetti and G. D'Antino, *Il cardinale Domenico Della Rovere, costruttore della cattedrale, e gli arcivescovi di Torino dal 1515 al 2000: Stemmi, alberi genealogici e profili biografici* (Cantalupa: Effatà, 2000), 221.

[24] See F. V. Massetti, *Pier Giorgio Frassati nel ricordo di un amico: Testimonianze riflessioni lettere* (Castelmaggiore [BO]: Tipocolor, 1984), 49.

Ordine nuovo, hard-core followers of Gramsci, to convince them that it was impossible to inaugurate a real new order without improving the morality of the masses. But he allegedly wanted to reach out also to the university students of *Rivoluzione liberale* to testify to them that it is impossible to establish a regime of true freedom without first having experienced the cost and the value of one's own interior freedom. Pier Giorgio considered interior freedom the first real conquest that should be proposed both to workingmen and to intellectuals in order to have a truly better world, true human and Christian progress under the protection of the peace that is truth, justice, liberty, and love, the peace that comes with a clear conscience, everyone's conscience.

10

FRIENDS

Friendship was a pillar and mainstay of Pier Giorgio's life. *Ubi amici, ibi opes*: "Where there are friends, there is wealth", Plautus wrote, and Blessed Frassati made this a rule of life. Of course he did not wait for friends to come to him; he sought them out, and most importantly he established solid, lasting ties: as an architect builds bridges to connect one riverbank to the other, so Pier Giorgio built bridges to bind hearts together. He was able to talk to others and to captivate them with his sympathy, his simplicity, his disarming spontaneity, his sincerity and purity of soul, without any pretense or hypocrisy. Pier Giorgio arrived at the bright border of friendship, which Saint Augustine calls "devotion of soul to soul", an unexplainable spiritual feeling that unites persons amiably.

Young men of the same age liked his company, not only because they were proud to have the son of the publisher of *La Stampa* as their friend, but because they discovered in him the gifts of a genuine individual, free of snobbishness, and, wherever he was, his presence inevitably and unequivocally reminded people of the things of God. Pier Giorgio distinguished very clearly between his true friends, to whom he gave himself entirely, and his mere acquaintances, because for him friendship was a truly serious, profound reality and no joking matter.

To his dear friend Marco Beltramo, who had brilliantly passed the examinations for admission to the Aeronautical Academy in Livorno, he wrote on November 4, 1924:

> The news made me glad, but it also saddened me. There is no joy without sorrow; indeed, for me this means, alas, that you will be far away, and I walked, thinking of the happy days we spent together hiking in the mountains. The one comfort, amidst such happy and yet sad thoughts, is the certainty that we are united by a bond that does not know distance and that, I hope, by the grace of God, will always unite us. This is the faith, the common ideal that you will be able to uphold in your career with the means that military life will provide and that I will endeavor, with God's help, to defend and uphold in my future life as a man.

These touching words pour out from a clear, extremely sensitive mind that is set on goods that are not merely human.

On May 18, 1924, in the town of Pian della Mussa in the Valli di Lanzo, Pier Giorgio and his companions founded the Society of Sinister Types (Società dei tipi loschi), a group of "odd" young men brought together in deep, close friendship by his initiative, under the aegis of prayer. Faithful to their schoolboy mottos: "Few but ready, like spaghetti", and: "Partnership of fully paid-up capital: paid up so much that none is left", they left an indelible mark, not only in the biography of the Blessed, but also as a model of youth formed in the name of the Lord, a model youth group that is still being imitated.

The objective of the society, whose designer, Pier Giorgio, knew how to make one soul out of many, was to rout "scruples and melancholy" from the heart of each one so as to "serve God with complete cheerfulness"; all this leads inevitably to the Augustinian reflection: "Indeed, there is no true friendship," Saint Augustine writes in book 4 of his *Confessions*, "unless you, O Lord, tie the bond between persons who cling to you by that love which is poured into our hearts by the Holy Ghost, which is given to us."

The "Sinister Types" addressed one another as *cittadini e cittadine* (citizens, male and female), or else they were called *lestofanti e lestofantesse* (swindlers, male and female), a mixed group, which was rather avant-garde for that era, when young men were strictly separated from young women both at school and during free time.[1]

Each one of them had a nickname. Pier Giorgio, the leader, was Robespierre, also called The Incorruptible; Marco Beltramo—Perrault; Gian Maria Bertini—*Gaffe*, because of his careless, clumsy exits; Franz Massetti—*Petronio arbiter elegantiarum*, because he dressed with great care and elegance; Isidoro Bonini (future president of the Istituto per la Ricostruzione Industriale)—Danton, because of his remarkable, spirited intolerance for authoritarianism, despite his gifts and imposing presence. And then there were "Araldus", "Figaro qui figaro là". . . . The female swindlers performed social duties: Ernestina Bonelli, called "Englesina" after she traveled to London, planned excursions; Laura Hidalgo was the secretary; Clementina Luotto, the oldest, who had the gift of gab, was the president.

The nicknames were inspired by a performance of the comedy *Il conte di Brechard* by Giovacchino Forzano that Pier Giorgio and some friends had gone to see a few days before the society was founded.

Once, in his parents' absence, he managed to bring them

[1] These were the members of the university group: Carlo Bellingeri, Gian Maria Bertini, Curio Chiaraviglio (nephew of Giovanni Giolitti), Antonio Villani, Antonio Severi, Isidoro Bonini, Franz Massetti, Camillo Pucci, Marco Beltramo, Ernestina Bonelli, Laura Hidalgo, Clementina Luotto.

home for a bit of harmless "merrymaking", as Massetti assures us. It was on July 27, 1924, and Pier Giorgio was staying in the city to study. His guest was Tonino Severi, and the two young men prepared everything, including the meals, and Pier Giorgio boasted of his own culinary skills to his friends, who did not take him seriously; then he challenged them: "I invite you to lunch tomorrow at my house, and you will see!" The invitation was well received. On the menu was a pie for twelve . . . and there were five of them. The Frassati's severe dining room was transformed, and the cheerful band of students sat down in their shirtsleeves. Pier Giorgio wanted a lasting record of that scene, and so we have a photograph documenting the hilarity: he is wearing on his head a paper hat folded from an issue of the satirical newspaper *Il Becco giallo*. Later on he asked to have the photographic negatives of that bravado performance in his possession, because a friend at the university had managed to get hold of them and jokingly threatened him, saying that he would send the negatives to his mother. The blackmail was negotiated, and the price was paid: forty-five lire to be deposited in the mountain-climbing account. On July 12 of the following year, Pier Giorgio was no longer among them, and the Sinister Types went to Oropa for a Eucharistic celebration in his memory; they collected forty-five lire, recalling the photo with which he had been "blackmailed", and gave it as a stipend for the celebration of Mass for the repose of the soul of their Robespierre.

He never preached from the pulpit, but humbly, with his formidable, disarming simplicity, he encouraged his friends to study and to make serious, responsible commitments; in particular, he sought to nourish their faith. He wrote from Turin on January 15, 1925, to Marco Beltramo:

Dear Friend,

May you have peace of mind: that is the wish that Robespierre extends to Perrault for the Holy Year; any other gift that may be possessed in this life is vanity, as all things of the world are vain. Life is beautiful inasmuch as our true life is beyond it; otherwise, who could bear the weight of this life if there were no reward for the sufferings, eternal joy; how could we explain the admirable resignation of so many poor creatures who struggle with life and often die on the front lines if it were not for our certainty of God's justice?

In the world that has turned away from God, peace is lacking, but something else lacking is charity, or true, perfect love. Perhaps if we all listened more to Saint Paul, human miseries might be diminished somewhat.

Yet his hope was always strong: "The future is in God's hands, and there could be no better way."

Pier Giorgio and Beltramo joined forces in the Terror Division, which was extremely active in making jokes; its motto was: *Terror omnia vincit* (terror conquers all things). The subdivisions were named according to the place where the Sinister Type happened to be at the moment: Acquatica, Talpinistica (if, for example, Pier Giorgio was in Pollone to prepare for an exam), Alpinistica, or Centro (Turin).

They periodically organized excursions to the mountains. The letters announcing them turned into proclamations that always concluded with terroristic embraces or a thousand terroristic cannon shots: "Boom! Boom!" One example can stand for them all. This was a letter written from Pollone on the feast day of Our Lady of Oropa (August 31, 1924), the 124th day of the new (non-Fascist) era. The Blessed was especially devoted to Our Lady under this title, and when he was in Pollone, he never failed to visit the majestic, monumental shrine frequently:

Third day of the fifth month, Year One.

Society of the Sinister Types.
Department of the "Agitated".
"Terror" Division.
Subdivision "Talpinistica".

Announcement:

To the future of the Terror, Citizen Perrault, a shot of the bombard!

We experienced great emotion upon receiving your postcard, worthy of the Terror; a terroristic shudder shook every fiber of our body, and an ardent desire took possession of us: the desire to thank you promptly for the nice postcard.

From our sister we learned that Englesina, the distinguished D.D.G. [*Dottoressa di giurisprudenza*, doctor of law], has left the remote ice sheets and the vertiginous steep slopes to return to cheerful Mondovì; but we learn also that she, notwithstanding the torment, like a brave *Sucaina*[2] obeying one of the *Sucain* commandments, confronted the cliff of the Aiguille du Midi and succeeded in overcoming every difficulty. Blessed is she who does not have to study and can devote herself to the mountains; there is nothing else for us to do for now but to admire her prowess and the rather beautiful photographs, but we have in our heart the hope, a great hope and a goal to conquer [the ascent in Grivola], and then we will write to the D.D.G. that we, too, did something this year.

We confidently await your promised announcement, and now, O most excellent Perrault, accept a fraternal and terroristic embrace from *Robespierre*.

---

[2] From S.U.C.A.I., Sezione universitaria del Club alpino italiano, University Division of the Italian Alpine Club.

And when he had climbed the Grivola, he wrote at the conclusion of his announcement: *Terror omnia vincit: Grivola victa est.* (Terror conquers everything: the Grivola has been vanquished.)

Pier Giorgio experienced much anguish and sadness because of the disbanding of the Society of Sinister Types, a break-up that resulted from forces beyond their control: everyone had set out on his own path, and with that the joy of youth would be gone. Aware of life now, he considered his student days all too precious and too swift to pass. This irreversible fact saddened and embittered him terribly; then, as always, he clung to the faith, the one anchor of salvation, which is capable of alleviating sufferings; the very principles of friendship are founded on it, and the ties of friendship could still be maintained, despite the passage of time, thanks to prayer. The Society of Sinister Types therefore turned into a Society of Prayer: Faith, Pier Giorgio said, "made us companions on wonderful excursions and caused our society to be built on granite foundations. And this is the sole comfort that we experience in the sorrow of having to part. If we did not have this hope, how could we keep on living, when we see that every human joy brings with it a sorrow?" He wrote to Laura Hidalgo from Forte dei Marmi on August 11, 1924:

Then when I think of our Society, doomed to break up miserably like everything of this earth, a sense of regret assails me: farewell to the wonderful excursions in the mountains; without Perrault, what will Robespierre do? A bond remains, however, which we hope with God's grace might unite on this earth and in the next world all the Sinister Types: that sacred bond is the faith, the one powerful bond, the one secure foundation; without it nothing can be undertaken. We received this faith in holy Baptism, and it made us companions on the wonderful Alpine excursions;

we hope that it will accompany us until the final day of our earthly journey and will serve as a bond by means of prayer to unite spiritually all the Sinister Types scattered throughout the globe.

His wish came true, too, for later generations thanks to the Societies of Sinister Types scattered throughout the world. Laura Hidalgo testifies:

> One Saturday evening . . . we were climbing from Oulx to Sauze, where we were to spend the night, so as to continue the next day through Kind. I asked him whether there was an early morning Mass in Sauze, "because I have to go to Communion." "What do you mean, 'have to'?" he asked me. "Tomorrow is the feast of our patron saint." "And otherwise you would not go? Then why did you say you had to?" I understood, because many times already he had spoken with me about this, and I replied facetiously: "You know very well what I think and in what sense I said 'have to'." "I know, but I do not like it", he replied rather seriously.

Those happy, faith-filled trips to the mountains were enlivened by sinister types of songs, and louder than all the other voices you could hear the baritone of the tone-deaf Blessed. Some tried to dissuade him: "Frassati, you're a terrible singer!", but he, with a smile, replied, "Patience: the important thing is to sing!" Cheer and good company went together perfectly with the way the whole group thought, based as it was on Christian union.

In the letters that he wrote during his last weeks, Pier Giorgio insisted on winning interior peace: "To possess this is certainly the best gift on this earth" (letter to Laura dated December 28, 1924). Little by little as he approached his final exit, he felt a growing need for an earthly peace, a reflection of eternal peace in Christ.

Pier Giorgio created a sort of prayer association, not only in his group of friends from Turin or Biellese, but also in Germany,[3] and to those with whom he managed to establish a deeper spiritual contact he would give a rosary made with the seeds of a plant with gray berries, called "Job's tears" and cultivated in his garden in Pollone. Pier Giorgio had some nuns make these rosaries, then had them blessed, and he assured his friends that they already had "all the indulgences".

The words dedicated to the theme of friendship that Don Montini wrote in 1927 to the FUCI council members were incarnated by Pier Giorgio:

> Our social life must be built with the cement of charity. Therefore, it is necessary to proceed gradually, starting with a foundation of the utmost charity: it is necessary to start with friendship. The little flock can be little in everything except friendship. Let us make sure, therefore, to acquire this virtue, which is a preliminary to our constructive work of friendship. . . . How do we engage one another to keep our word, to perform good works, to pray for each other? Without these hearths of unvanquished, heartfelt friendship, we cannot kindle the flame of the apostolate.

Pier Giorgio's flame drew nourishment precisely from the wealth of friendship that he knew how to create, elicit, nourish, and strengthen. "The memory of the wonderful trips in which our Society fully participated and of its resounding laughter has not yet dimmed among us, and we are already thinking sadly about the future. . . . The Society will inevitably, slowly disband, and we believe that the Ciamarello [a reference to one of the excursions] will be for us, as it were, the last sweet, sad remembrance of the years of our

---

[3] See P. G. Frassati, *Lettere*, ed. L. Frassati, preface by Luigi Sturzo (Rome: Studium, 1950), 327.

youth", he wrote to Marco Beltramo from Forte dei Marmi in August 1924.

Friendship had an immense value in Pier Giorgio's heart: "In earthly life, after the love of parents and siblings, one of the most beautiful sorts of affection is that of friendship; and every day I ought to thank God for giving me such good friends, who are for me a precious guide for my whole life."

The relations of friendship that he succeeded in establishing were intense; by being with his friends he improved, he asked for advice and prayers, often he exhorted them to do good and to increase their own faith. To Marco Beltramo he made an appeal: "May the peace of our Lord be always with you, so that every day when you possess peace you will be truly rich" (April 10, 1925): for him, spiritual wealth counted much more than financial assets or physical well-being or youth.

Marco Beltramo, one of Pier Giorgio's closest friends, and Antonio Villani, who was courteous and intellectual, were the only young men to be admitted to the Frassati house. To Marco he announced on November 4, 1924: "I always remind you that within three years, when you leave academia, one of the first excursions that you make will have to bring Robespierre on board, and then we can say that the Terror will reign, if only for an instant, over the vast kingdom of the winds." His relationship with Marco Beltramo was the strongest and most spontaneous; their shared tastes made their friendship dear and warm. Their trust was mutual and very great, without any ulterior motives.

The loss of that great friend was for Beltramo the cause of profound, immense sorrow. Probably his acquaintance with Pier Giorgio was a factor, as it happened also with other friends, in his decision to enter the friary of the Dominican Fathers in Chieri as a seminarian. A "Sinister", extroverted, original, and very big-hearted fellow, Marco found no peace within the walls of the friary when World War II broke out, and he felt it was his duty to take part in the conflict alongside the other Italian men. Therefore he abandoned his religious aspirations and courageously and boldly enlisted, performing deeds that, according to the testimonies of Laura Hidalgo's daughters, were worthy of a war hero and full of unconditional generosity. The master of the Sinister Types had taught a lesson.

11

BERLIN

In November 1918, rebellions of military detachments and German cities forced Wilhelm II to abdicate. On November 9, the Republic was proclaimed.

The new Social-Democratic government was headed by Friedrich Ebert, and the armed forces repressed the uprisings of the Spartacist League in Berlin. The Communist Republic of Bavaria was overthrown, also. While the national assembly gathered in Weimar approved a new republican, federal, and parliamentary constitution, the Versailles Peace Treaty, dated June 28, 1919, which was punitive for Germany, ratified serious territorial concessions, including the colonies, in favor of surrounding countries and imposed burdensome limitations on the armed forces and enormous reparations for the losses and damages sustained in the war; this increasingly nourished German nationalistic feelings of revenge, aggravating the mind-boggling economic and social crises that occurred thereafter. It was the start of years of extreme poverty, and there were frequent political killings by the hands of future Nazi masterminds such as Heinrich Himmler and Rudolf Hess, who came from the Freikorps paramilitary organizations, whereas in 1923 there was a failed attempt to rebel against the Bavarian government, the so-called Putsch of Munich headed by Adolf Hitler. With a keen nose for news and perfect historico-political insight, Alfredo Frassati perceived the Nazi threats against the Weimar Republic; he went so far as to predict the *Anschluss*, the annexation of Austria to Germany.

In that political situation, Giovanni Giolitti decided to appoint Alfredo Frassati himself as ambassador to Berlin, justifying his decision with these words: "I am convinced . . . that Frassati will do very well in Germany, because he knows Germany and the German people profoundly. Rather than send to Berlin a career ambassador, I preferred a man who, besides knowing the country well, knows life and is able to adapt to new times. In short, a practical man, a modern man."[1] Congratulations to the senator poured in from all sides, and among them figured a letter from the Association of the Subalpine Press that he had founded. It rejoiced because after Frassati's twenty-six years of uninterrupted and fruitful journalistic work, now Italy could proudly offer the first professional journalist ambassador.

Frassati left Turin and *La Stampa* (which he temporarily handed over to his faithful colleagues Banzatti and Salvatorelli, without ever losing sight of it) on January 22, 1921, the year that made the reputation of the dramatist Luigi Pirandello, who with his *Six Characters in Search of an Author*, burst onto the literary scene with the originality of his genius.

Alfredo had conveyed to his family and, therefore, also to Pier Giorgio his admiration for the German people, for their hard-working efficiency and their ability to confront problems from both a philosophical and a pragmatic perspective. He had learned to love Germany from the days when he was a law student at the University of Turin, when he decided

---

[1] L. Frassati, *Un uomo, un giornale: Alfredo Frassati*, vol. 2, pt. 2 (Rome: Edizioni di Storia e Letteratura, 1979), 233.

to take an advanced course in penal law in Heidelberg, where he stayed for a semester as an extraordinary auditor. After completing his degree with honors on July 9, 1890, he decided to travel to Germany again to attend courses in penal law. Therefore, his transfer to Berlin was not entirely traumatic.

He was proud of that appointment, but he was not happy to have to remain far from home and from his newspaper. We read in a letter sent to his daughter that January:

> Of all the sacrifices that Papa has made for you, the greatest is the sacrifice of having come to Berlin. . . . And that is no small sacrifice. To think that many people would be happy to be in my position. I, on the other hand . . . , almost with emotion [think] about my mountains. It is beautiful here, too. As I wrote to Mama, there are very beautiful beech trees right nearby us, deciduous plants of all sorts. . . . When Giorgio gets back, give him a nice kiss from me. And wish him well, very well, for me. . . . Greet everyone at *La Stampa* for me, and tell them that I will die before being able to accomplish one hundredth of what I accomplished at the piazza Solferino. But there I had both hands and feet free.

At Victoriastrasse 36, there was a run-down, disorganized embassy, and he turned it into a dignified, efficient place. The major task that this involved proved to be the receptions that the embassy was obliged to host, which Frassati could not avoid. Pier Giorgio experienced even more intensely the same impatience with social life, whereas the daughter, Luciana, was rather attracted to it. One day the chancellor Rofi saw Pier Giorgio in a hurry and asked him whether he was going to a certain party. The young man replied by giving an address in an alley near Alexanderplatz, in a district noted only for its poverty.

Many had heard about Pier Giorgio's generosity and there-fore asked for assistance and favors. He answered all letters and always sought to grant every request, and in the margins of the letters he used to write: "answered". One day with the temperature at 10° F, he arrived in Berlin with only his jacket on his back, because he had given his overcoat to a poor man. What an extravagant son the senator had . . . and what good could it do him to have an heir who used to take the flowers away from the drawing rooms so as to put them on the coffins of poor people?

In Germany he became acquainted with the Dominican Father Karl Sonnenschein, founder of the General Office for Work, of a circle for artists, and of the Catholic People's University, who was called "the German Saint Francis", the pastor of the Italian Catholics residing in Berlin and the spiri-tual guide of the students. The priest, known for his simplic-ity and his great charity,[2] struck up a very good relationship of mutual respect and sympathy with the young man from Turin and invited him to participate in the meetings of the mixed groups, made up of both students and workers. Pier Giorgio would have liked to imitate Father Sonnenschein, since he was attracted by his way of performing charitable work, but he understood that he would never succeed in doing so in Italy as a priest.

There had been a moment, before his experience in Ger-many, when Pier Giorgio had thought about a possible priestly career; he would have liked to talk about it at home, with his mother, but he lacked the courage; a decision like that would have been unthinkable. He spoke about it then with his father confessor, telling him: "My vocation is to

---

[2] Father Karl Sonnenschein left all that he owned to the poor and died in 1979 in extreme poverty. The funeral was celebrated at State expense, and all Berlin participated in it.

be a missionary, but I do not know how to tell my mother."
He therefore asked him to intervene by speaking about it
with the two nuns who used to visit the Frassati household,
Sister Angelica and Sister Celeste.

This is the account of Adelaide's cousin, Maria Rina Pierazzi: "One day Sister Angelica told me that she had taken
the opportunity of a walk in the garden with Signora Adelaide and had said to her: 'Signora, if Pier Giorgio were to
tell you that he wants to become a priest or a missionary,
what would you say?' And Sister Angelica related to me that
Signora Frassati stopped suddenly and said, 'Rather than see
Pier Giorgio become a priest, I would prefer that he take
his degree and then die!' "[3]

Pier Giorgio never learned of those terrible words, although scoldings were part of his daily routine. They took
every opportunity to humiliate him, making him understand
how little respect they had for him in the family, in the hopes
of being able to incite him to become more responsible according to their intentions and desires: to see their son make
a brilliant match. Not uncommonly the young man arrived
late for meals, especially because of his charitable work. He
would excuse himself and take his place at the table, and
the maternal rebuke would arrive punctually: "Always with
your head in the clouds; you remember to go to Mass but
not to come to dinner." He would not raise his head and
endured his own suffering in silence.

His mother, worried like his father about the continual
prayers recited by their son, decided to call on Father Tito
Zambelli, a Venetian refugee who had settled in Pollone,

---

[3] M. Codi, *Pier Giorgio Frassati: Una valanga di vita* (Casale Monferrato [AL]:
Portalupi, 2001), 68–69; see also L. Frassati, *A Man of the Beatitudes: Pier Gior-
gio Frassati*, trans. Dinah Livingstone, adapted and ed. Patricia O'Rourke (San
Francisco: Ignatius Press, 2000), 43.

who accepted the job of speaking to Pier Giorgio so that he would stop saying so many rosaries, especially at night. The family's custom was to recite the rosary only on the vigil of feast days; to exaggerate was wearisome, unseemly, and above all "dangerous".[4] To his question, "Is it true, Pier Giorgio, that when you are in your room you pray for a long time?" the young man at first gave no answer. Then, when the priest insisted ("Your Mother told me so. You are upsetting her, and she gets up in the night . . ."), he declared, "But I have so many prayers to say." "And who has ordered you to?" "No one. I just have to."[5]

The new ambassador admired Friedrich Ebert (1871–1925), leader of the Social Democratic Party, who had supported Germany's entrance into the First World War and, later on, the revolution on November 9, 1918, when the republic was proclaimed and he became head of the government. Opposed to the extremism of the Spartacists, he repressed their uprising with the help of monarchist military leaders. Without breaking continuity with Wilhelm's empire, he sought to assure Weimar Germany of stable leadership in confronting the moral and economic crisis. Ebert was worthy, according to Alfredo Frassati, of holding a place in the German Pantheon between Frederick the Great and Otto von Bismarck.

As one might have guessed, the ambassador found himself in the midst of a very delicate, complex German situation, in which political assassinations followed one after the other by the hand of nationalist extremists. Every possible means (newspapers, speeches, military anniversaries, sports events, and all sorts of associations) became a tool for spreading the

[4] Cf. L. Frassati, *A Man of the Beatitudes*, 44.
[5] Ibid.

nationalist ideology that accused men in the government of groveling before foreign opinion, thus reducing Germany to slavery. Frassati declared: "The constant drip of nationalism on people's minds is incessant."

Although completely absorbed by his new duties, he did not forget to report the most important facts to his own relatives, as demonstrated by the letter written from Berlin on June 23, 1922, after his meeting with Vittorio Emanuele III and Queen Elena, who were traveling through German territory during their trip to Denmark: "Dearly beloved, I write to you in haste because once again I am on the point of departing. This week was dedicated to the railroads: I was in Basel to meet the king and queen. They are very genteel, extremely genteel. I stood for more than three hours: I was invited twice to lunch and sat at the queen's left. I took advantage of the minister [that is, of the presence of foreign minister Carlo Schanzer] to visit Würzburg and Rothenburg." Moreover, he explains, alluding to a curious point of interest: "Tell Giorgio that I did what I could for his friend, but it would be better to have Don Sturzo recommend him. Immediately, I would say. I will travel on to Freiburg: if I can I will greet the family with which Giorgio stayed."[6] The dialogue between father and son was therefore started, and for the open-minded, brilliant senator, a man half belonging to the old nineteenth-century Piedmont region and half an Italian in step with the new times, Don Sturzo was not the Unmentionable. The family to which the ambassador refers is the Rahner family of Freiburg, to which Pier Giorgio was introduced by Father Sonnenschein on October 1, 1921. He remained in their house until October 25, 1921, was treated like a son, and there he had the opportunity to perfect his

---

[6] L. Frassati, *Un uomo, un giornale*, vol. 2, pt. 2, 440.

knowledge of the German language under the direction of the head of the family. During the conference of the Pax Romana in Ravenna, when a female student asked where he had learned German, he replied as follows with his proverbial humility: "In Berlin, where my father is employed."

Two of the seven Rahner children, Karl and Hugo, entered the Society of Jesus, and Karl became one of the greatest theologians of our time, the theologian of Vatican II. Father Karl relates:

> My father was a teacher at the German Institute. My mother used to host young students in our house so as to increase our income, and my father gave private lessons to pay for the studies of us seven children. Among the young guests of my mother in our house was Pier Giorgio Frassati. He was an exceptional, athletic young man: he was a mountain climber, a skier, and horseback rider; he was a cheerful fellow who was able to conduct himself in a lively, impetuous way with the other students.
>
> Every morning he rose early and went to church to hear Mass before the others in the family had risen. He made great efforts to help the poor. He thought of them until the last hours of his life. I remember the enthusiasm with which he recited the prayer of Saint Bernard to the Virgin from Dante's *Divine Comedy*: "Virgin Mother, daughter of your Son. . . ."
>
> He always used to recite the rosary. Maybe he will be declared a saint. That way I can say that I played sports in the Black Forest with a saint.[7]

According to his own biographers, Karl was influenced by the young Italian university student, who was three years older.

---

[7] See M. Staglieno, *Un santo borghese: Pier Giorgio Frassati* (Milan: Bompiani, 1988), 139.

Alfredo's letter to his sister-in-law Elena dated July 1, 1922, is undoubtedly of historic importance:

> I'm done with being a commercial traveler: I was quite tired of it. Imagine the trip! Berlin—Basel—Hildesheim, etc. Which means that I crossed the length and breadth of Germany four times in a few days. . . . The king was more than exquisitely courteous. On the return trip we were together for more than six hours: in Basel (at one o'clock at night) he got up to come greet me. I think that G[iolitti] has a major responsibility: it seems to me that at the time [referring to the First World War] I might have persuaded him about many things: but what happened, happened.

Pier Giorgio, who had been educated in the German language since his childhood and grew up in an atmosphere that was certainly not Germanophobic, considered Germany his second country and enjoyed staying there several times. He visited not only Berlin, but also Mannheim, Heidelberg, Koblenz, Frankfurt am Main, Bonn, Cologne, Düsseldorf, Baden-Baden, . . . and he liked to hike in the forest at Freiburg im Breisgau. He got along well with the people from there and went so far as to say (in a letter to Antonio Villani from Berlin dated November 19, 1922):

> I wish that school would not start again. I wish I had completed my degree so that I could remain in this beautiful country, where the people still are aware of their own responsibility and still have an upright conscience.
>
> Today more than ever we must regretfully acknowledge that the Christian poet Dante was and unfortunately still is right when he exclaims:
>
> > O Italy, you slave, you inn of grief,
> > Ship without helmsman in a mighty tempest,
> > Mistress, not of provinces, but of a brothel!

You can believe that we are well off here, where it is calm because we are far from our poor country, which has fallen into the hands of a band of rogues.

He confesses to Antonio Villani from Turin (January 10, 1923):

You can imagine that I left Germany with great regret because I am a great admirer of the character of the German people. Here in Italy the people change their opinions with every shift of the wind, and then there is no more freedom: I feel more like a stranger in Turin than in Germany.

I can no longer read the newspapers because it only makes me angry; I saw the disgraceful things that the French are perpetrating in the Ruhr Valley.

The occupation of that sector of Germany is disgraceful because it is ruining the most Catholic part of the German population, but, on the other hand, it will help Germany a lot because it will attract the sympathy of the free nations.

Now I am starting the studies that I interrupted, and in two years, if God grants me life, I too will work in the Ruhr and as a Catholic I will help the Germans as much as possible in their recovery, because I consider the war against France to be a truly Holy War, because France as a nation is the daughter of Darkness, the enemy of Peace.

So as not to be inferior to all the Communists throughout Europe, we Catholic university students in Turin are preparing a letter in protest against the infamy of the military occupation of the Ruhr; a letter that I will send to Signorina Schwan for her to forward to the Catholic ladies and gentlemen studying in Bonn.

I understand that words will do little good, but at least we will make them understand that the Catholic university students do not agree with the policy of the Italian government but, rather, are indignant against the European politics that will put an end to all nations.

What had happened in the Ruhr Valley? On January 11, 1923, troops from France and Belgium had occupied the German coal-mining region, the Ruhr, the center of the iron industries. The initiative had been made by the French premier Poincaré, under the pretext of German delays in paying reparations. The government of Chancellor Cuno reacted with a policy of passive resistance that aggravated the economic crisis, causing disastrous inflation in the country. This policy was suspended in 1923 by Cuno's successor, Stresemann. Thanks to Anglo-American pressures and the electoral defeat of Poincaré, France agreed to evacuate the coal-producing region in the summer of 1925.

Pier Giorgio felt desperately helpless: to his friend Willibald Leitgebel he explained that the Catholics in Italy had lost their freedom and that "with a bleeding heart" he was witnessing the Italian government's support of France; he was sure, however, that God would reward Germany for her cruel sufferings. With his hands tied, he could do nothing but help the poor directly and, in particular, the children of Berlin.

His Christian identity was for the Blessed a responsibility and a seal on life that must be taken beyond the borders of his own country, as was the case in Germany and in his support by public statements of the struggle of the Irish people who demanded "the independence of their own land and of their own spirit". He had also joined the international association Pax Romana, which united Catholic university students from all nations: the International of the Church confronting the Communist International.

Pier Giorgio actively participated in German social problems, and despite his distance from home, he seemed to find many elements in common with his political life as a student involved in the fabric of society. Moreover, he was perfectly well integrated into the German people, as he writes on January 23, 1923, to his friend Maria Fischer of Vienna, whom he had met at the Pax Romana congress in Ravenna: "I, who have traveled a lot through Germany, admire today more than ever the demeanor of the Germans. Today the German people are an example to all nations of true patriotic love and seriousness."

Pier Giorgio's decision not to enter the priesthood was made in Germany, of all places, thanks to Father Sonnenschein, who introduced him to many needy families. The young Blessed was deeply impressed by the freedom with which the German priest moved among his poor people, unlike the sometimes detached formality with which Italian priests related to them. In a foreign country, he understood that he was supposed to remain a layman and to carry out his Christian apostolate among the people, among those who were poor materially and in spirit.

The "friend from Germany", as he called himself, sent to Signorina Fischer the sum of ninety thousand Kronen,[8] which he had saved up from his earlier trip in German-speaking lands; he asked her to use the money according to the needs of her family and of their own acquaintances, specifying: "In all this my name must remain secret." In Vienna, as in many other cities of Austria and Germany, the rates of unemployment and inflation were startling; women and children were living without a roof over their heads, prey to hunger and desperation, and the Blessed witnessed poverty and privations. Pier Giorgio brought his breeze of charity to foreign lands as well, in areas that "do not count":

---

[8] The krone (crown), worth ten marks, circulated in Germany until 1924.

"His name, like his person, was unknown or almost ignored, whereas people spoke a lot about his sister as the one who held in her hands the social reins of the embassy."[9]

He fit in perfectly with German Catholic society, thus succeeding in establishing intense human relations and friendships. With company he used to drink beer, and he had bought himself a *Studentenpfeife*, a meter-long "student's pipe", at the price of fifteen Italian lire, which "can be smoked conveniently when one must study". Almost every day he would write to his mother, explaining: "With great joy I was able to hear the voice of my dear Papa."

His father met Benito Mussolini in March of 1922, the year of the march on Rome. The ambassador left the following written note:

> In the spring of 1922, my press office told me that the Berlin correspondent from *Il Popolo d'Italia* was asking me for an audience on behalf of Mussolini, whom he had met in the capital. Mussolini's polemics against me had never been intoned softly, and his followers, before and during Fascism, always did me the honor of listing me among those persons who had to be "removed from circulation, because they were always offending the national sentiment, whether they were named Albertini, Amendola, Frassati, Sturzo, Turati, Giovanni Conti, or De Gasperi, thus restoring to Italy the death penalty that the free republics of Europe and America employ so advantageously." I admit that for me it was not a distinct pleasure to have to meet with Mussolini, but I immediately understood that I needed to forget all merely personal circumstances. Mussolini came, there was a long discussion. He asked me what the situation was in Germany, and I made for him a summary of

[9] Codi, *Pier Giorgio Frassati*, 127.

my reports. . . . A serious situation with catastrophic consequences, both economic and political.[10]

Strongly opposed to Mussolini's warlike creed, Frassati's *La Stampa* was the only important Italian daily newspaper to disagree with Mussolini. With bitter regret, the ambassador lamented to his wife his helplessness when faced with the tragic events that were overrunning Germany: "It is a thankless, wretched task to foresee the catastrophe and to be conscious of not having delayed it for one second or mitigated it by a single milligram."

The gloomy German panorama did not stifle the nation's cultural activities: Berlin was the European center of theatrical activity, where the great Austrian producer Max Reinhard, the organizer of the Salzburg Festival, worked together with the dramatist and librettist Hugo von Hoffmansthal. The literature and the theater of the Roaring Twenties offered unsurpassable masterpieces to the world: Bertolt Brecht, Luigi Pirandello, James Joyce, Ernest Hemingway, Marcel Proust, Thomas Mann, and Italo Svevo . . . no other decade could boast of so many great artists, some of whom published their works only later, such as the Cantos of the American poet Ezra Pound or the novels of Franz Kafka in Prague, the author of the insecurity and helplessness of the individual in an absurd, uncontrollable world.

At the beginning of the First World War, Hermann Hesse had been one of the few writers in the German language to fight vehemently in favor of peace. Working for the Red Cross, he had considered it his duty and a "bitter necessity" to protest against the folly of war. His novels *Siddhartha*

[10] A. Frassati, "Ricordi di ambasciata: Ambasciatore di Mussolini", *La Stampa*, May 5, 1955.

(1922), inspired by Indian philosophical thought, and *Steppenwolf* (1927), a parable about the spiritual decline of the European bourgeoisie, took a clear stance in favor of the individual personality in an age of mass society.

Meanwhile, amid the dark clouds, promising news arrived in early November 1922: Pier Giorgio had passed a difficult exam, and his mother expressed her joy on the seventh of that month: "My dearest Giorgetto, your telegram just arrived, filling us with joy—bravo, my little son! Why did you never mention it ahead of time? Or did you not tell us that morning so as not to make us anxious? All day Papa exclaims that he can no longer do without it—the sky, the meadows, Pollone, etc.—but certainly we will see him here again in the spring. This is only my impression, though, and nothing else." Adelaide could therefore be affectionate, when she was calm and her desires were satisfied.

Weary, demoralized, and "fed up", the ambassador, who advocated a policy that, while preferring to maintain good relations with the Allies, did not admit that the salvation of Italy was connected with the destruction and annihilation of Germany, submitted his resignation the day after the march on Rome; his resignation was not accepted by Mussolini at first (November 4, 1922). He gave up a career as an ambassador because he could no longer represent a government he did not respect. Thus, after two years of enduring residency abroad, Alfredo Frassati was finally able to pack his bags.

12

LAURA

"The friend who encouraged you in mountain climbing will help you along the painful, difficult way to reach the summit where light, rest, and joy await us. Pier Giorgio's mother to Laura Hidalgo with affectionate memory. Turin, March 4, 1928": this is the dedication that Adelaide Ametis wrote in her own hand on the copy of the book *Pier Giorgio Frassati*, by Don Antonio Cojazzi, that was published in 1928, three years after the death of her son, which she gave to the girl that Pier Giorgio loved.

The Frassati family never liked to talk about this young woman, even after the death of Pier Giorgio. In Luciana's books, she is mentioned, nothing more. Laura always appeared as the one who aspired to enter the Frassati household but was rejected because she was beneath them. That was not the case. Through Laura's daughters, Stefania and Beatrice, we can now recover the thread of memory so as to become more closely acquainted with the secretary of the Sinister Types.

Laura Hidalgo was born on November 8, 1898, in Alessandria, but her father was of Spanish origin. She was a beautiful brunette with big eyes, highly intelligent, and very vivacious.

Laura was left an orphan at an early age. Her father, Stefano Hidalgo, after a brilliant military career in which he reached the rank of general of the light infantry, died in 1917 of diabetic gangrene, whereas her mother, Bice Coletti,[1] a school administrator and author, passed away two years later, at the age of forty-eight, of Spanish fever. Therefore, she had to grow up fast and care not only for herself, but also for her younger brother, Emanuele, a future engineer. Laura quickly became acquainted with the meaning of responsibility and the importance of confronting everyday problems.

She had a strong temperament, inclined to determination and not to compromise: facing life alone, even in its most difficult aspects, had refined and strengthened her character. She fit in perfectly with the Sinister Types.

She met Pier Giorgio in 1906, when his family settled in Turin on the via Avogadro 26, in the house where Pier Giorgio's paternal grandmother and uncle were living. When the future Blessed went to visit them with his sister, Laura often heard the noise they used to make in the staircases. Sometimes the children played together, but they did not get along very well, for one reason, because Laura was noticeably three years older.

She saw him again in their years in secondary school and at the Massimo d'Azeglio Lyceum. Someone who was about the same age as Laura, Gaetano Di Sales, recalls his classmate at the classical lyceum in a priceless testimony that we discovered in a parish bulletin from the church of La Crocetta (1984):

---

[1] Daughter of Nicolò Coletti, the brave patriot from the province of Caserta who sided against the Bourbon government, who after many transfers settled in the Piedmont in the city of Alessandria.

I remember as though it was today. There were four young ladies who came into the lecture hall together, wearing long black pinafores, after the boys. She was the first of the four, because she was shorter; she was poised, almost timid, with her face turned toward the others, as though she wanted to go unnoticed.

Our class made history. In that first year of the lyceum, our average age was fifteen. But there were also two students who were just thirteen. They were almost all "big guns". To mention just one: Piero Sraffa, who later was an economist at Cambridge. And of those who were mediocre, some through study excelled in other fields. . . . She, Laura, was at the same level as the best students. . . . She never made a bad impression. And in the literary competitions in honor of Umberto Cosmo, she was always one of the first. Some students also went to her house to do their assignments. Therefore I also remember her relatives: General Stefano, the commander of the stronghold in Kassala, commemorated in the dirges of the local people, to whom the Abyssinians paid honor by presenting arms (1896). Her mother, too, who used to come to open the door for us and then disappear. A thoroughly respectable family.

The young lady met Pier Giorgio again in the Catholic group named after Cesare Balbo, given the relations between the FUCI students and the women's group named after Gaetana Agnesi that Laura attended because of the religious initiatives and the spiritual exercises that it organized periodically. "And finally she struck up a fraternal friendship with him on the occasion of trips to the mountains."[2] She lived then at via Sacchi 24. In the same house, downstairs, lived her friend Maria Adelaide Chicco (who later had a son

---

[2] Congregation Pro Causis Sanctorum, *Canonizationis Servi Dei Petri Georgii Frassati: Positio super virtutibus*, vol. 2 (Rome: Tipografia Guerra, 1987), 41.

who became a priest), with whom she went almost every day to Mass. Maria is now elderly; shortly before Laura's death, she commended herself to her in these words: "You were always one floor above. From heaven throw a rope down to me and pull me up."

After successfully completing her secondary school studies, she took a degree in mathematics on July 13, 1920, and to commemorate the event several friends, among them Pier Giorgio, signed a manifesto sketched in pencil with cartoon scenes.

She became a professor as well as a university librarian on the via Po, and to supplement her income she also gave private lessons. The exuberant Pier Giorgio noticed her, and his initial sympathy turned into affection. This was at Mardi Gras, February 11, 1923, the year of the performance of *Il Paese dei campanelli* by Ranzato, which was an expression of the cultural climate of the *belle époque*: the operetta celebrated its splendors but also announced its decline. The Sinister Types organized an excursion to Il Piccolo San Bernardo, and on that mountaintop Pier Giorgio realized that he was in love. As Laura's daughters relate, he began to telephone Adelaide Chicco every day in order to talk with Laura, who had no telephone.

Did she know? It remained an undeclared love. Pier Giorgio did not mention his feelings so as not to trouble her. The journalist Maria Grazio Cucco wrote in *Famiglia Cristiana* in 1975:

> At a distance of more than a half a century, it is an almost incomprehensible episode, this conflict between romantic passion and reasons of state, or rather, in this case, the interests of the family. A useless cruelty. "I know," Luciana Frassati told me, "but then we did not think that Pier Giorgio's end was so near and that he too had a right to a hope

of happiness. Besides, our family was going through a very difficult time; our parents were on the verge of separating. Pier Giorgio had every reason to fear that he might accelerate the crisis by being headstrong. He sacrificed himself, as always, in silence."[3]

Stefania Gonella explains:

Our mother knew nothing. Pier Giorgio never acknowledged anything to her. But she was not in love. He was an exceptionally good friend, it is true. She always described for us his courtesy and his immense generosity; she was acquainted with other good young men who were sincerely devoted to Holy Mother Church, but what she said about Pier Giorgio was different because this was the son of Senator Frassati, and that made the difference: from a son of the *haute bourgeoisie* one expected a life-style more in keeping with his social class.

In an interview granted a year before her death, which occurred at the age of seventy-eight (October 28, 1976), Laura Hidalgo said that Pier Giorgio would never have married her. "And I am happy, in a certain sense, that he remained silent, sparing me regret for the grief that I would have caused him."[4] Laura was married on July 16, 1929, in the Church of San Secondo with Monsignor Giovanni Battista Pinardi officiating, to a fellow mathematician, Professor Giovanni Battista Gonella, who more than once helped Pier Giorgio prepare for his exams, and she moved to Genoa to follow her husband, who continued his teaching career there. Professor Gonella was born in Bologna on January 28, 1897; a member of Catholic Action, he was a fervent Christian like

[3] See M. G. Cucco, "Il capolavoro di Pier Giorgio", *Famiglia Cristiana*, May 18, 1975.

[4] Soon after the interview, Laura Hidalgo, while chatting about her old memories, suffered a sharp deterioration in the state of her health.

Laura, and he too was an orphan. Highly intelligent, he had taken his degree at the age of only twenty-one in 1918. In all ways entirely different from Pier Giorgio Frassati, physically and in his personality, Professor Giovanni Battista was reserved, taciturn, completely immersed in study. Timid, theoretical, and very kind, he found in Laura a highly trained, educated woman who loved books and authors like Thomas Mann, Thomas Merton, the Russian classics, and Saint Augustine. They had three children: Luigi, Beatrice, and Stefania. But Laura was widowed at the age of fifty: in July 1948, Professor Gonella suffered a heart attack after a demanding electoral campaign on behalf of the Christian Democrats. Laura found herself once again alone in confronting life, a spiritually intense life: it was no accident that she had become a Third Order Franciscan. Forty-six years of teaching helped her to raise her children, who gave her eleven grandchildren.

What did their mother tell them about Pier Giorgio? Stefania again answers:

> He continued to be the gentle, dear, generous friend. In her house, there was a photograph that always went with her, in which he is depicted on the mountain, alone, with his ice ax and a pipe in his mouth. When she socialized with him, she certainly did not think she was in the presence of a young man who one day would be raised to the honors of the altar. In those days, holiness was considered from a different perspective. The models of the Catholic Church were the giants, the ones involved in the great, extravagant enterprises. Turin was the scene of extraordinary champions of heroic virtue, and everyone talked about high-sounding names. Archbishop Giuseppe Gamba beatified Don Cafasso on May 3, 1925, and Don Bosco on

June 2, 1929. Pier Giorgio is an altogether different sort of Blessed. He lived an everyday lay sanctity, incarnate in simple little things. This sort of sanctity was not taken into consideration by the Church at that time.

The friendship that sprang up among the Sinister Types lasted over time. They lost their finest flower, but the other branches lived for a long time and were not forgotten. Pier Giorgio's best friend, Marco Beltramo, was the godfather of Beatrice Gonella, and Ernestina Bonelli, who came from a very well-to-do family, was her godmother. During World War II, at the time of the evacuation of the city of Genoa, Tina took in Laura's three children and their nurse because their house in Liguria had been destroyed in a bombardment, and they remained there from the autumn of 1942 until Christmas, when a house was found for them in Rapallo. Tina Bonelli, although very rich, was extremely generous and simple. Stefania goes on to say: "The Sinister Types were like that: united, loving beautiful, sensible things. A mixed group, which was avant-garde, despite the bigotries of that era and its notions of respectability." Clementina Luotto, too, the president of the Society of Sinister Types and also a teacher of Latin and Greek in Cavour, remained connected to her former friends. She died a few days apart from Laura Hidalgo.

Relations between the Frassati and Gonella families were always kept at a rather formal level. For Laura's wedding gift, the Frassatis gave a magnificent carpet and a silver platter. From time to time, Luciana used to call on Laura Hidalgo when she needed to for the questionnaires in her brother's beatification process, but nothing more than that.

One day Pier Giorgio, after a long description of a recent mountain ascent, showed his friend Franz Massetti a splendid photograph of himself standing on the summit. It depicted in the foreground Laura herself with an ice ax in her hand and the rope linking the party at her shoulder belt, and in the background the chain of snow-topped peaks. "Marveling at the beauty of the photograph," Massetti later said, "I asked him for a copy to keep in my album." At that request Pier Giorgio hesitated. As an expression of his utmost respect, he wanted to ask Laura first whether it was possible to grant his friend's request. She gave her consent, and the photograph was given to him.

Pier Giorgio and Laura spoke to each other using the formal Italian pronoun *Lei* (rather than the familiar *tu*), as was the case with all his female friends. But his love for her grew until the young man felt the need to speak about it with his sister, Luciana, who advised him according to the set rules of the family: she was not a suitable girl for him, and too many obstacles of a familial and social nature stood in the way of any possible engagement. Moreover, there was the pending threat of a definitive separation between their father and their mother, and a choice like that could have hastened the process. He spoke to her on December 18, 1924; what he confided to her was described in a letter that Luciana wrote to her fiancé, Jan Gawronski:

> Yesterday evening Pier Giorgio came to my room with his big brown eyes and told me that he was in love with a young lady whom I know. . . . Of course he said nothing to Mama because that would be the final blow. Poor boy, it was moving to hear him speak, given his activity, which we just do not discuss in the family. I told him to try not to see her: he assured me that he had already done so, and then added: "If I go to the mountains on Sunday and she

goes too, what should I do to avoid going? Should I telephone? Write her?" Poor boy.

I watched him, wide-eyed, and I told myself that it would take all his goodness, all his uprightness to act in that way: and I tell you the truth, I felt much, much lower than he. Then a set of arguments about his career, his ideals, the fact that he felt torn, because to everything he said he would add: "But I cannot, because I do not want to leave Mama."

It is necessary to remember this and to treat him with much kindness and sweetness, as though he had said: "Luciana, I am sick." Giorgio also told me that not only had he not yet said a word to her, but he had not even hinted.

To his closest friends, he then revealed his internal conflicts, and he clung to his prayers and his faith alone:

This is a major moment for me. The struggle is difficult, but it is necessary to try to win and to find our own little road to Damascus so as to be able to walk along it toward the goal at which we must all arrive. A little more effort, and I too will have earned the much-desired diploma; but then there is a whole problem that is much more difficult. . . . Will I be able to solve this serious problem? Surely the faith is the only anchor of salvation; it is necessary to cling to it steadfastly; without it what would our whole life be? Nothing! Or rather, it would be spent uselessly, because in this world there is only sorrow, and sorrow without faith is unbearable, whereas sorrow nourished by the torch of faith becomes so beautiful because it strengthens the mind for its battles.[5]

We do not know how Pier Giorgio would really have resolved his sentimental quandary if he had lived longer;

[5] A. Cojazzi, *Pier Giorgio Frassati: Testimonianze* (Turin: SEI, 1928), 276.

we know the arguments, but would the reality have corresponded to the theory? Probably yes, seeing that Pier Giorgio was an extremely serious, consistent person. His dilemmas, however, continued until the end, as he wrote to a friend:

> Dead? What does that word mean? If by dead you mean the common definition, then I am still alive, if my senses do not betray me. But if we take the word in its true meaning, then unfortunately not only am I dead but I have already been revived several times, only, alas, to die again. I would like to travel along the straight path, but at every step I stumble and fall. Therefore I exhort you to pray as much as you can for me, that I might arrive, on the day that Divine Providence foresees, at the end of my wearisome but straight path. Meanwhile, these days, I alternate my dry studies with marvelous readings from Saint Augustine. Until now my mind never experienced so powerfully the joy that has no end, because through these mighty *Confessions* one experiences a bit of the joy that is reserved for those who die in the sign of the Cross. Today I bitterly lament having often wasted my time and having waited to taste pure joys like this.[6]

Fifty years later, Laura Hidalgo, as a resident of a nursing home on a hill in Turin, would recall to a journalist from *Famiglia Cristiana* the young man who had loved her: "A good boy, quiet. . . . I remember that sometimes he seemed struck by sad forebodings. 'I will die young', he used to say. 'Oh, please', we would retort. 'You will grow old and will bring flowers for all the rest of us. . . .' When he died, what weeping. . . ."

They were acquainted from childhood, as we said, but Pier Giorgio's interest and tenderness emerged when he saw her

[6] Ibid., 276–77.

years later as an orphan compelled to shift for herself in her lonely existence. Although he had made no open declaration, Laura knew about his feelings. "It was clear that he had become infatuated. But there were the women of his family, who were so hostile. As if I, a general's daughter, were not of the same rank; and even higher than they", Laura continued in the same interview. In our opinion, she was still troubled not only by the Frassatis' rejection of her, but by the resignation of Pier Giorgio himself. "Only once did I set foot in the Frassati house, together with another girl from the group. They offered us tea in the dining room; Pier Giorgio's mother made an appearance for a few moments. Oh, I understood very well that we did not please her, that she found us ugly. But to us none of that mattered." It was an afternoon in the spring of 1923, and Laura, whose mind-set was completely different from that of the Frassati women, felt that they passed judgment on her: it was, as she herself said, a cross-examination by the mother. "We did not notice, therefore, that Pier Giorgio was watching her reactions with bated breath," Luciana explains, "like someone who is awaiting clemency or condemnation, and it fell to me, more than one year later, to impose the negative verdict on him."

One evening, Pier Giorgio confided to a friend: "I will not leave money to my children, because I am convinced that riches, instead of promoting their social integration, very often serve only to stir up their passions. I will endeavor to give them thorough instruction and a Christian education so that, if they want, they can acquire a worthy social position. But, once that is done, if I have any money, I will give it to works of charity and not to my children." Laura made no comment on that statement in the book given to her by Adelaide Frassati, but she clearly marked the passage with a line in the margin.

Love matured him psychologically, causing him to leave adolescence behind: he became a man, and his faith became stronger, more muscular. Until then he had observed and shared the sorrows of others, including those of his parents resulting from their lack of harmony, but now he experienced suffering firsthand. He was no longer the carefree youth; an awareness of life was ahead of him. Even his physical appearance showed this: the photographs from the last two years reflect a Pier Giorgio who has lost his childish features and whose expression has become more serious, deeper, more solemn.

He pours out his heart to his friend Isidoro Bonini (writing from Mondane on December 28, 1924):

Dear friend,

I am reading the novel by Italo Mario Angeloni *Ho amato così* [This is how I loved], in which he describes in the first part his love for an Andalusian woman, and, you can believe me, I find it very moving because it seems like the story of my love.

This is how I loved, too, except that in the novel the Andalusian woman makes the sacrifice, whereas in my case I will be the one sacrificed, but if God wills it, then may his holy will be done. Today I am going to Sauze d'Oulx to test the trail for the excursions of Giovane Montagna [an association of young mountain climbers]; tomorrow the company leaves for San Bernardo, and I am with them in spirit for two reasons: because San Bernardo was the birthplace of my shattered dream, alas, and then because there is found the one whom I loved with a pure love, and today in renouncing her I want her to be happy. I ask you to pray that God may grant to me the Christian fortitude to endure it all calmly and to you all earthly happiness and the strength to reach the Goal for which we were created. On the day of your graduation I experienced how true are the words of Saint Augustine, who says: "Lord, our heart is restless until it rests in Thee"; indeed, someone who chases after worldly joys is foolish because they are always fleeting and bring sorrows, whereas the one true joy is the kind that faith gives us, and companions who are loved in a special way through this powerful bond will always remain united even if the circumstances of life scatter us far, far apart. And so she will always be for me a good friend whom I knew in the dangerous years of life and helped me to continue on the straight path toward the Goal.

His love for Laura, the professional paths chosen by his friends, which would soon "scatter them far, far apart", and the approaching end of his own studies coincided; these three things saddened his life, as is clear from a sorrowful letter written to his friend Gian Maria Bertini on July 29, 1924, in which he confides the struggles his heart had to face:

I need prayers because I am going through a critical stage of my life—you understand, I am on the verge of leaving behind student life, which is beautiful because it is carefree, in order to undertake the arduous climb of life, a path that is, alas, very difficult especially since something in me has changed, something that forecasts a very severe storm.

Laura was the cause of the storm:

Our last excursion to La Ciamarella left me with good and sad memories that alternate endlessly in me. Unfortunately, I think it will be the last excursion I will make with the company, and this causes a bit of sorrow in me because I had befriended them, and then also for reasons that you know well. But if it comes to that final step, I will take it, with some regret on my part; the one thing I would want is that she should improve her condition and should live happily forever. My photograph album will be for me a sad reminder of my life. At any rate, I will confront the difficulties, I hope, by preparing myself in prayer and in the hope of one day or another going on to a better life.

My illness is such that no human intervention can stop it. Human intervention can give me remedies that may alleviate the crisis but not root out the cause of the ailment; faith alone can be my hope and comfort in my future life, and therefore I ask you to pray a lot for me that I may strengthen my faith each day and thus be able to have the fortitude to endure the difficulties that are being placed in my way in these final years of my youth. . . .

In a letter to Antonio Villani, he wrote: "And what are you doing? Will you come to spend Mardi Gras in the mountains . . . ? I was thinking of going, but yesterday evening I was totally in a crisis because I am leading a life that is not very good, and therefore I do not know whether I will go to the Piccolo San Bernardo, all the more reason because from now on I would like to be with the young ladies as little as possible."

A trip to the region of Quercianella, near Livorno, increased Pier Giorgio's love for Laura.[7] Luciana recalls:

[7] Forte dei Marmi, August 13, 1924: "Dear friend [Antonio Villani], on Saturday I took a trip to Marina di Pisa, but since it is only an hour by train from Pisa to Quercianella Sonnino, I decided to make an excursion first to call on Signorina Hidalgo.

"I met many charming young ladies and the house mother, who at all costs wanted me to miss the train at noon that was supposed to bring me to Pisa, and then I was to go to Marina di Pisa by streetcar. And so instead of returning on Saturday evening, I returned on Sunday after lunch. Of course, right now my relatives know nothing about this semi-academic modification; when I find an opportune moment to talk about it with my sister, I will tell her also about the particulars of that visit, but for now diplomacy and my mother's state of health, which is not too good, advise prudence. My studies, on the other hand, are going well enough, although I have to make an enormous effort in order to be able to concentrate in the few hours assigned to study:

Serious torments, sufferings, and renunciations occupied the short time between the trip to Quercianella . . . which I recall perfectly, and the day of his death. It tortured his mind cruelly to the point of the supreme sacrifice, the final "no" whereby he gave up before speaking to her . . . the girl whom he had chosen in the secret silence of his heart. But the thought of his future happiness could not overcome the anguish of his perturbed family.[8]

The days he spent at San Bernardo together with the company were wonderful for him: "Up there . . . one might say that I spent the happiest days of my past life" (letter to Signorina Hidalgo, dated December 28, 1924).

Laura received several gifts from Pier Giorgio: a gentian[9] picked near the Vittorio Sella shelter and a little rock brought back from the summit of La Grivola, reminders of his dear mountains; but the most important gift was the one he liked the best, the Letters of Saint Paul. They were in Latin with a commentary in Latin, two volumes bound together as one with a very carefully formulated dedication: "Easter, Holy Year [1925]. To the dear Signorina Laura Hidalgo, in a Christian spirit Pier Giorgio Frassati offers this book in Jesus Christ, so that Saint Paul may be for her a guide and

but I thank God that I have to study, otherwise my mind would wander to things that are happy and sad at the same time, and I do not know where I would end up."

[8] P. G. Frassati, *Lettere*, ed. L. Frassati, preface by Luigi Sturzo (Rome: Studium, 1950), 286.

[9] The gentian was sent from Cogne on September 13, 1924, with this message: "I send you a gentian picked near the Vittorio Sella Shelter as an homage from a Sinister Type to his secretary and from the porter to the cook and also because Abbot Henry says that 'young ladies are flowers', and therefore I think that every creature loves its like." On May 18, 1925, Laura and Pier Giorgio picked two gentians together and sent them to Clementina Luotto, the president of the Society of Sinister Types.

teacher on her earthly pilgrimage." Then came the Italian translation: "With this [volume] you can appreciate better the beauty of the Latin and understand better the philosophical connection . . ." (April 30, 1925), he wrote in the accompanying letter—"one of the very few that I kept," Laura later said when she was interviewed for the beatification process, "since I destroyed the letters that he sent me, as is my custom."[10]

Pier Giorgio also gave Laura a *Life of Christ* for Easter 1923, so that it might be "a consolation in the sad hours" of her life. When Laura had to take oral examinations, Pier Giorgio used to pray for her success; he even went to Eucharistic adoration at the Consolata Church right at the moment when she was being questioned.

During his evening prayers and the holy rosary, he admitted that he was distracted by his love: his spiritual suffering was continual. His love for Laura was controversial and tormented, which created for him a heavy, oppressive, unbearable spiritual crisis that sometimes made him feel he was suffocating. He wrote to Gian Maria Bertini in December 1924:

> Dear friend,
>
> when you read this letter I do not know what you might think of me; I smell right now all the stench with which I am reeking, and yet my weakness, my inconstant, insecure character drags me down.
>
> I would like to come with you, but my mind is too depressed, and I could not enjoy your company; it is more fitting for me, who until now have accomplished nothing, and if I have accomplished something it has been only buf-

[10] Congregatio Pro Causis Sanctorum, *Canonizationis Servi Dei Petri Georgii Frassati: Positio super virtutibus*, vol. 2 (Rome: Tipografia Guerra, 1987), 242.

fooneries. . . . I know what the better path would be: to remain at home and to devote myself in silence to study, but what I consider good I do not do because I do not have the will.

There was no conclusion to this letter, just a few confused ideas concerning his mental abilities at that moment.

I would love to attend your dinner were it not for the continual doubt that troubles my mind and the ongoing battle that torments my conscience, a battle to suppress my whole past with all my wicked acts so as to rise up toward a better life—I ask for your compassion and prayers so that I might soon find the strength to win this difficult but necessary battle. My boat is about to sink to the bottom in these last stormy waves of my student life. . . . In order to put certain plans into action it takes an iron will, . . . and I have a will that is too used to giving in. . . . I need prayers, because with them and through them alone I will be able to obtain grace from God.[11]

The suffering of unrequited love strengthened, completed, and perfected him. He himself revealed this superbly in words imbued with sanctity:

Today in my struggles I can only thank God that in his infinite mercy he willed to grant this sorrow to my heart, so that through these bitter trials I might return to a more spiritual life. Until now I have lived too materially, and now I need to reinvigorate my spirit for future struggles, because from now on every day, every hour will be a new battle to fight and a new victory to win. A spiritual upheaval ought to take place in me, and so this year I will dedicate myself to reading Saint Thomas Aquinas. Thus, immersed in those marvelous pages, every thought about the world will

[11] Cf. Cojazzi, *Pier Giorgio Frassati*, 277–78.

be dead, and I will experience glad days, in that joy that has no end because it is not human.[12]

On March 6, 1925, he felt the need to reveal his interior state to his friend Isidoro Bonini, and he wrote, in a sort of spiritual testament:

Dear friend,

[I]t is true that I avoided speaking to you about such a bitter concern, but I did not do so out of a lack of trust, but only because the question is now a thing of the past and it is better to say no more about it and, instead, to close that chapter of my life for good. Yes, the language of this letter will surprise you, but you must consider that something in me has changed: it is not my work, because, on the contrary, I did not apply even one of the energetic measures I announced to you before your departure from Turin. I was in the mountains many times with you and many times with others; but now I am convinced that being unable to achieve the Purpose, it is necessary to kill the seed that, if well tended, yields immense benefits but, otherwise, causes worries. In my internal struggles I often asked myself: Why should I be sad? Will I have to suffer and endure this sacrifice reluctantly? Have I perhaps lost the faith? No, thank God, my faith is still firm enough, and then we will support and strengthen it; this is the only Joy with which anyone can be rewarded in this world. All sacrifice has value only for the sake of this Joy; then, as Catholics, we have a love that surpasses any other and that, after the love that is due to God, is immensely beautiful, just as our religion is beautiful.

And then we see his love for Saint Paul:

This love had as its advocate the apostle, who preached it daily in all his letters to the faithful in various places. The

[12] Ibid., 283.

charity without which, Saint Paul says, no other virtue has value. Charity such that it can be the guide and direction of a whole life, of a whole plan of action. This with the grace of God can be the goal toward which my mind can tend. And then at the first moment we are alarmed, because it is a beautiful plan, but difficult, full of thorns and few roses, but let us trust in Divine Providence and his mercy.

He then continues with a statement that decisively refutes the theory, on which many have incorrectly insisted, that Pier Giorgio was quarreling with his family:

Pope Pius X of blessed memory recommended to young people the practice of Holy Communion, and I can only thank God every moment for having given me parents, teachers, and all my friends, who have all directed me by the royal road of the faith. Just think, what if at this moment when my mind is going through this crisis, I had the misfortune of not believing; it would be no use living an instant longer, and death alone perhaps would be a relief for all human suffering.

Love and death recall one another: Pier Giorgio was a romantic, not a rationalist; he lived very passionately, and there was no trace of nihilism in him. It was unusual that his jovial, cheerful character was combined with times of profound, long-suffering meditation; not without reason did the writer Piovene see in him "the mystery of joy and sorrow", while John Paul II described him as "the interior man [who] is able to admire the works of God in the external, visible world [and can] turn from this world to the internal, invisible one", thus discovering "the dimensions of the mind that reflect the light of the Word that enlightens every man".

In the same letter to Isidoro Bonini, to whom he confided much in his correspondence, he sketched the plan he wished to follow:

But on the other hand, for someone who believes, the controversies of life are not a reason for despondency. Rather, they serve as a correction and an energetic call to return to the path that may have been abandoned momentarily.

Well then, my plan is this: to redirect that special sympathy that I had for her and that was not deliberate toward the end at which we must arrive, in the light of charity, in the respectful bond of friendship understood in the Christian sense, with respect for her virtues, in imitation of her eminent gifts, as I have for other young women. Maybe you might tell me that it is foolish to hope for that; but I believe, if you will all pray a little for me, that in a short time I will be able to attain that state in prayer.

This is my plan, which I hope to carry out in the grace of God, even if it costs me the sacrifice of earthly life, though that is of little importance.

Pier Giorgio took it for granted that there would be no other loves after Laura and that the only union that could be accomplished was that of a Christian friendship with her "in the light of charity". He wanted to imitate Laura's virtues: "Believe me, the example of all three of them [Laura and his other female friends Clementina Luotto and Ernestina Bonelli] was very persuasive for me, especially at certain moments in life in which the flesh prevails over the spirit", he revealed to Marco Beltramo on April 10, 1925.

It is a real young man speaking, not a cold statue. His sanctity gets through to young people today because of the concreteness of his life; Pier Giorgio faced the everyday problems of all young men: the weariness of study, the joy and enthusiasm of being with friends, playing sports, communing with nature, the generation gap in his ideas as compared with those of his own parents . . . and then his healthy appetite, his desire to sing and have fun, his way of being authentic without pretense and hypocrisy, with a pipe in his mouth, a billiard cue in his hand, and a glass of beer.

Firm, stubborn, and extremely critical of himself, Pier Giorgio was bewildered: his rational decision to give up Laura collided with the aspirations of his heart, sacrificing his happiness in order to save his family: "I could marry her against my family's wishes, but to destroy one family in order to create another would be absurd, and there is no chance that I would think of doing that", he once said, as Don Cojazzi relates in his biography. But Laura Hidalgo put a question mark beside that sentence, right next to the infinitive "to destroy".

The family situation was extremely tense and difficult, with his parents on the verge of separating. Luciana Frassati explains clearly and resolutely:

> The silence between the two of them was heavy with rancor, and it was not easy to move in that atmosphere where Mama's exasperated sensibility had reached the point that it was impossible for her to relate in any way: she behaved like the healthiest person in the world, and yet we had long since become firmly convinced that we were committing a crime if we caused her even the slightest disappointment. Every little incident took on enormous dimensions in that mute, irremediable battle of father against mother.[13]

Despite the very pat answers that Laura always gave about her sentimental indifference toward Pier Giorgio, a mystery remains as to what the young woman, who was a Third Order Franciscan and a Vincentian Lady of Charity, really experienced on account of her friend Pier Giorgio: the

[13] M. Codi, *Pier Giorgio Frassati: Una valanga di vita* (Casale Monferrato [AL]: Portalupi, 2001), 186.

knowledge that the Frassati family had "rejected" her from the outset must have upset her pride somewhat, but one thing is sure: the story of the love between Pier Giorgio and Laura has no parallels with that of Francis and Clare.

After speaking about it with his sister, Pier Giorgio confided in Don Antonio Cojazzi, and the priest recalls as follows the result of that sad discussion:

> He came to visit me once when he was back in Turin for exams, and he told me everything in a long conversation. I remember how he was persuaded when I pointed out to him that the so-called rights of the heart, in such matters of engagement, must keep in mind other more sacred rights. Christianity is not stoicism; it commands neither indifference nor the destruction of feelings, but intends that the demands of the heart be kept within due limits. Without being able to agree with her, I told him all that his mother was thinking.[14] He wept, but with that indescribable gesture of assent that was typical of him, he bowed his head as if to say, "I obey!"[15]

The final testimony that records Pier Giorgio's affection for Laura dates to nineteen days before his death; in it he longs for resignation so as to renounce her entirely, but it is a very difficult struggle. To Marco Beltramo he confides on June 15, 1925:

> Dear friend,
>
> I expect from one day to the next to arm myself with a resolve that will give me the strength to put an end to my final trouble: since now I am close to reaping what I have sown. Alas, the days go by, and, even though I notice some

[14] At this point Laura Hidalgo underlines the whole sentence, implying that the expression "without being able to agree with her" did not correspond to the truth.

[15] Cojazzi, *Pier Giorgio Frassati*, 278.

sign of improvement in me, I see the persistence of the Beast in me that wins out over the Spirit in combat. I see the prayers of my friends as the only powerful aid that can help me regain the upper hand over my animal nature, and therefore I trust especially in your prayers.

"Close to reaping what I have sown": Pier Giorgio is speaking about his long-desired baccalaureate degree, but the expression seems to foreshadow his imminent death.

The emotional crisis continued. From time to time it seemed to be overcome, but those were only short pauses. In his last letter to Beltramo, dated June 22, he writes again: "Thank you . . . for the prayers that you promise; they are all the more appreciated because above all else they are most helpful, especially for someone who is taking a serious step."

A theory that until now has not been taken into consideration was suggested by a friend of Pier Giorgio, Franz Massetti; indeed, it should not be underestimated, and we agree with it.

His anxieties resulted not so much from fear of causing pain or more trouble within his family and of breaking the tie of charity that bound him to his relatives, particularly to his mother, as from the fear of failing to correspond to the invitation of grace.

If the feeling of tenderness for that young woman had been for him a real sign of the divine calling to matrimony, it would have brought serenity, peace, and happiness to his heart as a gift from God, which then would have entered as a grace, without turmoil, together with the prudence and constancy that proceed from the things of God, into the hearts of his dear relatives, in the same way in which the other riches of his life had made their way little by little or were gradually making their way. His mother would have been convinced that the companion whom she begged God to send for her son could only be the one chosen by him in advance and that Pier Giorgio could not give up a grace that would not be his own alone but one shared with the other person.

His fears had much deeper roots; they resided in the depths of his heart in a conflict with himself and had repercussions also in the hearts of his relatives, aggravating the hidden conflict.[16]

This, in our opinion, is the true key for interpreting that unhappy love that was born and died at the same time. If he had heard a real call to matrimony, Pier Giorgio would have knocked on the door of his house and would have declared his intentions courageously, even though the young woman had not been well received. Had he not succeeded in going to Communion every day, despite his mother's disapproval? Had he not joined a party that was opposed to his father's liberalism? Did the heir of the founder of *La Stampa* not throw himself into the fray, amid thrashings and threats? Did the son of the senator and ambassador to Berlin not regularly visit the poor districts of Turin? Did he not disappear every day for purposes that were often unknown to his relatives and that would be discovered only afterward, with his death? . . . In short, when he believed something, he believed it and acted accordingly. He was obedient to his parents, but more obedient to God, who was uppermost in his thoughts, surpassed his intentions, and came first before his own plans.

One day his father held up to him as an example an acquaintance of theirs, saying, "He is such a fine young man that he would marry anyone his father wanted." He

---

[16] F. V. Massetti, *Pier Giorgio Frassati nel ricordo di un amico: Testimonianze riflessioni lettere* (Castelmaggiore [BO]: Tipocolor, 1984).

replied in no uncertain terms and without any other comment: "Well then, he is a big blockhead."[17]

Here, then, is how the many uncertainties, the many doubts and worries can be explained. He was not convinced of that love: it was a strong attraction, but not sufficiently deep to follow that path in reality. His wise friend Franz goes on to say:

> If he did not become a priest, if he did not go off to the missions, if he could not go work among the miners and perhaps would have to be the manager of his father's newspaper, it would be not so much because of the will of men as by order of the One who enriches with his gifts those whom he calls, so that among men they might always and everywhere be faithful witnesses of his love.
>
> Now this affection for a particular creature that seemed to point out to him a different path clearly appeared to him as something contrary to his true vocation, and he wished to remove it from his mind and heart.

But human weakness is strong, and doubt troubled Pier Giorgio's efforts, and therefore he incessantly asked for the help of his friends' prayers.

Massetti sees the mother, who knew nothing about her son's feelings, as an instrument of Providence, and in the cool reception that she gave Laura, who was introduced to her as one of the FUCI members and a companion on excursions, Pier Giorgio found proof that the path that he was to follow, to which the Lord called him, was quite different. His mother, therefore, in light of these considerations, no longer appears as a cruel, egocentric figure, but rather a means of defense and the involuntary, unwitting guardian of her son's vocation to aspire to greater charisms. Franz continues:

[17] Cf. Codi, *Pier Giorgio Frassati*, 185.

Thus the priest in whom he confided could only note with surprise his determination to put out of his mind and his heart his particular feeling of affection for that creature; this was not a renunciation made simply for familial reasons or for other human motives, but the decision of a soul that, contrary to that feeling, had rediscovered its true vocation: the call to give himself totally and unreservedly to God for others.

The uncertainty looming over his future was very much on his mind as well as in his letters. Perhaps it is not trying to read too much between the lines to say that he wanted to know what plans God had for him and therefore was uneasy, troubled, disturbed; it seemed that life was slipping out of his hands. He was listening for the invitation of grace, but it seemed not to arrive. He wrote on December 16, 1924: "I hope with the grace of God to continue on the path of Catholic ideals and to be able one day, in the state that God determines, to defend and propagate these unique truths." His Christian vocation was a strange one, ahead of its time, better suited to our contemporary situation, with the social commitment of Catholics after the council, their dedication to volunteering, direct and active participation in the institutions and programs of the Church on the part of the laity, their missionary apostolate. . . . Toward the end of his earthly days he seemed to reap the fruits, and all that he had done until then appeared to him to add up to something inconclusive and fragile. He said that he had been capable only of "buffoonery", as if to say that he would have liked to do much more for the kingdom of God, humbling himself and not taking into consideration the fact that sanctity is not gauged by the number of things that one has done, but by one's being and essence. This then would finally explain those moving words, which would be inconsistent had they been dictated solely by his family's rejection. Pier Giorgio was a saint, not a weakling:

> Well then, my plan is this: to redirect that special sympathy that I had for her and that was not deliberate, toward the end at which we must arrive, in the light of charity. . . . This is my plan, which I hope to carry out in the grace of God, even if it costs me the sacrifice of earthly life.

Death was a constant, recurring thought of his. The statement that he made one day to a friend who asked him what he would like to do "as a grown-up" after his studies, remains a mystery: "I do not know; a priest, no, because that is too great a mission and I am not worthy of it; marriage, no. The only solution would be for the Lord to take me to himself." [18]

[18] Ibid., 130.

13

"A TREMENDOUS
MOUNTAIN CLIMBER"

"With every passing day, I am falling madly in love with the mountains; their fascination attracts me",[1] Pier Giorgio declared. He was immensely, boundlessly enraptured by them, and up there it seemed to him that he was closer to God. Verses transcribed by him and dedicated to his mountains were hung with thumbtacks over the door of his room and on the cupboard to accompany Dante, Saint Paul, and the updated list of exams that he had passed. And even before he began his studies of engineering, he avidly collected minerals. He often returned from trips to the mountains loaded down with stones that he had extracted with his mineralogist's hammer. He arranged them in a display case in his studio, under lock and key ever since the day in which someone gave him a little mineral sample with traces of gold. Pier Giorgio's mineral samples, each one bearing a name in Latin, were classified in Pollone by Professor Antonio Cavinato in 1961, and all were donated by Luciana Frassati to the Politecnico, but then they disappeared along with the display case that contained them.

[1] P. G. Frassati, *Lettere*, ed. L. Frassati, preface by Luigi Sturzo (Rome: Studium, 1950), 174.

His hyperactive nature led him to leave very early in the morning and to return home very late in the evening, busy as he was with group meetings, the poor, Masses, and Eucharistic adoration. At home he would study, write to his friends, read the daily papers and pamphlets. In the mountains he used to take dozens and dozens of photos with his Kodak camera. He was also a collector of butterflies, which he kept in boxes and catalogued (*Satyrus statylinus, Acherontia atropos* . . .), and of stamps from all over the world, and he owned hundreds of copies of art works from every museum in Europe, mainly of a religious character, but also some appealing to other tastes, such as a few disturbing works by the Austrian painter Gustav Klimt, a lover of symbolism, gilded backgrounds, the palette of colors typical of Japanese painting, and the abstract absolutes of Byzantine mosaics, which indicate that he had a well-formed, mature, critical taste in art.

He was gifted and versatile in sports; he used to ski for fun and because he was convinced that it is necessary to strengthen the body with sports while young "so as to be able to adjust to the pains of old age". Mountain climbing and skiing were his favorites. But he was skilled also in horseback riding, as a bicyclist, at the wheel of an automobile, in a sailboat, and in canoeing, which he often did along the Po River.

Upon returning from his trips to the mountains, he used to tell the domestic servant Maria Miletto: "The trip went well, the snow was good, more or less, but it was so beautiful in the middle of all that white that I wished I did not have to return so soon", and, instead of resting from the exertions of the trip, he liked to hoe the garden in Pollone; in particular, he had chosen one part that was never without sun, where flowers and vegetables were grown.

He never forgot to put his camera in his backpack, thus allowing friends, family members, and posterity to admire splendid views, landscapes, moments of joy and of spiritual recollection. It is impressive that in these photographs, each accompanied by a caption, he appears with a modern, contemporary face that has no suggestion of the past, as we sometimes observe in the looks of companions and friends who are connected with their era (physically speaking as well).

"Son of the everlasting snows", as his sister described him, he did not restrain his enthusiasm for the Alps; he went so far as to write impulsively: "Mountains mountains mountains, I love you." The whiteness of the snows was reflected, he sensed, in his overflowing soul: "I left my soul among the white snows, and I hope to find it white again next year."

In his final days, the mountains became his oxygen. The engineer Pasquale Marino recalls:

> One day we were at the Porta Nuova station, waiting for the arrival of an ecclesiastical authority. I saw him look dejectedly at a little train that had slowly started moving. "What are you thinking about, Frassati?" I asked him, seeing him so silent. "I would like to be on that train", he replied. "I have a great desire to see the mountains again and to ski a little on the snow." "Go on! . . . You always have one thing on your mind!" "What can you do, Marino? Our Alps are so beautiful that I would stay there for months on end if I did not have other things to worry about."

In his collection of membership cards for the groups and associations to which he belonged, including his card for the Italian Touring Club and besides his driver's license (obtained on April 24, 1924) and his license to bear arms, there was also his card as a member of the Italian Alpine Club, which he joined in 1918. The club had been founded in 1863 by the famous finance minister Quintino Sella, together with others who loved the mountains, and this initiative was applauded by Alfredo Frassati in the *Gazzetta del Popolo della domenica* on March 13, 1887:

> It was Quintino Sella, a believer and a mystic, the man who was moved to tears if at Oropa he saw the processions of the faithful coming down from the mountains, it was he and none other who was to invent mountaineering; such a beautiful, pure idea could spring only from that candid soul made holy by patriotism and religion. . . . He would see in the future the contempt, the mud that would be thrown at him by men who lacked the intelligence to understand him; he faced the monster that frightens everyone, unpopularity, and understood that only in the sublime regions of heaven could he restore his temperament as a native son of Biella. . . . They have told us so many times that up there, in the blue skies, there is another great and beautiful homeland, where they live happily and forget the anxieties, the hatreds, the resentments, and the worldly passions that continually shatter our soul, wrapped in the terrible sackcloth of doubt . . . where one lives only to love, where one sees again those for whom we wept so much when we lost them on earth. When we are in the mountains . . . the faith of our early years returns, pure and beautiful, with sad and holy memories, the image of our dear departed returns to our mind, with their words and their prudent counsels . . . the soul returns shining and resplendent, just as it came from the hands of God, an innocent butterfly; there only one passion remains, the passion for what is good; only one instinct, for greatness; only one aspiration, to immortality.

These are strong words, intense feelings that his son Pier Giorgio experienced profoundly when, immersed in his contemplation of natural masterpieces, he aspired to climb ever higher, battling at every step against ice, crevices, and obstacles, ascending with his hands, opening passages for himself now with his hatchet, now with his pickax. In the mountains he followed the rough ways of the mountaineers, for whom he had the greatest esteem, and it was no accident that he collected figurines depicting their heroic deeds. In 1921, when he became eligible for the draft, someone told him that he would make a good officer. Pier Giorgio retorted: "I want to be a simple soldier; I do not even want to become a corporal. I want to live close to the Alpine soldiers."[2]

> In the fresh air of the Alps my brother found the world that he kept hidden within himself, which I myself, his sister, still have not entirely discovered. The world that brought him close to God. . . . Pier Giorgio was himself, and anyone who has not seen him intent on conquering the summits cannot have understood him fully. Mama, however, used to lament that "He would never make progress since he was with people who did not know how to ski." And that was true. If there was a person who fell and was perhaps incapable of overcoming the hardships of the mountains, Pier Giorgio kept close to him, adjusted his skis, and helped him. He acted so spontaneously that the generous act seemed natural to everyone and almost obligatory.[3]

When he was acting as guide, Pier Giorgio used to say: "Robespierre is passing: either death or Scotland! Out of the way!" With the same youthful impetuosity he attacked the summits, and when he conquered them, the witnesses heard him say: "Oh! How great and wonderful are the works of God!"

[2] A. Cojazzi, *Pier Giorgio Frassati: Testimonianze* (Turin: SEI, 1928), 178.
[3] L. Frassati, *La piccozza di Pier Giorgio* (Turin: SEI, 1995), 19.

Laura Hidalgo relates: "On the last trip to the Rocca Sella, Pier Giorgio at one point was skiing, and I remember that I was the one holding on to the rope. I shouted: 'Our Lady, help him!' He calmly said, 'Why bother Our Lady about such a little thing?' Signorina Reyneri was surprised by that reply and repeated her impressions to Beura, who said to her, 'But do you not know that Frassati is a saint?'"

Brave yet prudent, in the most critical Alpine passes Pier Giorgio joined expert guides like the famous Aldo Pellissier, who in the 1950s still remembered that agile, fearless young man and his enthusiasm for the natural spectacles for which he thanked God out loud; or like Luigi Carrel, nicknamed Carrelino, his contemporary, with whom he was very much on the same wavelength and from whom he learned many mountain-climbing techniques. He knew the most daring maneuvers and would climb or descend vertical walls or overhanging rock faces. He then amused himself in particular by making the double-rope descents that were necessary to get over crags on a mountain ridge. As the saint of the summits and of the mines, he aspired to reach the mountaintops in the freedom of the wind and the sky, and at the same time he desired to plumb the depths underground, where the darkness and the air are imprisoned by earth and rocks.

Pier Giorgio was very fond of Oropa, and the engineer Domenico Morelli remembers as follows one of the trips that he made together with him: "On returning with several companions from an excursion in 'his' mountains, we passed by the Shrine of Oropa. We all went into a café: all except Pier Giorgio. He had disappeared without saying anything. We looked for him; he was in the little church praying unostentatiously but unabashedly. He said nothing to disapprove of our indifference, but his silence and his example were more eloquent than any reproach." When they arrived in Oropa, he used to say: "First let us greet Our Lady, and then we will have a snack", and it was not uncommon to see him bring flowers for his Black Madonna. Flowers were his passion; he always got some on the occasion of family festivities, and he frequently brought them to Our Lady in church.

As we know, he belonged to SUCAI, the association of university students who were members of the Italian Alpine Club; every Thursday evening they met at 9:00 at the Caffè Alfieri at via Po 9. The motto of the group was: "We are an invincible mountaineering company", and they had eleven commandments:

You shall never wash your face.

You shall not bring alcoholic beverages, but if you have some, humbly give them to the older members.

Where the chamois [a mountain antelope] has its doubts, there the reign of SUCAI begins.

Where a SUCAI member wants to pass, there is a way.

If you are surprised by a storm, ride it out and let it bring you home; if there is a blizzard, very carefully put it back into a little box.

You will count the hours by the sun and by the stars like the Shepherd Kings.

You will gather salt [*sale*] on the ascents [*salite*], pepper from the remarks of the Older Members, and for lack of anything else you will season your food with the air of the summits.

The Mountain is your Queen.

Always go on foot, but if you find a railway car make use of it.

If you are musically inclined, practice the double bass,
   since that is the only instrument suited to a SUCAI
   member.
Exaggerate prudently. Remember that all the cliff faces
   in the world are not worth a human life.

He was very protective of the young women, lending
his services for the humblest tasks, such as greasing boots,
adroitly smearing the terrible grease with the heat of his
hand. The engineer Riccardo Bordi recalls:

> I put on the cape that he had immediately lent to me when
> he learned that I lacked one and would not have been able
> to participate in the excursion. I had accepted, thinking that
> he had another, but then he was left without one. "As you
> see," he told me, "I am not cold!" And indeed, besides his
> bag, which was the most voluminous, he always had on his
> shoulder belt some other bag, taken from someone in the
> company who was more tired and could not manage it. I
> remember him making mayonnaise in a few minutes, in a
> competition with one of the young ladies on our excur-
> sion, with the bowl immersed in the snow, and celebrating
> his success with shouting and endless laughter.

Once a female companion on an excursion, Angela Mon-
tafia, came down with a sudden illness; she recalls "the spontaneous courtesy with which he obliged me to take several
lumps of sugar with cognac at a moment when I was about
to give up the excursion because of weakness. Not only
did he carry my bag and skis, but by his authority he obliged
the company to stop until I had completely recovered from
the indisposition. And the director of the excursion became
the cook, too, quickly mixing pasta and cheerfulness in great
quantities."

His cheerfulness was infectious during one evening party at Sauze d'Oulx, as he let loose with a series of jokes, satires, songs, and melodies to the strains of an accordion—performances that provoked violent reactions on the part of his sister, Luciana, "who scolded him roundly".[4]

Laura Hidalgo, on the other hand, recalls the twelve hours in which they were held up in a train because of the snow. "In the pleasant warmth of the car, we heard the dear, toneless voice of Pier Giorgio and did not suspect that he had thought up that means—as he later explained—of getting rid of a terrible headache that had come on because, despite the cold and staying awake, he did not want to break his fast so as not to miss Communion in the morning."

He was the one to sound reveille, saying, "Hurry up, hurry up, time for Mass!" They all washed with icy water and then quickly followed him downstairs to the chapel in the hostel of the Piccolo San Bernardo, where they saw him praying in such a way that he seemed to forget that he was together with his friends, reciting the server's prayers at Mass in his calm cadences. He also served Mass in the summer huts at around three or four o'clock at night. Don Domenico Massè remembers him as follows: "I particularly recall one of the excursions of Giovane Montagna in which I had him as a generous, tireless companion in the ascent on the Levanna Orientale. . . . Upon arriving at the top, we found the note left by three mountain climbers who had perished shortly before. Immediately he knelt down with one of his friends, a certain Loretz, and asked me: 'Don Massè, let us recite the *De profundis*' [a psalm traditionally prayed for the dead]. Less than two weeks later, Loretz, too, lost his life in the mountains, the victim of an accident."

[4] See ibid., 96.

Starting in 1923, reminders of death occurred insistently and became, along with the approaching end of his studies, a leitmotiv in his letters. From Pollone he wrote to his friend Antonio Severi on August 13, 1923:

Did you read about the tragic end of poor Loretz the lawyer? He was killed in a disaster at the Château des Dames. . . . That is the fate that will befall me some year, and so the moral of the story is: when you go to the mountains, you have to put your conscience in order first, because you do not know whether you will ever return. Despite all that, I am not afraid; in fact, I want more and more to go mountain climbing, to scale the most difficult peaks; to experience that pure joy which you have only in the mountains.

He then salutes his friend in Jesus Christ and adds "Pax Domini sit tecum" (May the peace of the Lord be with you).

While remaining faithful to the Italian Alpine Club [CAI], Pier Giorgio also joined the Giovane Montagna, an association of mountain climbers founded in 1914, which had a strongly Catholic spirit and offered the possibility of mountaineering on Sundays, with attendance at Mass; furthermore, it accepted young women also as members.

Besides being in great physical shape, Pier Giorgio was self-assured, and this enabled him to achieve exceptional results. His friends remember him in the nostalgic songs of the valleys or else on his knees speaking with God, his first and last thought of the day. In those moments, his "manly figure" seemed to disappear, "and he was completely transformed in the ecstasy that brought him close to God, so as to make him worthy of the only reason for being, to work."[5] The painter Falchetti remembers:

[5] Ibid., 49.

He had come to say hello to me in my studio before leaving for the mountains. I can still see him before my eyes as I saw him then. In his full mountain-climbing gear, he was magnificent: so handsome that I not only made him pose in the middle of the studio, admiring him from every side, but I leaned out from the terrace so as to be able to see him again in the street, carrying his bag and with his skis on his shoulder. He wore a full hunting jacket, a dark shirt, loose-fitting trousers with brightly colored Scottish socks, a Scottish beret over one ear. . . . Among the many fellow mountain climbers in the city, you would have picked him out first: sturdy, strong, determined, with his skin tanned by the sun, with thick, exuberant facial hair, despite having shaved, in complete contrast with his gentle smile and his childlike eyes, just as his somewhat subdued, forthright, rough, masculine voice contrasted with his pure, unspotted soul. You could see in his eyes his joy in living, his happy heart, his vision of the lofty snows glistening in the sun, of the wild slides down the steep slopes, in the solemn silence, where cries of joy echo through the endless valleys, under beautiful skies transparent to the vivid colors of the dawns and fiery sunsets. But even more you could read in his face his joy in the simple, healthy life of roughing it; the joy of fatigue, almost a return to the ancient customs of our good forefathers.[6]

On July 25, 1923, he tackled Monviso with Marco Beltramo and with the ice ax belonging to Antonio Villani. The plan was: on the 24th, stay overnight at the Quintino Sella hut, on the 25th, scale the eastern rock face of Monviso; on the 26th, the Visolotto; and on the 27th, the Granero. Their conquest of the coveted peak is faithfully recounted by Marco Beltramo:

[6] Cojazzi, *Pier Giorgio Frassati*, 193–94.

We were supposed to leave together from Turin, Giorgio and I, by the 5:00 train. Our friend Gilli . . . a CAI guide and a member of the Cesare Balbo circle, would be waiting for us in Crissolo at around noon. That evening we counted on sleeping at the Quintino Sella hut. Of course I missed the train and did not catch up with Giorgio, who left alone; I arrived that evening at around 6:00. I learned from Gilli that that afternoon they had visited the grotto of the Rio Martino, above Crissolo, and then had carried some wood. That night Giorgio and I slept at the inn in Crissolo. Before going to bed, we recited the rosary together; it was the first time that I prayed with Giorgio, and, before falling asleep, we chatted for a long time. The following morning, Giorgio led me to the grotto of the Rio Martino, but once we got down there, our flashlight went out, and a return in the dark was impossible. We had three matches in all; two went out, and we struggled for a while to light the third. That evening we slept at the Quintino Sella, and I fell asleep almost immediately, but first I heard Giorgio reciting the rosary. The following day when we left at dawn, Gilli asked us whether we would welcome to our party a young villager from Crissolo; of course we agreed. The ascent presented no problem, but on our return, about two hours' distance from the hut, that young man slipped and fell, spraining an ankle. We took off the shoe and massaged the foot, but the pain did not stop. Gilli then thought of using the mule that went down every evening from the hut to Crissolo, to transport the injured young man to the village. Giorgio immediately ran on ahead to make sure that the mule waited, and little by little we carried the young man to the hut. There Giorgio came to meet us, exhilarated, fresh, and well rested, as though he was just back from a nap and not from a difficult climb, and to my surprise he said that as soon as he had performed his task, sweating and panting as he was, he had bathed in the nearby lake. Then when I pointed out to him the imprudence of his action, he replied, smiling and thumping his chest, that a mountain climber was not afraid of such things.

On September 14, 1923, Pier Giorgio enthusiastically scaled Mount Grivola in the Valle d'Aosta (13,022 feet). With the FUCI members, he spent Carnival season in 1923 and 1924 at the Piccolo San Bernardo. Often the Sinister Types had the necessary foodstuffs transported on a little donkey, and it was nice to see that young party, especially Pier Giorgio, interacting with the valley dwellers, staying at the shepherds' huts or in the Alpine cabins that they used for their stops. "These Alpine climbs", he said, "have a strange magic in them so that no matter how many times they are repeated and however alike they are, they are never boring, in the same way as the experience of spring is never boring but fills our spirit with gladness and delight."[7]

On the occasion of the twenty-fifth anniversary of the image of Our Lady of Consolation that had been brought to the peak of Uia di Ciamarella, Giovane Montagna organized an excursion with seventy-eight members and several priests. Pier Giorgio was in charge of guiding that excursion, and on the mountaintop the man of the eight beatitudes served Mass.

After his death, the German-language newspaper *Österreichische Alpenzeitung* (Austrian Alps Newspaper) devoted an extensive article to him, which said:

> To those who disdain sports, [Pier Giorgio] makes it clear that sports can be connected with the loftiest spiritual de-

[7] L. Frassati, *A Man of the Beatitudes: Pier Giorgio Frassati*, trans. Dinah Livingstone, adapted and ed. Patricia O'Rourke (San Francisco: Ignatius Press, 2000), 132–33.

velopment. How he reached that height is the mystery of Parsifal. It tells those who only superficially like sports that training is ennobled only by the aspiration to goals that are worthy of mankind and by the coordination of values. His figure rose to great heights that transcend nationalities, and it is rooted in universal depths. Even German-speaking mountain climbers turn their thoughts to the tomb in Pollone.

He would have been quite capable of joining the academic group of Italian mountaineers, in search of notoriety, but he preferred mountain climbing pure and simple, introducing friends to this sport, and supporting them in their first ascents. Here, too, he gave instead of receiving. The strongest emotions experienced by Pier Giorgio were in the mountains: the panoramas that presented themselves to his view from the lofty peaks overwhelmed his soul, and the desire to repeat the sublime experience of those moments was very strong and insistent. As refreshment after his Alpine exertions, Pier Giorgio used to eat with a hearty appetite, and if there was no fondue, he liked to have hot tea with bread and jam (he was especially fond of chestnut spread). He would take jam with a convenient teaspoon with the SUCAI emblem; we saw it jealously preserved by Laura Hidalgo's daughters.

Luciana says: "Like our mother, who was incapable of resisting hunger after a certain hour and was obliged to have someone bring milk, coffee, and biscuits to her room after having dined, Pier Giorgio had a formidable appetite. Although he was by no means greedy, he liked healthy, substantial foods and disliked dishes that were complicated or too insipid. How humiliated he was when, as a child, they would serve him at dinner a thin, thin soup! He used to say: 'But that is broth for sick people!' "[8] Nevertheless, even though he did enjoy eating, Pier Giorgio was willing to fast, both so as to be able to go to Holy Communion daily (at that time it was necessary to observe the fast from midnight on) and in the season of Lent.

We believe, and not mistakenly, that Pier Giorgio truly experienced moments of sheer happiness among the Alpine peaks and of pure contemplation amid the enchanting scenes of unspotted creation. Being an obedient young man, he yielded to his father when he wanted to scale Mont Blanc, but the senator dissuaded him from such a dangerous undertaking.[9] During his final ascent (he made forty-four in all, thirty-nine of them in the last four years of his life) of the Lunelle di Lanzo, on June 7, 1925, Pier Giorgio was photographed clambering up a rock face, looking upward, with the intention of reaching the peak; on the extraordinary picture he wrote: "To the top."

To Franz Massetti, who preferred the sea, he never stopped telling stories about his mountain-climbing expeditions, the wonders that he observed or encountered, the difficulties that were overcome, the joys experienced, and the inebriation of the descent on skis, which his agility and skill enabled him to make faster and faster. Massetti testifies: "He meant to transform his athletic accomplishment into a triumph of that vitality of his which he received as a gift, and on the peaks that he had victoriously conquered, before the spectacle of Creation contemplated from above, this vitality was expressed in an intimately joyful song of praise and thanksgiving to the Creator, the giver of every good thing."

---

[8] L. Frassati, *Mio fratello Pier Giorgio: La fede* (Rome: Edizioni Paoline, 1954), 115.

[9] Cf. P. G. Frassati, *Lettere*, 175.

Not all his friends were capable of climbing up to the mountaintops that he reached, and they were not always all together on their excursions. He missed them in those moments of happiness and gave voice to his regret about their absence. For him, friendship was sharing, a participation in his own being. He wrote to Antonio Villani from Turin on July 9, 1923: "Dear Tonino, yesterday I was at an altitude of 11,483 feet to breathe a bit of fresh air. . . . Sunday was then one of those magnificent days, and my thoughts turned from the glacier to my distant friends; I wished they all had been here to enjoy that marvelous spectacle with me."

The mountains were for him a gymnasium for the body, but above all a smithy where he forged his soul for lofty spiritual summits, with his glance always turned to the heights, directed toward "our true Homeland to sing the praises of God". And up there, at a distance that gives a new perspective on all human inadequacy and misery, he used to recite the *De profundis* for those who had died in the mountains. The more difficult the mountain-climbing expeditions of that cragsman were, the more he demanded of his strength and abilities, so much so that in 1924 he decided to purchase an insurance policy with the CAI for benefit of his sister in case of his death or total permanent disability.

John Paul II, during his visit to Turin on April 13, 1980, called Pier Giorgio "a tremendous mountain climber". And on April 12, 1984, at the Olympic Stadium in Rome, he pointed to him as an example for the athletes of the world, inviting them, too, to be peacemakers.

Today his name stands in the Valsorey range at Le Rocher, at an altitude of 10,367 feet, in the Valle d'Aosta (July 4, 1926); on August 14 of that same year, two "teeth", or sharp peaks, in the Grand Combin range were named after him also (at an altitude of 10,800 feet). The entirely basalt peak

Pier Giorgio Frassati is found in the Fitz-Roy range (9,500 feet) in the Cordillera of the Argentine Andes; so it was baptized by the Salesian explorer Don Alberto De Agostini of Pollone on January 1, 1936: he was accompanied by Luigi Carrel, who had not forgotten the heroic climbs he had made with Pier Giorgio. Also dedicated to him are many mountain paths both in Europe and in South America, the land where he would have wanted to work and carry on his apostolate.

In Italy, from north to south, along routes for mountain excursions that are of particular natural, historical, and religious interest, there are various paths named after Pier Giorgio Frassati, an idea that started with the international Pier Giorgio Frassati Association and the Italian Alpine Club.

No one would have been more deserving than the group of mountain climbers to carry the mortal remains of the young Blessed, on June 30, 1990, from the cemetery in Pollone to Oropa. After a brief stop in front of his house and the vigil in the local parish, the coffin, escorted by *carabinieri* (Italian gendarmes), ascended to the Sanctuary of the Black Madonna, to the chapel where so many times he had been seen leading the praises and intercessions. Black feathers were the best homage offered by the mountain to its very faithful, valiant, intrepid standard-bearer, who had brought the "terror" of Robespierre to the wide kingdom of the winds.

14

THE VIGIL

After the interval he spent in Germany, Alfredo Frassati was contacted by Mussolini. *Il Duce*'s initial hatred for the senator turned into an esteem dictated by the circumstances: "Your work was highly appreciated by the German government, which, through the president of the republic, recently expressed to Count de Bosdari its regret about your departure from Berlin and recalled the close, cordial collaboration that had been renewed between the two countries by means of Your Excellency" (Rome, January 27, 1923). The tone here is quite different, therefore, from the one used in his famous "rants" against Frassati. Not only that: he would have liked to employ the senator again as a diplomat and even offered him the embassy in Moscow. (At the same time, by rewarding him in that way, he would have succeeded in removing from one of the most widely read daily newspapers in Italy the journalist he most feared.) But the senator declined "indignantly", as he himself had to say.

From 1924 on, the steadiness of *La Stampa* began to waver, and the main offices of the daily paper were guarded by gendarmes and law enforcement agents, while groups of Fascists sought to bring their violence into the building on via Davide Bertolotti. But the most alarming episode was when some Fascists broke into the Frassatis' villa on corso Siccardi on June 22, 1924, when a handful of aggressors found themselves confronting, not the senator, but Pier Giorgio. The Blessed himself relates the incident to Antonio Villani:

Dear Tonino,

I write to you to reassure you: you will read in the newspaper that yesterday we suffered a bit of devastation in our residence at the hands of the Fascist pigs. It was a cowardly deed and nothing more. We were sitting tranquilly at table at a quarter to one when we heard someone ring the doorbell. Mariscia went to see who it was and saw from the window a rather well-dressed young man; then, thinking that it was a friend of mine, she opened the door a little. He immediately asked for "Commendatore Frassati"; after hearing a negative reply, he threw open the door and then, shouting "onward", entered the house together with five other men. We were eating tranquilly when we heard Mariscia's scream; my first thought was of thieves, but then as soon as I reached the entrance hall and saw one of them trying to pull off the telephone receiver, I immediately thought of the Fascists, and at that moment the blood ran faster through my veins. I rushed over to that rogue, shouting "scoundrels, cowards, assassins", and I landed a punch on him. Bravely, as soon as the crooks heard a man's voice, they went for the door of the house and ran out headlong, followed by me and Italo [the chauffeur]. Outside they found an automobile that was waiting for them. Meanwhile, they had succeeded in breaking 2 mirrors. After that there were comings and goings of inspectors, gendarmes, examining judges, the royal prosecutor, etc. Too late; now I think they dare not do anything more, particularly since they arrested Mariotti, one of the heads of the assassins' department.

They are a shameless lot; after the events in Rome, they should not let anyone see them anymore and ought to be ashamed of being Fascists, but instead they continue to give evidence of what they always were and will be.

This, now, is their last hurrah, the brave deeds of their death throes, because now the government is so rotten that unless the surgeons intervene promptly and cut off the part that has become gangrenous, there will be no more hope of saving even a little. We are fortunate that today we can glory in the fact and boast of always having been opposed to that party, made up of a criminal association of thieves, assassins, and idiots: in a word, Fascism itself.

And now I leave you; I have poured out my soul to you, knowing that you have the same ideas as I, and I leave you shouting

> Viva Matteotti! Viva liberty!
> Viva Christian Democracy!
> Down with tyranny!

Pier Giorgio, a spotless, fearless knight, writes as he thinks, and from his words the reader can tell all his youthful exuberance and enthusiasm for fidelity to his ideas.

Alfredo Frassati, who was in Pollone at the time, when informed of the incident, telegraphed indignantly even before leaving for Turin:

To His Excellency Federzoni,
Ministry of the Interior, Rome.

I notify Your Excellency of what they tell me in a telephone call from Turin: My house, with my sick wife and my son present—in broad daylight—was invaded, mirrors were broken, etc. I am certain of the honesty of your intentions, but they will remain such only as long as the current directors are in the prefecture and police headquarters.

I await your energetic measures, which will sound the alarm for everyone that the hour has come to safeguard the citizens with the strict application of the law. Regards.

Federzoni did not delay in sending a reply, but he attributed the incident to the clear opposition of *La Stampa* to the government:

I must nevertheless frankly point out that the attitude of the newspaper *La Stampa* exceeds the limits of an objective chronicle of events and of what ought to be a loyal, calm opposition to the government and to Fascism and, instead, manifestly tends to foment unrest in minds and to embitter public opinion, making it more difficult to return to normalcy.

The prefect was suspended, and the Villa Frassati began to have police surveillance: for several long months, five or six *carabinieri* encamped temporarily in the entrance hall or on the stairs. "Uninterruptedly shadowed and . . . under discreet surveillance, Frassati may not have liked letting the police headquarters know about some of his sentimental escapades!"[1]

Alfredo was enthusiastic about his "magnificent creature" —a prelude to the eye-opening events of one year later; on June 23 he wrote to his daughter:

My dearest Luciana,

I am happy that I was not at home because, between Giorgio and me, we would have killed someone, and that would not have been good, although you know my opinions. I enclose for you the account in the newspapers, and so you

---

[1] L. Frassati, *Un uomo, un giornale: Alfredo Frassati*, vol. 3, pt. 2 (Rome: Edizioni di Storia e Letteratura, 1981), 123.

will be amply informed about it. I was not wrong in telling you that at the moment things are better abroad.

I ought not to love this land, and I ought to be able to live without it! And you know that I cannot.

Your brother behaved marvelously well: he is indeed a magnificent creature. What self-possession: he tried to lead Mama away [from the commotion] and struck hard. Afterward he was calmer than before. I told him: Bravo, Giorgio, on every occasion do your duty. As if I had said to him: buy the newspaper for me. Imitate him in many things, and you will find yourself happy in life.

It was part of Pier Giorgio's nature to consider as normal acts that to most people appear extraordinary, just as he never considered his demonstrations of his faith, his overflowing charity, his total self-denial for the cause of the Gospel, his athletic courage, or his bold opposition to undemocratic regimes to be heroic acts. It was absolutely natural for him, as a serious man, to act in a way consistent with his own values and principles. His mother, on July 1, proudly stated in a letter to Luciana: "It is understandable that my maternal heart should exult when I hear such praises of P.G.! Now when wicked, excommunicated people tell Papa that P.G. is a 'bigot', he will be able to reply that bigots know how to do their duty at the proper time."

And so the son who had a screw loose and was a bit of a rebel, the student preparing to take a degree who frittered the whole day away with his friends and with prayers for a God who gained him no advantages at home, now gave great satisfaction to his parents, appearing on the stage of international news: the London *Times* and many German newspapers dedicated columns to reporting his deeds. Even the long-time rival *Il Corriere della Sera* could not remain silent and printed an article headlined: "Vandals break into house of Sen. Frassati: Many aggressors put to flight by his son."

On the second anniversary of the march on Rome, Frassati's daily paper wrote without any hypocrisy: "The story of these last two years is being ended . . . by the Fascist government in a series of lost opportunities; no other government ever had so many or such good ones." When the senator declared Mussolini complicit in the assassination of Giacomo Matteotti, the dictator decreed the death sentence for his newspaper. From that moment on, the life of the publication was suffocated, and some newsstands were even forced to stop selling *La Stampa*, a daily newspaper that in 1925 had print runs of almost four hundred thousand copies, despite confiscations, censorship, and public and private incidents of violence.

In 1924, Luciana was engaged to Count Jan Gawronski, first secretary of the Polish delegation to The Hague. The event alarmed Pier Giorgio; he was happy for his sister, but at the same time he thought of how this would change things in the family: "Just as every rose always has some thorn, so too unfortunately my joy in seeing my sister happy is combined with the bitterness of separation, because unfortunately Italy will no longer be her land. Now I will have to fill the void that my sister will leave at home: I will do my best" (letter to Villani dated December 16, 1924). Never as then did he appreciate the ties of affection that he had with Luciana.

He shouldered full responsibility for keeping together his parents' broken marriage and chose to remain beside his mother so as to support her in her difficult trial. In June, Adelaide wrote as follows to her daughter:

> Pier Giorgio does not know how to talk, but he knows how to act courageously, promptly, simply. God grant him

a companion who is able, like him, to seek *quae sursum sunt* (the things that are above). Papa, on his return, embraced him emotionally: certainly it provides great calm and great strength to have him with us. He, so childlike, is more of a man than many. I wish to pray to God that it will be granted to me always to be close to him, in all dangers.

Pier Giorgio will always be wonderful in all his actions, because he does not think of himself but spontaneously thinks about others, as his great, good heart prompts him. May God bless him!

In recent days, Pier Giorgio seemed to have abandoned the caprices of his youth, but also his political interests, disappointed also by the Popular Party, which, in his opinion, could have done more. With greater knowledge, he immersed himself in everyday reality: "Time passes terribly fast . . . the years go by, and we grow old, and therefore we have to exercise a bit of judgment."[2] What remained were the problems in his family, his uncertainty about the future, his unshakable faith, and his true spouse, charity.

The Holy Year in 1925 opened for Pier Giorgio with a toast together with his beloved family; then he went to the Church of the Holy Martyrs and prayed there for the peace of Italy and "for us . . . we hope for a strong will, so that we might soon complete our baccalaureate degree. I am happy to conclude my career as a student in such a beautiful year."[3] On January 25, Luciana was married in the church of the metropolitan curia in the presence of Archbishop Gamba. Pier Giorgio commented as follows on the wedding in a letter to Marco Beltramo dated January 25, 1925:

[2] P. G. Frassati, *Lettere*, ed. L. Frassati, preface by Luigi Sturzo (Rome: Studium, 1950), 176.
[3] Ibid., 207.

The ceremony is magnificent; a civil wedding is comical in comparison; I would hope that in the near future civil marriage will be abolished completely and only Church weddings will be performed and, at least as a transition, that both will be valid in the eyes of the State.

However, while I am glad because my sister is happy, even more so because her husband is good in the sense that you and I understand, on the other hand, yesterday evening the separation was terrible. You can imagine: my only sister, the companion of my childhood: to see her leave for such distant shores was for me a blow to the heart.

Another blow was added to his torments: he had to follow his father's plan to have him hired by *La Stampa*, certainly not to work among the miners . . . Disoriented, Pier Giorgio was going through his dark night of the soul and wished more than anything else to know and understand God's will for him.

As a wedding gift for his beloved sister, Pier Giorgio chose an old ivory crucifix found by a dealer in antiques, which he had blessed by the cardinal of Turin. His family members told him that it was inappropriate and not very welcome. Therefore, Pier Giorgio made up for it with a more worldly gift that was suitable and in keeping with the Frassatis: a silver tea service, worthy of taking its place in the spouses' official display on the billiard table at the villa. The crucifix, left in a corner and wrapped in a crumpled newspaper, later became the most precious object in Luciana's life, and in 1939, at the time of the German invasion of Poland, it was the one thing that the couple salvaged in their hasty flight from Warsaw.[4]

---

[4] See L. Frassati, *A Man of the Beatitudes: Pier Giorgio Frassati*, trans. Dinah Livingstone, adapted and ed. Patricia O'Rourke (San Francisco: Ignatius Press, 2000), 127–28.

The sister, too, gave her brother a gift: one thousand of the three thousand lire received from Grandmother Frassati. Delighted with that bank note, Pier Giorgio immediately set it aside for the Saint Vincent de Paul Society and the Cesare Balbo circle, five hundred for each, to be distributed to the poor. Luciana received thank-you notes from the two organizations that benefited because Pier Giorgio did not forget to tell them where the money came from.

At the station, at the moment when he left her, he was trembling all over and broke out into desperate, uncontrollable weeping that, besides alarming the bystanders, greatly upset Luciana, who, in an effort to console him, told him that she would soon return to Turin. And she had to keep her promise because of the death soon afterward of their eighty-six-year-old grandmother, Linda Copello, who had been ailing for several years. Pier Giorgio felt the full weight, at home, of "serving for two". Luciana's marriage, indeed, had burdened her brother with the responsibility in a tragic role play, which incidentally had already been evident in their mother's disclosure on the day in Berlin when the eighteen-year-old Luciana had confessed her love for an Italian official: "If you marry Lazzarini, you will be responsible for our [that is, the parents'] separation."[5] Those words were unfair, imbued perhaps with a form of selfishness: the choice of herself to the detriment of her children's future. "And our father used our mother's hypersensitivity as another argument to prevent Pier Giorgio from doing what he wanted. Our father built up his arguments to dissuade Pier Giorgio from his vocation by predicting that he would become a fanatic, useless for *La Stampa* and to his family, if he continued frequenting religious organizations."[6]

[5] Ibid., 152.
[6] Ibid.

Pier Giorgio wrote a very tender letter to Luciana on April 10, 1925:

> Write to me often, so that at least in that way the enormous void that you left among us can be filled. First, while we were living together every day, I could not sufficiently appreciate everything that you are to me. But unfortunately, now that many kilometers separate us; now that we have had to separate, not for a few days, but for life, and will only see each other from time to time, I have understood what a sister means in a household and what emptiness her absence can leave.

A modern mystic, Pier Giorgio Frassati is the link between nineteenth-century holiness and that of the current generations. He in fact had inherited the tradition of the subalpine saints of the 1800s, identifying himself with their work of defending the faith, through his profuse charity among the marginalized; but he did not stop there. He understood the need for a new system: confronting human experience and performing charitable work in every area: family, school, workplace, the press, politics, the economy, sports, so as always to defend social freedoms by seeking to enliven the movement to form associations, understood as Christian friendship for the sake of applying Catholic social teaching. The era of de-Christianization had already begun, and Pier Giorgio guessed the weapon with which to confront it: the marriage of faith and work must no longer be viewed as a pair of concepts restricted solely to the ghetto of charitable work and relief efforts, but should be extended to all human realities: "Faith and hope cease with our death; love or charity lasts eternally, and I think that it will be even more alive in the next life." He constantly yearned for "that joy that has no end because it is not human".

Our Lady, "fixed goal of the Eternal Wisdom" [Dante, *Paradiso*, Canto 33], constantly showed him the way to Christ. The thought of death accompanied Pier Giorgio daily. For him it was not a dismal foreboding but, rather, a continual call to be vigilant and ready for his final encounter with the Almighty, the highest aspiration of his mind. The young Blessed thought that every day had to be lived out well and intensely: the concrete, practical manifestations, even the simplest ones, were a mere translation of one's interior reality, of one's own conscience, for the sake of an asceticism that is acquired moment by moment.

On August 20, 1923, in notifying his friend Severi of the death of his uncle Pietro, he expressed himself as follows: "You can be sure that life must be a continual preparation for the next life, because one never knows the day and the hour of our departure." Some thought that he was joking when he touched on the subject of death, but afterward they inferred that he actually had a presentiment that he would very soon leave this earth. He wrote to Villani on July 19, 1923:

Tonino, dear friend. . . .

On Monday my sister took her degree in law, defending a thesis on public water works legislation, and the whole panel gave her the highest marks and awarded her the degree *cum laude*.

Today I was at the funeral of a man with a degree in literature, a friend of Bertini's and a correspondent for *La Nazione* in Turin. He died of consumption at San Luigi Hospital, and today I saw him before they put him into the box. He was in a pitiable state; I was able to remain in the room for only two minutes, because he was almost decomposed and therefore it was better not to stay any longer. However, that sight was salutary for me. I reflected and thought that I, too, in a few years will be in that state; I, too, will arouse the same feeling of compassion mixed with revulsion, and yet sometimes I have been ambitious. But for what: inasmuch as death, that great mystery and the only just judge, having no human respect at all, will dissolve my body and in a short time reduce it to dust. But besides the material body, there is the soul, to which we need to dedicate all our efforts, so as to be able to appear before the Supreme Tribunal without guilt or at least with only minor faults, so that after having spent a few years in purgatory it can enter into Eternal Rest. But how are we to prepare for such a great passage, and when? Since no one knows when Death will come to take him, it is very prudent every day to prepare for death on that same day; therefore, from now on I will try each day to make a little preparation for death, so as not to have to find myself unprepared at the point of death and have to lament the beautiful years of youth that were squandered from a spiritual perspective.

This awareness is disconcerting for someone who is twenty-two years old, but such reflections allowed him to perceive a spiritual dimension rich in nutrients for a soul that had grasped not only the principal values but also the ultimate purposes of earthly existence.

We are now on the eve of his death, and without asking himself whether or not his son had consented, Alfredo Frassati told his friend, the lawyer Arturo Garino, to draw up the official decree employing Pier Giorgio in the administration of the newspaper. Not a month passed, and then the pitiless sickle carried off Pier Giorgio, harvesting a large part of his father's life.

On June 20, 1925, the future Blessed was present for the translation of the new Blessed Giuseppe Cafasso to the Shrine of Our Lady of Consolation. Some witnesses report that, when the urn passed in front of the platform where he was stationed to watch the long procession go by, they saw him on his knees, extraordinarily recollected. "Certainly no one will ever know what grace he asked of God through the intercession of Blessed Cafasso, but perhaps it is not difficult to guess, knowing how much he was suffering and how worried he had been, for some time already, about the dreaded separation of his parents. He had said that he was willing to sacrifice his own life to avert that catastrophe. His sacrifice, accepted by the Lord, had now resolved every problem."[7] The chambermaid of the Frassati household, Ester Pignata, of whom Pier Giorgio was very fond, relates:

> One evening I heard the mother scream; I do not know why or what happened, but I know that her voice was very loud, and I heard it from my room: I do not remember the words, but I know that the young master came out very sad. She was terribly nervous in that final time: I had never heard her scream that way, and her sister tried to calm her. I remember very well what it was about, because every evening I went to bring them a thermos full of milk. One evening she told me: "Ester, I am just desperate", and made some hints about the senator, so that I understood the reason for her desperation (rumors were going around that the senator was in a relationship and that he wanted to separate from his wife). Certainly that lady was unhappy, and although she was kind she was unbearable.

Everything was condensed into the space of a few weeks: the senator's decision to "enlist" his son in *La Stampa*, Adelaide's psychological collapse, the final days in the life of Grandmother Ametis (Adelaide's mother, Linda Ametis Copello), and the tragic death of Pier Giorgio.

---

[7] M. Codi, *Pier Giorgio Frassati: Una valanga di vita* (Casale Monferrato [AL]: Portalupi, 2001), 371.

Adelaide could not bear the idea of the public consequences of a separation between herself and her husband.
She spoke about this to her sister Elena, who was alarmed by
her nervous and psychological conditions and also brought
up the subject of her need to recover in a private hospital;
moreover, she spoke to her friend Alda Marchisio and to
her son, who was extremely upset by it.

Pier Giorgio saw Franz Massetti for the last time on June
30, 1925; he had decided to make the rounds to greet his
closest friends, as though to say goodbye to each of them.
He carried with him the recently published life of Saint
Catherine of Siena by Jørgensen. "I have a sharp pain here
in my spine", he said suddenly to Franz, who did not pay
too much attention to that complaint, thinking that it was
a sprain caused by an effort made in his last excursion in
the Alps. They were joined by another friend from FUCI,
Giuseppe Grimaldi, who was also a member of the same
Saint Vincent de Paul conference as Pier Giorgio and Franz.
The Blessed opened his book and dwelt on two episodes:
the first related the saint's mystical encounter with Jesus; he
explained that Catherine, at the Glory Be, turned to Jesus
at her right, saying "Glory be to the Father, to You, and
to the Holy Spirit." The second spoke about Catherine's
mystical nights with her Divine Spouse. Pier Giorgio, after
pausing for a moment, turned to Franz and called him by
name; then he said: "Here, you see, even during her lifetime Saint Catherine had the gift of seeing Jesus." Another
pause, and he added: "We, though, must wait until we go
to heaven", and "I envy her." It seemed that he no longer
wanted to leave his friends. Then, awakened from his med-
itations, he realized that it had become late, he said goodbye
and climbed the stairs. Once in the street, he called him:
"Franz, Franz . . .", so as to see him again. Massetti recalls:

I appeared at the window; he greeted me merrily, as always, and said to me: "A Dio", "Farewell." It was the Tuesday of his final week.

At this distance in time, recalling now the slightest details of that encounter, I have the deep conviction that Pier Giorgio had from that moment on a clear presentiment of heaven's precise warning and with docility confidently abandoned himself into the hands of the One who was inviting him and would sustain him.

Italo, the chauffeur of the Frassati household, relates:

A week before his death, I said to him jokingly: "Master, where to on Sunday?" And he replied: "To go on an excursion in the mountains." I immediately expressed my feelings as follows: "Happy are you, Master, that you are full of life and health and enjoy that! There is never any lack of funds, the automobile is at your disposal, and the driver is ready. What more can you ask?" I had not finished speaking these words when he said to me verbatim: "You, Italo, are still the same madman; but what if you knew that I wish I were eighty years old?" "But why?" was my response. "Because if I were eighty years old I would die sooner and would go right to heaven." And I said: "What would the group do without Robespierre?" He answered that he would wait for them all in heaven.

Some time before the end, Pier Giorgio grew thin, and his father reproached him: "I saw you with a friend. You looked just like a scarecrow in comparison to him. How can you go around like that so raggedly dressed?" His cousin Rina Maria Pierazzi, too, noticed that something was not right about his physical appearance, and since she could not ask him a direct question about the state of his health, she limited herself to saying: "Your jacket is too big", and he, smiling, said, "That is true: too big. . . ."

He had asked Laura Hidalgo to embroider for him on a bookmark these prophetic and blunt words: *Pulvis et umbra sumus* (We are dust and ashes), and on the excursion to Rocca Sella on May 17, 1925, in thanking his companion Elisa Reineri, who had bandaged for him a finger scraped on a rock, he had declared: "The first of us to go to heaven will help the other to climb up." He desperately wanted to live and to love, to love beyond time and fleeting earthly realities. He lacked the time to accomplish all that he hoped to do, and death came to free him from conditions that were too heavy for his free, very intense spirit.

Death did not catch him unprepared. His interior life was already that of an adult Christian. He had long since encountered the living, concrete person of Christ. Pier Giorgio had understood that Christianity was neither a theory nor an ideology, not fanatical thinking or a fashion, not just a set of moral norms and good advice, not even a religion in the literal sense of the term, but rather an extraordinary, unheard-of event that had started the history of a new man, the new man that was in him.

15

SISTER DEATH

Six days were enough to carry him off, from Monday, June 29, to Saturday, July 4, 1925. Scarcely a week to conclude a full life, one so complete as to leave an everlasting imprint. He had told his dearest friends: "The day of my death will be the most beautiful day of my life!"

His departure enlightened the minds of those who had never understood him. And his death is commemorated with chilling lucidity in a long, relentless chronicle, almost a familial indictment, by Luciana Frassati. Her account, which is not cloaked in rhetoric but is instead lean, tragic, and intense, goes back more than fifty years now and was composed "as expiation for a wrong that continued, in apathy, until a few hours before he passed away, when, thinking that we loved him, we dared to judge him."[1] In dramatic words, Luciana presents to us the image of a Blessed who waited for Sister Death alone, as he had wanted to be alone in performing works of charity.

For months Pier Giorgio had been warning: "Death can arrive from one moment to the next. The virtue of a Christian is to be prepared always, every day, to welcome it." And

---

[1] L. Frassati, *Mio fratello Pier Giorgio: La morte* (Rome: Edizioni Paoline, 1952), 11. The following recollections of Luciana Frassati concerning her brother's death are taken from the same volume.

his day arrived on the morning of his feast day, when the Church commemorates Saint Peter. Although he had rested well the whole night, he did not wake up right after dawn as he always used to do but, inexplicably, slept until nine. That delay, which ought to have said a lot about a young man usually ready to jump out of bed like a spring, meant nothing to anyone. They were all distracted by their own concerns, including Luciana, who was living "like a society lady with whom death is not compatible, not even with her feelings; and I was still thinking of the duties, the needs, and the ambitions of my career."

Together with his sister he went to visit a cousin, Silvia Torello, who shortly before had entered the convent, and then he went to Communion. He returned home tired, weary. He went into the kitchen, told the maid that he had a headache and a backache, and asked her to buy him some pills. Since this was an unusual request, the woman became suspicious: "Do you want to see the doctor?" "No, no," he hastily replied, "Mother is already so worried about Grandmother. My sickness will pass." Grandmother Linda was, in fact, dying.

In the early afternoon hours, he asked his sister to lend him thirty lire to give to his poor people: "And so we remained for a few moments in the room, in front of each other: he with his request on his lips and then with some money in his hands and great sadness on his face, until he embraced me. It was the last kiss and the last 'thank you' that I had from my little brother. . . . The only consolation today for the terrible remorse that I was the only person in the house to think for a moment about his feast day. . . ."

Pier Giorgio went out again. He was restless. He arrived at a house on via San Massimo where he had an appointment with several companions, among them Marco Bel-tramo, who immediately noticed changes in his friend. "Do you feel ill?" "I think that it is a case of muscle poisoning. Too much activity in these last few months." Then one of his companions remembered the date, and, therefore, a bottle of wine was uncorked to celebrate Pier Giorgio's name day; as Luciana Frassati declares, "he invited them all to toast, and he himself drank to his own health. . . . At home that evening, silence. He did not say a word, nor was it our custom to question him or to share in his life outside the home, except for what directly concerned us."[2]

Nothing is known about how he spent that night. On the morning of the 30th, he again woke up late. He went to Mass together with his sister, who was brought back to the sacraments by their grandmother's worsening condition. When he returned home, he sat down at the table in the study and, by sheer will, opened his books, but he had to close them a little later because he could not manage to concentrate. He felt exhausted. After being tormented year after year by studying, it was now time for him, who loved vast open spaces, the freedom of the plazas, and the mountains, to close the volumes and the lecture notes definitively.

He went out to meet a friend. "If God calls me, I shall willingly obey", he kept saying. He returned home at midday, paid a visit to his grandmother, then sat down at table, and his mother announced to him: "They are talking about you from the pulpits. Don Borla said so." The priest had been a regular guest at the Frassati house for years; he was the boys' religion teacher and therefore a reliable source. "All of it nonsense", was Pier Giorgio's lapidary response.

[2] Ibid., 24–26.

Simple and humble as he was, that sort of talk disturbed him; he was set free by the poor little girl who arrived every day at lunchtime, and Pier Giorgio served her some food.

Besides his back and his head, his teeth ached, and therefore, while waiting for the mathematics library to open, he asked Bertini to go with him to see the dentist, Doctor Garelli. But he did not call on the doctor, who might have noticed the poliomyelitis that was attacking him. He had brought a walking stick with him because he was unable to stay securely on his feet for a long time, and therefore he sought relief by standing now on one foot and then on the other. He arrived at the library and in the reading room met Laura for the last time, who was still convalescing from a fall in the mountains. He joked with her and, showing her the walking stick, said, shaking his head, "See, we are old, there is nothing left to do about it . . . it takes patience!"

That afternoon his friends organized a boating excursion: he appeared on the Po River as never before, an exhausted rower. He then bought a round of beers, and, after a visit to Saint Joseph's College, where a Christian Brother was supposed to speak to Bertini, he drifted aimlessly until beneath the National Gallery; too tired now to walk because of the pains that were becoming more acute, he decided to take the number 9 streetcar.

His proverbial appetite abandoned him that evening. Although it was an effort, he met with some friends of the family. Then he went to Maria the maid to ask whether the bar was open; that was his way of ordering a cup of coffee. "I will have some coffee so as to feel better; we hope to be able to get better and to be able to study." This obsession with study still weighed upon him in the final days of his life. He went directly up to his room; he asked Mariscia for an aspirin, and the tablet was brought by his mother. Then, hoping to sweat it out, he closed the door to his room without complaining so as not to worry anyone, leaving all with the idea that it was a simple case of the flu.

> Meanwhile, he sweated in his room; he was still only Pier Giorgio Frassati, the son of Senator Frassati and of the painter Ametis; the brother of the wife of the Polish secretary in The Hague; he had nothing of his own but his badge from Catholic Action, the membership cards from Nocturnal Adoration, and the pawn tickets of the poor.
>
> What if he had spoken about death? That night everyone, ourselves included, would have clapped their hand on his shoulder smiling. And therefore we let him sweat it out: a fine, useless, tortuous sweat with the windows open.
>
> And so perhaps we missed our second chance to save him, or at least to understand him. The following morning the dawn entered through the wide-open shutters, without our hearing it, and it brought news that now everything was finished.[3]

Pier Giorgio, lying on his deathbed, spent the night with the windows thrown wide open. At 7:30 Mariscia arrived, whom he had informed the previous evening that he had to arise "at all costs"; but once he had awakened, he said, "I am not well. I slept little last night, too." Worried, the maid took his temperature: 101.8°.

Adelaide Ametis went to visit her son in his room, but her mind was on her mother in the next room, and therefore she limited herself to saying: "It will be necessary to give him a purgative." Two hours later, Doctor Luciano Alvazzi Delfrate arrived at the house to visit Grandmother Ametis; then he went to Pier Giorgio's room and found that the fever had risen to 102.2°. This was his diagnosis: "Armpit

---

[3] L. Frassati, *Pier Giorgio Frassati: I giorni della sua vita*, 3rd ed. (Rome: Edizioni Studium, 1990), 52.

temperature 102.2, throat somewhat reddened, complains of headache, sense of exhaustion in his limbs, back pain especially in the sacral region. Diagnosis: rheumatic pains." Treatment: aspirin.

At midmorning, Luciana went to greet him, and he made a request: "Please go and bring from Reviglio the photographs from the last excursion." He rested a bit, at lunchtime some soup was offered to him, which he refused, and he took the purgative salts with a sip of broth in the hope of recovering quickly. But immediately afterward, he had an unexpected attack of vomiting; at the sight of that Luciana was very worried, recalling what their mother used to say when they were children: "Woe, if vomiting goes together with fever!" Frightened, she went right to her mother and was surprised to hear her say: "Let him take a purgative and do not complicate matters at a time like this." Luciana sorrowfully declares:

> Thus even in his final days, through our fault, his secret and silent life continued. In effect he gave up consolation, sympathy, the comfort of a familiar hand holding his, and of a person dear to him who would be nearby as he sadly awaited death; even his final hours remained a secret between his soul and God.
>
> We were already completely ignorant about his life: his poor people, his evenings of prayer, his letters, his long, painful torment. We did not know who he was, beyond his birth certificate and his career as a tenacious student, and therefore we left him to toss and turn his head on the pillow, and one after the other we all walked out of his room.[4]

The only one who remained with him was Mariscia, the German chambermaid, who admonished him: "To get well

[4] Ibid., 60–61.

quickly you are taking too many purgatives, and then they do you harm", and she added: "But now you will get better." At that point Pier Giorgio burst out laughing. Then, becoming serious, he said: "I am losing too much time; only a few days are left before the exams." He asked Mariscia for a cigarette, but to safeguard him from who knows what effects, she refused him. Meanwhile, the pains in his spine were becoming acute, and paralysis was running its implacable course.

When Luciana went to visit him, he wept because of their grandmother and invited her to pray for her. Shortly afterward, a maid brought news that now the grandmother was about to leave the world. Pier Giorgio therefore got up, wrapped himself in a large checkered shawl and by an enormous effort reached the room of the dying woman. Pale, exhausted, unable to stand on his feet, he knelt down beside the bed and folded his hands while holding a rosary. The grandmother and the grandson said farewell to each other in her last moment of consciousness, while everyone continued to be mysteriously indifferent to him and his condition. After he left the room, he said: "Tomorrow morning I will tell Doctor Alvazzi to give me an injection that will get me up. I have to be well for the exams." Those accursed exams were still tormenting him during the last hours of his life.

He fell asleep, but at ten Maria called him to bring him again to his grandmother, and so he was able to witness her final breath. "I am sorry. Poor Grandmother", Maria remarked, and Pier Giorgio replied: "Why poor Grandmother? I am thinking about Mother, about those who remain." Every two hours or so, he would stand or kneel beside the dead woman's bed, even though he was increasingly fatigued and feverish. During one of his vigils, his mother caught him praying and therefore advised him to go back to bed. Pier Giorgio told her: "I cannot sleep." "Say the rosary, you will fall asleep." Pier Giorgio smiled sadly: "I've already said one", and presented his cheek for a kiss.

He leaned unsteadily against the walls, and no less than three times that night he fell on the cold floor. At four he heard Mariscia moving about in his room. "Are you awake?" he asked softly, and when he saw her, he said: "I have never felt like this." The maid told him to go back to bed, but he asked her: "Go telephone the Boniscontros at the pharmacy and tell them that as soon as Doctor Alvazzi arrives they should send him up to me." She replied, "It is not yet five o'clock, wait a little more." Luciana Frassati sarcastically comments: "Mariscia was like one of us, someone like the others who had rested that night and the evening before had shed their fine tears at the death of our grandmother."[5]

He waited for an interminable three-quarters of an hour and then repeated his request to the maid. When Pier Giorgio caught up with her, he was visibly upset and his legs were unsteady. He let the woman ask the operator to complete the call and then took the receiver: "Please, when Doctor Alvazzi comes, tell him to come immediately to the Frassatis' house, because the senator's son is not seriously ill but is not well, he did not sleep all night." His walk back was tragic. Pier Giorgio passed in front of the billiard table, sat down on the edge of it with his legs swinging and said to Mariscia: "Doctor Alvazzi has to give me an injection. When he comes he will give me a strong dose, and everything will go well." The Blessed stretched out full length on the green cloth, with his eyes fixed on the ceiling: "I have never been like this", he repeated in the pale light of

[5] Ibid., 72.

dawn, abandoning himself to suffering, twisting, and turning in a spasm of pain, his lips pressed together and his hands
clenched.

He went back upstairs by himself, his body swaying like
a reed in the wind, and several times he hit his head against
the gleaming plate glass protecting the paintings by Michetti
"that lined the hallway, as though to ridicule you". "There
was someone who heard your head slam against the picture
frames and the glass, there was someone who heard that
dull noise that forever defined our remorse." He managed
to reach his bed: "It did not even occur to him to forgive
our indifference, since to him it was natural that we should
behave that way."[6]

The daylight arrived, and the city began to come alive. It
was seven o'clock. Pier Giorgio once again asked Mariscia
to send Italo to call the doctor. "Wait," the maid said again,
"the doctor kept watch with your grandmother until late.
Let him rest." His mother arrived, and he repeated to her
the same request, only to hear: "Italo had a fever; we should
let him sleep. The doctor will come."

It was broad daylight, and then, after the umpteenth request from her son, Adelaide Ametis finally sent someone
to call the doctor. Meanwhile Pier Giorgio wrapped himself up in his plaid shawl and, in the restlessness of his illness, wanted to change rooms; he went to stretch out on
one of the two beds in his mother's room. "That sudden
desire seemed to be a childish action, and indeed it was, at
least in part: weakened by the disease, he heard again the
calls of childhood, and perhaps the memory of a time when
our mother's character had not allowed us to be children

[6] Ibid., 75.

completely made him hope that at least in his final days his
need for affection would be resolved and satisfied."[7] But no
one approached him, not even Adelaide.

While his terrible disease took its course, everyone else in
the house was thinking about the thousand things required
by the funeral, for example, changing their clothes, and in
his room, to which he had returned, his mother threw open
the baroque Piedmontese wardrobe. She pointed out two
suits: "We will have them dyed black, and you will be set",
but Pier Giorgio did not answer, and Luciana disapproved
of his conduct: he seemed aloof from their preoccupations,
indifferent to their anxious concerns.

He had another bout of vomiting, and again Mariscia was
the only one who stayed near him. The painter Falchetti
and his dear friend Marco Beltramo called on him; with
the latter he recited the *De profundis* together with the priest
who had gone to bless the grandmother's remains. Then,
before saying goodbye, Marco promised that the next day
he would bring a book that was easier to read than the one
about Saint Catherine of Siena.

That Thursday Pier Giorgio expressed the desire to eat
some ice cream. "Our house, however, was a miserable bar-
racks: for whatever reason, he got no ice cream . . . so as
not to transgress the cold rules of the official protocol, not
even in the face of death." Instead of ice cream, they gave
him a frozen egg custard, which was already prepared in the
kitchen. An hour later they brought him, as he requested,
breakfast rolls and coffee with milk. Mariscia asked him to
sit up in bed to eat, and for the first time his response was
harsh and curt: "I will eat like this, lying down. Enough!"
But the maid would not give up and tried, uselessly, to lift

[7] Ibid., 81.

him up by the armpits. In order to put an end to those tor-turous demands, he turned on his side and sat up on the edge of the bed. Mariscia tried to put on his slippers, but they fell to the floor. Irritated, the woman said: "You will catch a chill if you keep joking like this!" Unfortunately, it was no joke; his feet were already inert because of the paralysis and did not obey the commands of his mind, and therefore they gave way to the slightest weight.

Toward evening, Pier Giorgio tried to get out of bed but failed and fell to the ground. Mariscia found him stretched out and could not manage to lift him up alone. The family members were in the room set up for the wake, attending the ceremony for the closing of the coffin, and therefore she asked for help from a relative of the Frassatis, Andrés Seitun.

Thursday night, Mario Gambetta, a cousin who had come from Albisola, kept watch over him, and a room next to that of the Blessed was assigned to the guest. Luciana writes: "And I behaved worse than my mother, because although I was not tired from the wake for the dead woman and not overcome with grief, I immediately went to bed, nestled among the blankets and let a distant relative keep that envi-able watch instead of me."[8]

The patient was bathed in sweat, and Mario Gambetta helped him change his drenched garments, but Pier Gior-gio's movements were now stiff like those of a wooden man-nequin; yet he asked Mario not to mention anything to any-one.

At five o'clock on Friday, all the Frassatis arose to get ready to leave for Pollone so as to accompany the hearse to the final resting place. Mariscia came into Pier Giorgio's

[8] Ibid., 98.

room at around six and awakened him, after endless hours of insomnia and suffering, to ask him how he was feeling; his grandmother was about to depart from that house forever, did he want to be present at the farewell? "I cannot," Pier Giorgio answered, "I do not even know whether I am well or ill, but I fear a bit worse." He repeated the same thing to his mother. "But there was no one who could understand him, and the only voice that spoke up reprimanded him, the same scolding as on Thursday, when he was accused of acting like a baby and not being of any help."[9] When it was time to leave, Adelaide, who had already adjusted her hat on her head, allowed her sister to persuade her and decided, due to the great weariness that tormented her because of the repeated nocturnal and daytime vigils at her mother's sickbed, not to go to Pollone but to remain with her son.

When they were alone, Adelaide, less a prisoner now of her mannered formalities of etiquette, found tender words to say: "My little boy, my baby, do not be sick; I am afraid." Whether he was dreaming or it was just his childlike nature, Pier Giorgio asked: "When will I get better, Mama?" seeking in his mother the sense of security that every son wishes to find. "Wait . . . today is Friday . . . Saturday . . . : you will get up on Sunday." Then she added: "You will have to wear mourning." "Poor Mama, I am causing you this trouble, too." "But this sickness of yours is nothing; I just need to rest." And after adjusting the pillows under his head, she stretched out beside him, with her head close to his. He protested, saying that she too would catch the contagious disease. "Do you not know, my boy, that mothers never catch the illnesses of their children?" Thus, in a quarter hour of love and compassion, mother and son experienced some of the most beautiful moments of their lives.

[9] Ibid., 104.

Later Doctor Alvazzi arrived. He came in smiling and immediately asked Pier Giorgio how his last excursion had been: he knew that it went back to June 7 at Le Lunelle. But the joviality quickly disappeared from his face. He began to interrogate him, with curt, anxious questions. He thoroughly examined him. At one point the physician said: "Get up." Pier Giorgio admitted: "I no longer can."

The diagnosis fell like a guillotine on everyone's head: "Flaccid paralysis of the lower limbs, absence of patellar [knee] reflexes, palsy of the upper left arm. Unable to sit up in bed due to weakness of the muscles of the torso. Irregular breathing due to incipient paralysis of the diaphragm and the intercostal muscles. Completely conscious. Catheterization." It was an acute ascending form of arteriovenous, infectious poliomyelitis. In those days the word poliomyelitis or "polio" terrified all mothers of families in a sort of collective psychosis; many children had been struck down more or less seriously by it.

Several years later, another layperson, this one an extraordinarily vivacious young woman, would also fall victim to poliomyelitis: Benedetta Bianchi Porro. On December 23, 1993, John Paul II promulgated the decree on the heroicity of her virtues. She was born on August 8, 1936, in Dovadola, in the province of Forlì. At the age of a few months she was struck by the disease, which caused the impairment of one of her legs. Sensitive, intelligent, very pretty, and jovial, at age thirteen the girl was forced to wear a corset to prevent a malformation of the spine. But the disease progressed. At the age of seventeen, without attending school, she passed the entrance examination and enrolled in the university, first in physics and then in medicine. In late 1956, after many surgical interventions, there were signs of diffuse neurofibromatosis, an invasion of small tumors that paralyzed the nerve centers of her sensory and motor activity. Since the disease was progressing, she was forced to give up her plans for a baccalaureate degree. She needed just one more examination.

Immobilized in a wheelchair, she was surrounded by the affection of many friends, who assisted her and encouraged her to live and to hope. She died at the age of twenty-seven on January 23, 1964, leaving an indelible memory of herself. Many aspects of her life recall the spirituality of Pier Giorgio Frassati: her love for the Eucharistic Jesus, her great humility, her belief that one's body is the temple of the Holy Spirit, her ecclesial sense (that is, her love for the Church), and, last but certainly not least, her charity, which Benedetta defined as follows: "Charity is living in others." For both of them, then, creation was a divine book, and love for nature became a perpetual praise of God, a "praised be you, my Lord" of the Franciscan tradition. Their freshness of life, self-giving to family and friends, enthusiasm for all forms of art, sensitivity to the maternal warmth of Mary, and an irresistible and irrepressible interest in others inevitably led them to be called lay apostles. Tried by suffering, they accepted the cross with resignation and hope, knowing that it is the path for the redemption of every being: "Now that suffering dwells in me, everything in me has been purified", Benedetta used to say, and "the cross takes on an appearance that we would not have expected." So it happened, too, for the young man Pier Giorgio, who, even before reaching the goal posts, passed his soul through the fire that transformed it into molten gold.

Pier Giorgio was living the last hours of his life, and his head was now immobile. He told the maid in a weary, distorted voice: "Mariscia, adjust the pillows under my head, I want to find a more comfortable position." It often happens that in serious situations, those who are well stiffen in the presence of the sick, as though not admitting the harsh reality that upsets the usual routines, and Mariscia behaved like that: "Do not talk that way," she exclaimed, terrified, "it will frighten your mother." But now, although Pier Giorgio's will could no longer be dominated and controlled, his body was falling into the arms of Sister Death: "I cannot [do it myself], I cannot manage it", was his reply.

His mother wanted her son to receive the Viaticum, and so as not to give any hint of the seriousness of his condition, she told him: "Go to Communion for your grandmother." "But I will on Sunday", he replied, referring to his hope of being up and around on the day that his mother had mentioned to him. "No, it is better for you to do it now. You will do me a favor if you obey me." "I cannot, I drank some milk a little while ago." "That does not matter; you are sick." "Well, then, as you wish, Mama." Don Giorgio Formica arrived; he was the only priest with whom Pier Giorgio had had differences in their ideas and practical approaches.[10] He made his confession, and, after receiving absolution, Pier Giorgio asked him without any anxiety: "Is my condition serious?" The priest answered that the doctors had not yet made a pronouncement, and then the Blessed made him promise to tell him if his condition should worsen. Everything was prepared for the Eucharist. Pier Giorgio insistently asked them to place on the table the silver candlesticks that had been used in Berlin for official dinners, while on the altar they opened a small case containing the image of Our Lady of Seggiola that Benedict XV had donated to a lottery of the Cesare Balbo circle and that

---

[10] The Milites Mariae group that Pier Giorgio had founded in the latter half of 1921 in the parish of La Crocetta had greatly worried the assistant pastor, Don Formica, who did not look kindly on such an innovative initiative made up of laymen, and he did all he could to hinder it.

Pier Giorgio had been fortunate enough to win. After the Communion service, Don Formica left, and Pier Giorgio asked: "Mama, give me something to drink so that no particles of the Host remain in my mouth."

Professor Micheli arrived and pronounced the final death sentence. Luciana recalls:

> With a sort of malice toward myself, I made him explain to me, later on, the significance of that terrible remark, and I learned that Pier Giorgio had died by the silent working of a minute germ that hides in the mucous membranes of the nose and throat and then in the circulatory system so as to establish itself, optimally, in the nervous system. It seems that the virus travels this path more easily in the circulation of strong individuals than in that of the weak: its insidious nature is more likely to kill those who are called to life than those who are rejected by it.
>
> When they told me that the lethal stage of the disease is infectious, many obscure things were suddenly clear to me. I understood that Pier Giorgio, as Professor Micheli then repeatedly told us, must have caught the disease during his visits to the poor in the most squalid part of Turin, and since the infection could easily have spread, I could tell that it was a sign from the Almighty that he had rejected us all.[11]

Doctors Alvazzi, Micheli, and Ganna consulted with one another, and all three reached the same conclusion. Adelaide had already taken steps to tell her sister, Elena, to return to Turin because she felt lonely and needed them all. But the aunt did not believe her and insisted on having additional news; then Adelaide said that Pier Giorgio was well, that she was the one who needed assistance and company.

---

[11] L. Frassati, *Pier Giorgio Frassati: I giorni della sua vita*, 118.

Professor Micheli's automobile parked in front of the main entrance to the house gave the first sad signal to those who arrived from Pollone. Pier Giorgio experienced hunger, for the last time. And after he insisted repeatedly, the doctors soon agreed that he could swallow something. Mariscia lifted his head and Sister Angelica served him, offering him one spoonful of egg custard after the other. Then they gave him a cup of coffee with milk.

One possible gleam of hope might still have been the poliomyelitis serum that was available only at the Pasteur Institute in Paris. But an unexpected storm that had been unleashed over the Alps cruelly prevented both passage by rail and also travel by airplane. Ferrarin himself, who was the commander of the airport in Turin, refused to attempt the flight. The physicians administered to him an intravenous injection of ovatrophin; in his left arm the liquid went nowhere, kept back by the paralysis; in his right arm it managed to make its way.

Pier Giorgio called Luciana and told her to go to his study to bring him the wallet in the inside pocket of his jacket. His sister went in a hurry; on the table she found the lecture notes for the next-to-last exam and the missal already opened to the Gospel for the following Sunday. From the wallet she took out a pawn ticket. Then, while still in the study, she took a box of injections, a calling card, and her brother's pen. Pier Giorgio told her to forward the ticket as soon as possible to his friend Grimaldi, who was supposed to accompany him on the usual weekly visit of the Saint Vincent de Paul Society to the poor. He wanted to add a note to it. Luciana tried in vain to have him dictate the message to her (in the book by Cojazzi it says that his mother also offered to help), but with superhuman effort he tried to write it himself: "Here are Converso's injections.

The ticket belongs to Sappa; I forgot it; redeem it at my expense." Then Luciana went to bring him, at his request, his alpaca jacket and took out the contents of the pockets. The Blessed selected one small sheet of paper and handed it folded to his father: "Take this, Papa; it is to be published in *La Stampa* tomorrow." It was an announcement of a pious work to be listed in the Saturday charity column.

The opportunity to see Pier Giorgio one last time was denied everyone, even the archbishop of Turin, Cardinal Gamba; their wish was overridden "by the stubborn inclination of his relatives not to let into the house anyone who might 'disturb' Pier Giorgio", as Luciana Frassati later put it. When news of their friend's serious condition reached his friends from FUCI, they gathered in prayer with Don Carlo Borgatello to implore grace.

During the endless time of his suffering, punctuated by the tolling from the nearby bell tower, he would have liked to fall asleep so as to have a little rest, but the pain in his limbs was indescribable; then he asked for an injection of morphine, but the physicians refused. His mother drew near and whispered to him: "It is not possible; it would harm you. Offer to God your suffering, your inability to sleep, and your desire to, for your sins, if you have any; if not, then for those of Papa and Mama."[12]

Don Formica returned, and Pier Giorgio told him: "I feel much more exhausted: much, much more." "Giorgio, what if your grandmother were calling you to heaven?" "How happy I would be!" But then, in a flash of concern: "And what about Papa and Mama?" "Giorgio, you will not abandon them; from heaven you will live in spirit with them. You will give them all your faith and your resignation; you

---

[12] A. Cojazzi, *Pier Giorgio Frassati: Testimonianze* (Turin: SEI, 1928), 298.

will all continue to be one family." "Yes", was his reply. From that moment, every time Don Formica entered the room, Pier Giorgio's eyes followed him and the priest murmured: "Courage, Giorgio." Luciana relates:

> To Mariscia, who had come into his room and had asked how he was feeling, he had gestured with his hand, as though to say: "So, so." Immediately afterward, with the last glint of his old cheerfulness, he again made at her the funny face with which he always used to tease her.
>
> When the woman told us about this incredible leave-taking we were stunned: he was doomed to die, and he still managed to smile, just as he had tried the whole day to console Mama and Papa, who were sitting on one side of his room with their eyes fixed on the wall to hide their weeping; just as he had thanked the doctors and whoever had come by to help him with looks so intense as to move them to tears.

Professor Pescarolo arrived, too, and offered a glimmer of hope: contrary to what the other physicians had said, he did not rule out the possibility that the disease might limit itself to affecting the peripheral zones without attacking those that are strictly vital. He prescribed absolute peace and quiet. If by four o'clock in the night his condition had not deteriorated, they could begin to believe that he would be saved.

Alfonsina Morra, who had assisted his grandmother for a month and a half, arrived to keep watch over him. Together with her, Sister Michelina of the Franciscans sat beside his bed,

> . . . while we left him once again to go to our rooms.
>
> Courage, keep your eyes wide open tonight, O pious ladies, even though they are weary from many days of little sleep: this is the last night that he will live, that he will see the electric lights turn on, the last time that he can hear the

sound of nocturnal steps on the asphalt and the passage of the streetcar in silence.

Watch him well, therefore, and let us sleep in our beds, let us enjoy the rest that we seek and do not deserve. As of tomorrow evening we will have enough to be sorry about; we will have our whole lives to repent of it.

It seemed like the script of a Shakespearean tragedy; it had all the redolence of one, and not one of those who continued to live found serenity again.

Toward two o'clock at night, Pier Giorgio called Sister Michelina to his side. He had not yet had any sleep, and his strength was failing him. "Help me to make the sign of the cross." Now his right arm, too, was almost completely paralyzed. As Sister Michelina began to recite the ejaculation, "Jesus, Joseph, and Mary", Pier Giorgio interrupted her and wanted to continue by himself: "I know, I know", because he did not want anyone else to pronounce the rest of it: "May I breathe out my soul in peace with You." As it was nearing four o'clock, the Blessed asked: "Will God forgive me, will God forgive me?" and with an anguished cry, he said, "Lord, forgive me, forgive me!"

Four o'clock passed, and his condition began to deteriorate. All his senses were extinguished, and Don Formica arrived with the blessed oil. "Giorgio, your soul is beautiful. Jesus wants you to be with him. Jesus loves you." Alfredo Frassati was standing in a corner of the room so as to experience the beginning of a new interior life; with his face turned toward the wall, he listened to the words of Doctor Pescarolo and cried like a baby. His whole existence was crumbling right in front of him. The sacrifice of his son was being accomplished before his incredulous eyes. It was a sort of holocaust consummated within the walls of that house in which rancor, selfishness, hostility, and lack of understanding had dwelt together, that house that for the Blessed had been mission territory, between his father's agnosticism and his mother's sterile religiosity, mission territory to which he could bring peace and harmony, mission territory where he could lead his relatives closer to the truth.

Alfredo continued to weep and called him desperately in the absurd hope of delaying the separation. At six o'clock, the family members went up to the Church of La Crocetta to pray. "It was a desperate act to ask for a grace we did not merit, and yet we tried."[13]

At nine, Pier Giorgio's heavy breathing stopped, and his right side was completely paralyzed, too. His forehead no longer needed to be dried. The oxygen tanks came and went to help his breathing, which became increasingly difficult in that slow agony. His glassy eyes from time to time brightened tenderly. His facial muscles contracted more and more spasmodically while he gasped like a drowning man, desperately trying to take in gulps of air.

With the 3:00 P.M. express train, the anti-poliomyelitis serum arrived, and at 4:00 a lumbar injection was administered to him. He seemed to improve, but the paralysis also ascended to his lungs. Down his suffering, lank, and ruined face streamed big, mysterious tears, the only sign of life. Then a gesture as though to point at something in front of him, perhaps the picture of Our Lady from which his eyes no longer turned away.

It was a torturous, difficult end. "When he found the strength necessary to go back to the bedside, Papa, now unrestrained in his sorrow, shouted so desperately as he called to his son that the nun had to ask him to stop for fear that Pier Giorgio would hear him. And who can say that he did

---

[13] L. Frassati, *Mio fratello Pier Giorgio: La morte*, 139.

not hear him, considering the tears that ran down his face until the final moment of his life?"[14]

While his legs became ever colder, his heartbeat weakened, and his face took on the appearance of a corpse, artificial respiration was administered. "Seven o'clock sounded on the great timepiece, while through the corridor outside the room passed a mysterious breeze."[15] His mother supported his head, while Luciana, kneeling beside the bed, held his hand and his rosary. She noticed a final grip, a final salute. And when he expired, outdoors, as the sun was about to set, a band struck up a very sad funeral march behind the hearse of a police officer, while the faithful maid of the Frassati household, Ester Pignata,[16] hurried into the kitchen to write on the calendar: "7:00, irreparable misfortune. Poor Saint Pier Giorgio! He was a saint, and God wanted him with him!"

That tragic year 1925, which is remembered for the opening of the first highway for automobiles in the world, the Milano-Laghi Motorway, and for the turn taken by the Italian State toward Fascism and the end of democracy in that country, carried off an explosion of life, the gleaming fragments of which continue to rain down today on the stories of personal deeds and individual souls.

[14] Ibid., 142–43.

[15] Ibid., 143.

[16] One day Pier Giorgio had said to Ester Pignata: "The path of the honest is the most difficult, but it is the shortest one leading to the path of heaven."

16

THE TRIUMPH

The contortions of pain disappeared from Pier Giorgio's face, and his features relaxed. They dressed him in black: it was his suit for social occasions, which he did not like to put on because it meant attending a party or a reception (which he always tried to miss); or else he would respond as follows when his family insisted: "It is enough for me to arrive in time to greet the people as they leave." The one time that he had gladly worn the suit was on the occasion of the Eucharistic Congress in Turin, when the task of escorting Jesus in the Blessed Sacrament was entrusted to him. At the behest of the archbishop of Turin, Cardinal Gamba, on his black suit was pinned not only a crucifix but also a relic of then-Blessed Giuseppe Cafasso.

The body was arranged in his room, which was decorated with flowers. The florist herself, Vittoria Asinari, who had served Pier Giorgio so many times, wanted to place pink gladiolas beside him, as a reminder of the festivities sponsored by FUCI. Adelaide had asked her to prepare a wreath of Alpine flowers, but it was impossible for her to find any.

Franz drew near to adjust the tie, as he used to do every time his friend put one on with the inexperience of someone who cared little for that type of elegance. For two consecutive nights, his friends kept watch over him. At his feet had been placed the rhododendrons he had gathered in the mountains: his favorite flowers from his Alpine peaks. There were also gardenias to recall the friendship of his female companions. Meanwhile, the eulogies and acknowledgments began. For the members of his family, it was a real revelation: large quantities of letters and telegrams arrived.

The painter Falchetti, struck by the serenity and peace of that face, traced its features in a drawing and asked the sculptor Edoardo Rubino to make a death mask; the latter confided: "Such purity emanated from that very handsome face that I was overcome with emotion, and I refused to cover it with plaster, and I told my instructor to leave off." Dismay was on the face and in the words of everyone.

Let us read the obituary announcement in *La Stampa* on July 5:

> That young man, only twenty-four years old, strong and healthy as an Alpine trooper from our valleys, and good with the moving goodness of a little saint, was snatched away from life and from his family by a death that was slightly less than lightning-swift, as though it were horrified by its own ruthless work. . . . We cannot recall Pier Giorgio without thinking of what was the homeland of his soul, the unearthly source of his thought, and the sure refuge of his higher existence. . . . He lived in the truth as though he had never departed from it. . . . There was in him a vein of mysticism so pure and deep that from his early years it had made him a stranger to every comfort and to every fortune in life. Born in the midst of wealth, Pier Giorgio Frassati had the Franciscan spirit of poverty. His hands were not made to gather but to distribute. . . . His soul was not made to enjoy but to see others enjoy. . . . He was heavily involved in life, as though he were already a mature man, with the moral fortitude and righteousness of

the old Piedmontese school: the soul of a boy in a manly character. . . . He walked in justice with the same forthright, steady pace, without delays, without stopping, without lagging. His Christian conscience placed an abyss between the fate of his body and that of his soul; yet they opened our eyes and our minds as though they were fused in one expression: it was enough to see his face to anticipate the few decisive words of his speech; his speech was the clear mirror of his sentiment and spirit.

Even when he was twenty-four years old, on the eve of taking his coveted degree in engineering, the older editors, the ones who long ago had held him on their own knee or taken him by the hand on walks along the streets and through the gardens and over the hills, considered him a little like the baby and the boy of a former time.

The managers of the daily newspaper decided to allocate a thousand lire for "the poor protégés of Pier Giorgio Frassati" and donated the money to the Cesare Balbo circle at the university.

His mother's sorrow was wordless, his father's weeping—inconsolable. Adelaide, unable to make any claim to words of comfort for herself, was closely attentive to Pier Giorgio's friends.

The death affected all Italy, and the grief in Turin was universal: the fame of the Blessed had spread much farther than the reputations of his parents: "The letters we received then and, even more, what was later told us about him by his unrecognized friends and all the unknown beneficiaries who gradually turned to us were such an impressive and sublime revelation that it overwhelmed us as much as his death."[1]

---

[1] L. Frassati, *Mio fratello Pier Giorgio: La morte* (Rome: Edizioni Paoline, 1952), 148.

The funeral, a veritable triumph, was held on July 6, and, contrary to the wishes of Pier Giorgio's parents, the young men of FUCI, after a long discussion, obtained permission to carry him on their shoulders from the house to the parish church of La Crocetta: at nine in the morning, the coffin glided away from the villa[2] that was first devoid of appreciation and then devoid of Pier Giorgio. Neither Alfredo nor Adelaide nor Luciana had noticed the light that reigned in their dwelling or the immense gift of having beside them such a noble and extraordinary creature. They had to lose him in order to meet him.

The crowd was immense, and in order to process in front of that whole multitude of persons that invaded the via Marco Polo and what was then called corso Orbassano, the FUCI members had to slacken their pace. Then a very strange thing happened. During a change of the pallbearers, the bier swayed and Alfredo Frassati, with desperate tenderness, helped prevent it from falling. It is quite probable that the incident occurred because of the weak shoulders of the FUCI member Francesco Manara, who was already struck by a terminal disease. A few months later, when Francesco was laid out on his deathbed, his friends noticed on his black suit the mark left by Pier Giorgio's coffin.

Giolitti, who had been informed the previous day in his native region of Cavour, wept and sent a telegram to Alfredo: "I read the dreadful news. I am terrified by it as though one of my own children had been struck down. I find no words of comfort. I embrace you." The statesman did not go to the funeral because, he said, he would have been unable to

---

[2] At 70 corso Galileo Ferraris, a memorial stone reads: "A steady calm of humility, / Pier Giorgio Frassati / lived here, / only to deposit / in Christ's lap / the human sorrow / and the joy / of his dying. / April 6, 1901–July 4, 1925."

restrain his emotion and someone in his position could not allow such a display.

The editor of *Il Momento* wrote in a column that was reprinted by *La Stampa* that Pier Giorgio was and "will remain in our memories everlastingly as one of the finest and sincerest figures in the Catholic youth movement". The referendum of grief over the Blessed's demise was unanimous, and all the major daily newspapers joined in the sorrow: even the *Vossische Zeitung* in Berlin announced the death with considerable emotion:

> He was an especially likeable young man and showed an extraordinary interest in all German political and economic questions. During his stay in Germany he had endeared himself to his contemporaries and to all who regularly visited the Frassati household. For these reasons, in Berlin the sorrow of his parents, who were struck such a cruel blow, is felt and shared in a particular way, especially in the political and diplomatic circles in Berlin, which have a pleasant memory full of admiration for the Frassati household.

Thousands of people came from all parts of the city, especially from the poorest districts, drawn, not by the family name Frassati, but by the given name Pier Giorgio. Streetcar traffic was stopped to allow room for the crowd, from which many individuals emerged to try to reach the hearse and touch the coffin. So it happened with one old blind man, who was guided to it and, once he arrived, made the sign of the cross over himself, while the people murmured: "That is one of his many beneficiaries." An uncontrollable tide was moving through the La Crocetta district: old and young, poor and rich side by side.

His sister writes: "As I was following the hearse, I just could not be hopeless. It seemed as I walked that I was lifted above the earth, taking part in a triumphal procession.

It seemed to me as though we had walked behind Pier Giorgio all our lives."[3]

The people were praying and weeping; emotions ran high in a way that was deeply involving and stirring, just as he had been: the humble youth who was nevertheless a leader. Marco Beltramo's father, a Catholic but certainly not a fervent one, found himself reciting the rosary in the midst of a group of people.

When the coffin was set down in the church, in front of the altar, his friends placed their pallid faces against it and remained there motionless for several minutes. The reporter from *La Stampa*, Ubaldo Leva, admits:

> It was my turn to "serve" [as a journalist] at the funeral of Pier Giorgio. I would like to say something about that funeral. I would like to say it was the most moving and edifying funeral that I have attended, either as a journalist or as a private person; not the most solemn, no, as an official ceremony, but the most vivid, the warmest, the most human—I would almost say the most beautiful. Even now, after such a great interval of time, I am overcome with tenderness and bewilderment in remembering it. . . . On no other occasion have I wished so much to be, not a poor, plain old journalist, but a writer. . . . I have never seen and will never again see so many tears at a funeral.

The gate at *La Stampa* on via Davide Bertolotti was closed for the first and only time on the day of the funeral. No famous person had died; the one who had died was a student, at the dawn of his responsibilities in life; in the eyes of those who did not know what had made up that life, the scenes that followed one another that day were a mystery.

[3] L. Frassati, *Mio fratello Pier Giorgio: La morte*, 149.

Archbishop Giuseppe Gamba supported Don Antonio Cojazzi's idea of gathering information and testimonies about Pier Giorgio Frassati so as to compose a biography[4] for the edification of the faithful, especially of young people. Pier Giorgio's mother, sustained by her sister Elena, dedicated herself to the task of gathering documentation on her son.

On July 7, 1925, the day after the funeral, in recording some impressions for a newspaper in Turin, Don Antonio Cojazzi wrote: "Some verses from a ballade by Déroulède come to mind: 'They will speak of him for a long time, in the gilded palaces and in the squalid garrets.' Because he will live longer than the glories that are based on power or wealth or cold intellect. I will write his life when, according to the Gospel, much of what is unknown will be made plain and what is hidden will be revealed." Don Cojazzi was right in saying that people would speak about him for a long time: at his death, the extraordinary young man named Pier Giorgio left not a void but an abyss. Archbishop Giuseppe Gamba sent a heartfelt letter to the same Don Cojazzi:

> You have guessed my thought! Just last night, as I kept vigil, I was thinking about our Giorgio, who absorbs all our thoughts these days, and I said to myself: it is necessary to write his life; he will be a great model for our young people and a protector, now that he is in heaven! But who will be able to draw the dear young man from life and propose him as a model to our young people? Would you believe it? My thoughts turned to you: Don Cojazzi will be able to do this work, and how well he will be able to do it, since he was Giorgio's tutor and knew him so well! Happy coincidence! The following morning I read in *Il Corriere*

---

[4] According to Rina Maria Pierazzi, the biography was corrected by Umberto Cosmo at the behest of Alfredo Frassati.

your very fine article, in which you invited people who knew the dear Departed to send you any information they have for the precise purpose of writing his life! Imagine how delighted I was by that! Allow me, therefore, to thank you for the holy thought and to encourage you as well as I can to complete as soon as possible this project, which will be not only very welcome but also very useful to our young people, whether FUCI members or not; since Pier Giorgio Frassati was a model for everyone, having in his young years passed through all the dangers of the world, which, rather than harming the purity of his soul, made him a Christian hero.

Pier Giorgio was placed, temporarily, in the chapel of the Delleani family in Pollone. Two years later, his remains were translated to the family tomb, which Adelaide intended to adorn personally with copies of frescoes by Fra Angelico; on the marble slab, beneath the name, was engraved the question: "Why do you seek the living among the dead"? (Lk 24:5).

Turin wore mourning: there were no flags at half staff, but there were truly many who understood that no one could ever be a substitute for Pier Giorgio Frassati. The street-cars, the churches, the streets, the poor attics of the city, the Polytechnic, the youth groups no longer saw his smile, his courtesy, his unique presence: saints are not interchangeable numbers; when they die, they cannot be replaced, and their memory spreads like leaven over time instead of fading.

The publicity that surrounded Pier Giorgio praised the integrity of his life, as opposed to the easy attractions that could result from the social class to which he belonged and which that ambience could offer him on a silver platter. And precisely this adversarial view, the fact that he went against the current, his rebellion against conformity in his manners and in his thinking, was the basis for its immediate success. Therefore the Salesians made Pier Giorgio known as a model for the younger generations, and there were many who began to assign to their own son the name of the young man of the eight beatitudes. Catholic Action and the Saint Vincent de Paul conferences had the same intention of spreading news about Pier Giorgio's sanctity. Since the Great War was over, the Catholic movements were revitalized for a comprehensive apostolate.

Catholic Action and FUCI were the two movements most committed to presenting the figure of Frassati to young Catholics. Pope Pius XI promoted in a particular way the world of the organized Catholic laity, even offering them examples of sanctity (facetiously nicknamed "saints in suit coats") drawn from the younger generations of the Catholic movement. Thus, after the lull in the thirties and forties—when the Italian regime had gagged Catholic organizations, forcing the ecclesiastical authorities to exclude all those who had participated in some way in the Popular Party—the figure of Pier Giorgio emerged from the sacristy to exert the full force of his fascinating charisma.

With the end of World War II, Catholic lay associations, stimulated by the plan for Christian civilization devised by Pius XII, turned their attention to social concerns. Catholic Action saw an increase in its membership, and in this atmosphere of rebirth and euphoria many biographies of Pier Giorgio were published, side by side with other figures, such as Aldo Monelli, a seventeen-year-old who had been shot by the Nazis in Cuneo, Blessed Alberto Marvelli, who wholeheartedly imitated Pier Giorgio in everything, and Teresio Olivelli, who resembled Pier Giorgio in his stubborn will, jovial spirit, and passion for sports, although he followed a different ideological path.

When a young provincial Italian Catholic sacrifices his life for his ideals of freedom and justice, often the story of his life is written and he is compared to Pier Giorgio Frassati; in some cases, the biography is even entitled: *The Pier Giorgio Frassati of . . .* followed by his place of origin.

And so we arrive in the 1980s, when Pier Giorgio is presented as a layman dedicated to practical charity, service to his neighbor, and the social and political liberty of his native land. Now he is the man of the eight beatitudes, the one who mingled with the people and brought the word of Christ by living an ordinary life with extraordinary trust and faith, heroic in his everyday routine, the herald of sanctity in volunteer work.

Famous writers and thinkers have left firsthand testimonies of him: Papini, La Pira, Don Sturzo, Cardinal Lercaro, Rahner . . . and they did so for two sorts of reasons: first, because the illustrious Frassati family was well known; second, because Pier Giorgio was truly fascinating. Karl Rahner wrote:

> When I look back at the years after the First World War, with their many initiatives and movements in the world and Church of the time, and I recall the impression that Frassati made on me then (when I knew much less about him than I know now), I have to confess frankly that I thought of him as just one among many Christian young people in the Catholic youth movement at that time. There were so many of them. . . . There were plenty of young Christians like him at that time, thank God, in Germany, France, and Italy.
>
> However, I am convinced that few of them coming from

the liberal environment of the high bourgeoisie became like Pier Giorgio Frassati.[5]

Thanks to the extensive documentation that reached Don Cojazzi and the Curia in Turin reporting many graces and conversions obtained through the intercession of Pier Giorgio Frassati, on July 2, 1932, Cardinal Maurilio Fossati, archbishop of Turin, initiated the first ordinary informative process, which was concluded on October 23, 1935. But in 1943 Pius XII ordered that the cause be set aside (*reponatur*), due to calumnies regarding the Blessed's association with young women and to his alleged resuscitation and subsequent despair in his coffin. Therefore, everything was shelved in the archives, and there were no plans to proceed further; therefore, the case should have been closed. Upon the death of her mother, which occurred in 1949, Luciana began to compile thousands upon thousands of testimonies, to write biographical profiles, to collect her brother's letters, sending it all to the Vatican, to the then Substitute in the Secretariat of State, Monsignor Giovanni Battista Montini. Luciana carried on her activities against her father's will and that of Don Cojazzi himself.[6]

The Franciscan Gaetano Stano was then assigned to review the material collected by Jesuit Father Molinari, and the cause was again allowed to move forward. In 1978, Paul VI confirmed the introduction of the cause, and the apostolic process began in Turin on July 16, 1980, in the presence

[5] K. Rahner, in the introduction L. Frassati, *A Man of the Beatitudes: Pier Giorgio Frassati*, trans. Dinah Livingstone, adapted and ed. Patricia O'Rourke (San Francisco: Ignatius Press, 2000), 15–16.

[6] Marcello Staglieno maintains that he was perhaps "jealous of what she might be able to write". See M. Staglieno, *Un santo borghese: Pier Giorgio Frassati* (Milan: Bompiani, 1988), 189.

of Cardinal Anastasio Ballestrero, Father Molinari (the postulator of the cause), and Christian Brother Gustavo Luigi Furfaro (the vice-postulator), and it concluded one year later on July 21.

On December 21, 1989, John Paul II, who in Poland already knew about, esteemed, and loved the Italian student, promulgated the decree regarding his heroic virtues.[7] Pier Giorgio became a Blessed on May 20, 1990, on Saint Peter's Square in the presence of a multitude of young people. And for the first time in liturgical history, on July 4, the Church began to celebrate the name Pier Giorgio. On July 16, 1989, when the Holy Father, who shared with Pier Giorgio a passion for mountain climbing, visited the tomb in the cemetery of Pollone, he had this to say: "I, too, in my youth felt the beneficial influence of his example and, as a student, was impressed by the power of his Christian witness. . . . The peculiarly incisive character of his witness springs from the radical nature of his adherence to Christ, from the clearness of his fidelity to the Church, and from the generosity of his missionary commitment. He offered to all a proposal that even today has lost nothing of its attractive force." Pollone welcomed him with the words that the Blessed had written to Mario Bergonzi: "I wish I were in your position to see the Holy Father every so often. You know how I love the pope. I would like to do something for him. But since I

---

[7] The miracle through the intercession of Pier Giorgio Frassati that has been recognized by the Church had taken place long before. It was the year 1934, and Domenico Sellan of San Quirino di Pordenone, afflicted with Pott disease, a terrible form of tuberculosis of the bone, was cured in a short time; an elderly priest who had visited him at the end of his life had entrusted to him a picture of Pier Giorgio and had invited him to recite the prayer on the back. The cured man lived another thirty-five years in poverty, collecting rags and scrap iron, but in good health and always grateful to Pier Giorgio, whom he continued to invoke in prayer.

cannot, I pray every day that Jesus might give him many consolations and blessings. Long live the pope! *Viva!*"

Several times during his pontificate, John Paul II returned to the figure of Pier Giorgio Frassati with words fraught with conviction and emotion like these (May 5, 1996): "Today believers—and especially young people—have an urgent task to accomplish. Their job is to preserve the smile of the world—of a world that is sometimes furious or disappointed or bored, and needs to meet cheerful, smiling persons who can face the future. May the example of Blessed Pier Giorgio Frassati enlighten you."

His sister, Luciana, who had lived with the constant memory of her brother while striving for his beatification and the exaltation of his virtues, began very humbly in the 1950s to admit that their family had not understood, while he was still alive, what it meant for a creature to be filled with God. And when prose was not enough to communicate her nostalgia, regret, and tears, Luciana started to write intense, hermetic, powerful verses like these, entitled "July 4, 1925":[8]

> Arch of the bridge over the deserted valley
> pours out sorrow over having lost you
> with no return from the ice that hardens
> not only December, thickset with high peaks,
> but also this torrid July of tears.

Hers was a life amid everyday anxieties, spent in remembrance of her brother so as to keep his example alive and to raise him up to the throne of heavenly glory, in contrast to his earthly experience, when he was humiliated and his

---

[8] These verses are quoted from the volume by L. Frassati, *Sole in miniera* (Genoa: Marietti: 1988).

choice of love for God, for Mary, and for the poor remained unknown.

Luciana wrote from Berlin in 1921: "Dearest brown-haired Brother . . . you know that your worldly sister likes movement . . . company. The Good Lord willed that I should be nothing but a fault and you—many virtues. What are we to do? You will pray for me, and I a little bit for you, but from my heart; and so let us live."

Every year, on all five continents, new groups named after Pier Giorgio Frassati come into being: cultural associations, parish groups, institutes, oratories, training centers. It is not possible to make an exhaustive survey of these Frassatian cells, such as the Frassati Society of Texas, directed by Reverend Timothy Deeter. One that is outstanding for its vitality and adherence to Pier Giorgio's academic and spiritual ideals is the Society of Sinister Types [Società dei tipi loschi] in Grottammare, in the province of Ascoli Piceno.[9]

Foundations, schools, rest homes, student centers, communities, oratories, a university in Poland, churches, and nursing schools in Rome are some of the institutions affiliated with the Blessed, who is also present on the Internet in Argentina, Paraguay, Brazil, Canada, Spain, Cameroon, and Australia; we find a group of lay Third Order Dominicans at the friary of Santo Domingo Ocaña (Toledo), mountain

---

[9] The group, which was formed in 1933, is directed by Marco Sermarini, who has been a criminal defense lawyer for thirty-seven years. Its principal objective is to live Christianity as a personal relationship with Jesus Christ according to Pier Giorgio's spirit of simple freedom. There are members of the Sinister Types who have baccalaureate and graduate degrees or none at all. Sermarini explains: "We are normal people who live the realities of everyday life with the lamp of faith always lit, following the example of Pier Giorgio." They have an Italian-language website: www.tipiloschi.com; their e-mail address is: tipiloschi@hotmail.com, and they distribute a monthly newsletter: *Vivere! . . . e non vivacchiare* [Live, and don't just barely get along].

huts dedicated to him, such as the one in Krynica (Poland), groups of blood donors, volunteer associations. . . . Americans are enthusiastic about this Italian Blessed; many religious take his name, and since nuns cannot call themselves Sister Pier Giorgia, they choose the name Sister Maria Frassati.

From week to week, new "sinister types" spring up. On April 6, 2001, to celebrate his one hundredth birthday, the International Pier Giorgio Frassati Association in Rome invited all the institutions and groups that share Pier Giorgio's name to participate in a special initiative: between 6:30 and 9:00 in the evening, one hundred places scattered throughout the world were to hold a short prayer meeting, while lighting a candle in front of his image. Many, many more little lights than that were lit.

17

"NOW EVERYTHING
IS CLEAR TO ME"

Four days after his son's death, Alfredo wrote to his mother[1] a letter filled with anguish, a torment that was to continue for thirty-six years, until his death:

> Giorgio was a saint, everyone recognizes it today. . . . The impression made by his death here in Turin was equal to his goodness. Never has the city seen [such] a crowd singing with one voice the praises of a dead man. But poor Pier Giorgio is no more, and my life is finished.
>
> I had too much in the world: until the age of 57 I had everything. Now I am the poorest of the poor. I go begging in the world; no one can give me even the smallest part of what has been taken away from me.
>
> I kiss you, dear Mama; let us look forward to joining him soon. Your Alfredo.

Pier Giorgio, misunderstood during his lifetime, was the source of much worry and impatience and now, after his death, was the cause of desperate and inconsolable lamentation.

An unexpected obituary appeared in the July 8 issue of *La Giustizia*, written by the famous socialist Filippo Turati, who had not been personally acquainted with Pier Giorgio

---

[1] Giuseppina Frassati died later in 1933.

yet had understood his moral caliber, guessing that this was not an ordinary Catholic:

> He truly was a man, that Pier Giorgio Frassati whom death carried off at the age of 24. . . . What we read about him is so new and unusual that it fills with irreverent astonishment even those who do not share his faith. Though a rich young man, he had chosen work and goodness as his lot. He believed in God and professed his faith with a public display of worship, understanding his faith as an army, as a uniform that he wore in confronting the world, without exchanging it for the usual garb of convenience, opportunism, and human respect. A staunch Catholic and a member of the Catholic university student group in his city, he defied the facile scoffing of the skeptics, of the vulgar and the mediocre, by participating in religious ceremonies, processing with the archbishop's baldachin on solemn occasions. . . . He acted as he believed, spoke as he thought, and did as he said.

In other words, complete consistency. Pier Giorgio, who in his serenity and peace understood the importance and seriousness of life, used to say: "With charity one can sow peace among men: not the peace of the world, but rather the true peace that only faith in Christ can give us, by making us his brethren."

Now it was clear that his death opened the eyes of his mother and father, but relations between them continued to be rather cold; each one seemed to lead his own life, enveloping it in individual isolation.

On July 16, the prelude of a death sentence arrived at *La Stampa*: the official warning that listed the newspaper's "mortal sins". In one month, Alfredo Frassati lost his son and his newspaper; distraught, he left Turin, took refuge with his daughter in The Hague, and from that city wrote a impressive letter to his sister-in-law Elena (August 25, 1925):

Dear Elena,

You are right: we can no longer make any predictions about ourselves—not only cannot but must not. Life is really finished: every day that passes I see the abyss more clearly: the first few days seemed less burdensome to me. I still have him in my heart: no one understood what Pier Giorgio was for me: my pride, my passion: I saw in him in reality all the fine qualities that I had dreamed of having myself, that I did not have, but I saw also in his stubbornness and kindness my own character, which is stubborn but not wicked; I saw in his affection for the humble my affection: it seemed to me that in him was multiplied a millionfold the little bit in me that was not wicked.

For some time now I have wept no tears that were not for him; it seemed to me that something told me that I had to separate from him, but I felt that I was the one who had to walk away.

Did I never tell you the vision that I had at the archbishopric on the day of Luciana's wedding? Ask Alda about it. When I entered the room where the altar was, instead of it I saw a coffin: a coffin that was to destroy *everything*—just what, I did not know, I did not see or hear, but I understood: everything. And for the first time in my life, I felt that I was giving way; for one second, maybe less, but I lost consciousness of it; it did not reoccur to me even when Giorgetto died, not even while I was following his coffin, not even when the earth swallowed him up. A strange thing, is it not, my dear Elena? Incredible if I had not said it first. The coffin was his: the "everything" that it was to destroy was his death and my marriage: only that, only that, only that. Farewell, my dear Elena. Wish me well, pardon and endure my faults; let us be united at least in facing misfortune. Farewell, farewell.

Alfredo copied out a letter sent by Pier Giorgio to his sister so as to keep it with him always; the original was dated February 14 of that same year:

You ask me whether I am happy; well how could I not be? As long as faith gives me strength, I will always be happy! Any Catholic cannot *not* be happy: sadness should be banished from Catholic souls; sorrow is not sadness, which is a sickness worse than any other. That sickness is almost always produced by atheism, but the purpose for which we are created points the way for us, a path sown with many thorns, but not a sad way: it is happiness even when it leads through sorrows.

From September 29 to November 2, 1925, *La Stampa* was sequestered and its publication interrupted. Frassati was compelled to resign as publisher of the newspaper, entrusting the management thereof to Giovanni Vitelli and Giuseppe Colli. The following year, the assassination attempt against Il Duce on October 31 in Bologna became the pretext for a new suspension of the publication of the daily in Turin and of eighteen other newspapers. Mussolini now wanted to get rid of Frassati for good, since he was the extremely inconvenient manager of a newspaper that categorically refused to endorse the Black Shirts. So it was that Giovanni Agnelli acquired the entire ownership of the newspaper (he had already owned one-third together with Riccardo Gualino), and on December 30, 1926, the Nuova Società Editrice reported the news of the change of ownership. Agnelli did not allow Frassati ("although I had asked him—I am not ashamed to say so—with tears in my eyes") to have the following two lines published in the daily: "As of today I leave the management of this newspaper and hand over ownership thereof." And the newspaper ironically continued to appear

with the Frassatian motto *Frangar non flectar* (Let me be broken, but let me not be bowed). Nor was the senator's final wish granted, when he left the headquarters of the daily
paper that had seen him tirelessly compose headlines and
columns, namely, to leave free the study and the armchair
that he had intended for his heir. Years later Frassati would
write:

> Thus for more than two decades *La Stampa* was subjugated
> to Fascism: but Fiat's business steadily increased, despite the
> fact that Fascism had suppressed all freedom and had vio-
> lated the entire Albertine Statute, the masterpiece of our
> *Risorgimento* [Italian unification] and the logical conclusion
> of the heroic work of thinkers and soldiers.
>
> The newspaper unconditionally supported Fascism, and
> not only the Fascism of the first style, which had still kept
> an appearance of constitutionality, but even when power
> was totally usurped by Mussolini, as the founder and head
> of the republic of Salò, which was at war with the legiti-
> mate authority, represented by the king.[2]

Unfortunately an ominous parade of jackals began, who
presented themselves as alleged friends of Pier Giorgio. Taking advantage of his parents' sorrow, many made off with
objects that had belonged to the Blessed, which were "taken
away, inexplicably unbeknownst to Mama".[3] Others called
on the senator to ask for assistance and favors, and some of
them began magnificent careers. The ninety-year-old Father
Giuseppe Mina, a Consolata missionary, recounts: One day
I went to the Frassati house to pick up a portrait of Pier
Giorgio destined for a Catholic Action center to which I
belonged. I remember very well Signora Adelaide's recep-

---

[2] "Open Letter of Alfredo Frassati", *La Nuova Stampa*, September 26, 1945.
[3] M. Codi, *Pier Giorgio Frassati: Una valanga di vita* (Casale Monferrato [AL]:
Portalupi, 2001), 375.

tion, full of pride for her son: "His education, she said, had made him autonomous." The group of "friends" kept expanding beyond all bounds, and the father and mother, desperate in their misfortune, were unable to discern and evaluate, since they had always been in the dark concerning Pier Giorgio's dealings. "Now, for such individuals, it was enough to have been 'friends of Pier Giorgio'. It was enough to ask in his name, and everything was granted", Rina Maria Pierazzi later said. Elena Ametis also noticed these abuses and the enormous outlay of funds by Alfredo Frassati to aid the false friends of his son.

Some time before then, Pier Giorgio had knocked on the door of all the relief organizations in Turin seeking hospitality for two children who urgently needed shelter. As a last resort, he tried the Cottolengo, but their doors did not open, either; therefore, he said to his friend Bertini: "As soon as I am able to dispose of my father's riches, the first thing I will do is build a large building for children who need it." Death carried him off before he was able to put his plans into action. His father would be the one to have a large wing for homeless children built, which is still named after Pier Giorgio today, in the Piccola casa della divina provvidenza (Little House of Divine Providence), as his son had wished. As a rule, the Piccola casa names divisions and wings after canonized saints; but an exception to the rule was made for Frassati, since the request came from Cardinal Gamba himself to the superior of the house: "Blessed Cottolengo and Pier Giorgio are two great friends of the poor, they are two saints . . . and it is good to have two saints standing by."[4] Today, Cardinal Giuseppe Gamba and Blessed Pier Giorgio are laid to rest in the cathedral in Turin, one opposite the other.

[4] Congregatio Pro Causis Sanctorum, *Canonizationis Servi Dei Petri Georgii Frassati: Positio super virtutibus*, vol. 1 (Rome: Tipografia Guerra, 1987), 207–8.

"Life is sorrow and sadness. Now I can say with Brunhilde: *Alles ist nun mir klar"* (Now everything is clear to me).[5] Strong words from Alfredo Frassati, who changed his way of life and set aside his desires for power, his ambitions for ever greater profits; everything now appeared to him as vanity, and he looked at others with a more sympathetic eye; he became open to charity, in the footsteps of his son, and he dedicated his beneficent works to his Giorgetto.[6] At the same time, he aided his journalists from the old *La Stampa*, who were scattered in a sort of diaspora.

Eight years after Pier Giorgio's death, Franz Massetti returned to the Piedmont region to celebrate in Pollone a Mass on the tomb of his friend, and he stayed as a guest of the Frassatis for several days. "One day," he relates, "the senator invited me to go out for a short walk in the neighborhood of the villa. I remember the moment, which was difficult for both of us. The presence of the friend called to his mind the memory of his son. He felt the irrepressible need to give free expression to the sorrow that was now being renewed over the loss of the one in whom he had placed so many of his hopes, the one support, he now understood, on whom he could always safely rely." He began to speak about his beloved Pier Giorgio and started to weep inconsolable tears. "More than once I had seen Pier Giorgio weep when he was moved by sorrowful cases, especially of children left without any support. I got the impression of hearing again the intonation of the son in that of the father: the same sobbing, the same tone of voice. At that moment they were as similar as two drops of water."

[5] Letter from Alfredo Frassati to his friend Spartaco Fazzari from the year 1926.

[6] Cf. F. V. Massetti, *Pier Giorgio Frassati nel ricordo di un amico: Testimonianze riflessioni lettere* (Castelmaggiore [BO]: Tipocolor, 1984), 105.

Frassati walked across the estates in Pollone, and he always had one and the same destination: the cemetery. This obsession would lead to the conversion of his soul. In 1927 he wrote to his friend Spartaco Fazzari (the "Calabrese bandit", as Pier Giorgio used to call him with a smile): "To my immense discredit I do not believe that there is an afterlife. But he [Pier Giorgio] believed in it: and so it is as though there really is one. . . . Do you remember his smile? If you knew, dear Spartaco, how alive my anguished nostalgia for him still is today! And you can be sure that while I am writing you these few lines, the tears are running down ceaselessly. And I have shed so many!" Alfredo leaves us a precious legacy of words in which his bitter sorrow is laid bare and all the repressed feeling of the preceding years bursts forth in exalted emotions (November 4, 1926):

Dearest Luciana,

[A]ll days are sad: all days are full of tears: but you are right; these days are the saddest of the sad: holydays, days of funerals: the very sad day of his death: today. Just this minute we returned from the parish church. We took the route that he used to walk every morning, so full of health, so serene, so full of faith. For me it was painful to the point of agony to walk where he walked. How sorrowful it is to live now, Luciana. I pray to God, and you, too, pray for this fervently, that among all the sorrows of life just one will be spared you: the sorrow of surviving your children.

Being an imposing, extremely active man, Alfredo felt as though he were going mad in that tunnel of anguished solitude; only a job would be able to distract him from his relentless thoughts. Then he had the courage to ask for a demanding, difficult task that would completely absorb him, so as to resist this "disintegration". He neither wanted nor asked for recompense,[7] and, if there were any, it would go toward increasing the large sums that he already planned to leave to charity. So it was that Senator Frassati became the president of Italgas in 1930; the appointment came directly from the king and from Il Duce, who indeed had removed Frassati from the helm of *La Stampa* (we know how carefully Mussolini employed the media to make propaganda for his regime), but at the same time, aware of the senator's qualifications and talents, knew he was capable of solving the problems of a company in financial difficulty.

Several years passed: Frassati worked eagerly, while Pier Giorgio continued to be uppermost in his thoughts. In 1945, he had the satisfaction of once again being owner of the newspaper *La Stampa*, but only for a short time.[8] Subsequent disagreements with Fiat did not allow calm relations in their joint ownership of the newspaper, and after a legal dispute that concluded in 1955, Frassati yielded his share to Agnelli, while continuing to collaborate with his articles. He was the president of Italgas until the age of ninety, and, besides being an honorary ambassador, he was also a member of the Italian Constituent Assembly as well as a senator by right, appointed by a decree dated April 22, 1948.

The senator's return to the Church was slow but inexorable. An extremely important role in this spiritual journey was

[7] See letter dated October 7, 1932, by Senator Ettore Conti, president of the Banca commerciale.

[8] Senator Frassati writes: "I was not looking for millions; I just wanted guarantees that from then on the line taken by the newspaper would no longer have to be that of the two Fascist decades, inasmuch as the sole duty of *La Stampa* was to defend the national interests and not those of Fiat, which was powerful and easily capable of finding suitable means of safeguarding its legitimate interests without subjugating the newspaper to them."

played by Giovanni Battista Montini, the future Paul VI, who was proclaimed Venerable by Pope Benedict XVI.[9]

In 1959, FUCI held its congress in Turin, which opened on September 1[10] with the inaugural lecture by Cardinal Montini, then the archbishop of Milan, who had already been called to be part of the College of Cardinals by Blessed Pope John XXIII and with whom Frassati had been acquainted in Rome as the Substitute of the Secretariat of State, accompanying him every so often on walks in the countryside. The former curial official began his talk as follows: "There is someone here whom I see yet who is not visible, although he is present." With his eyes he sought out Pier Giorgio: "the face of a handsome, vigorous student, whose features our young people have studied in recent years and whose manly goodness they have meditated on: a model of an ideal brother." With great enthusiasm he presented the figure of Pier Giorgio Frassati, whom he had not known personally, although loud echoes of a life entirely spent in ascending had reached his ears; several witnesses still say today that the future pope could not have known some of the details unless he had heard them from the senator's own words.[11]

But on that day, Montini did not limit himself to remembering Pier Giorgio publicly: he went in person to greet his father by visiting the headquarters of Italgas, as a demonstration of his true and lively interest in the young man

[9] Paul VI was more recently declared Blessed by Pope Francis.—TRANS.

[10] That same day Alfredo Frassati wrote a previously unpublished note: "Dearest Eminence, I will never forget this day. I know for whom you came to visit me, though performing an act of humility. Thank you, thank you. I kiss your ring; pray for me, I need it so much. Yours very devotedly, Alfredo Frassati."

[11] The testimony is of Doctor Cornelio Valetto, who personally knew Senator Frassati (he often saw him in Turin in the rectory of San Lorenzo).

of the eight beatitudes and in the sorrow that had utterly
scarred Alfredo Frassati. This enlightened and significant
visit is recalled as follows by President Frassati's secretary,
Lucia Busca:

> The senator had boundless admiration for Cardinal Mon-
> tini, and such an honor, such tact and benevolence, had
> left on him a truly profound impression and given him a
> very special joy. Their conversation lasted a long time; their
> goodbyes were moving and affectionate.
>
> Overwhelmed with emotion and extraordinarily happy,
> the president did not even try to hide his tears. No sooner
> had he taken leave of the prelate than he called me into
> his office and asked me, "Did you see Cardinal Montini?"
> When I answered yes, he added, "Well, you have seen the
> future pope! Because Cardinal Montini most certainly will
> be pope. I will no longer be here; you will be; you will see
> him as pope. And on that day you will say: 'Behold, my
> president was also a prophet!'" I emphasize the word *also*
> with a malicious smile, and it was plain that his indomitable
> personality was already reemerging in his awareness of his
> own gifts, even though it had been subjugated for a mo-
> ment by the presence of the man destined for the glory of
> the triple tiara.[12]

In the archives of the Archdiocese of Milan, in a file
dedicated to the correspondence of Cardinal Montini with
laypeople, invaluable unpublished documentation was found,
which is reprinted here as an appendix; it confirms Senator Alfredo Frassati's journey of faith and his return to the
Church.

Alfredo had already been a widower for eight years—to
be precise, since June 18, 1949 (Adelaide Frassati died five

---

[12] L. Frassati, *Un uomo, un giornale: Alfredo Frassati*, vol. 3, pt. 2 (Rome: Edizioni di Storia e Letteratura, 1981), 492.

years after her sister Elena Ametis), when, at Christmas of 1957, he wrote frankly and cordially to Montini: "I follow your brilliant career with joy, and a thousand times I have planned to tell you in person all these sentiments of mine. But I am, as Your Eminence knows, a solitary. . . . But one day I will conquer this fear. . . ."

The archbishop responded very warmly to Frassati's greetings, inviting him to a meeting.

In his letters to Montini, Frassati often mentions the "distinguished Canon Bosso": he means Father Giovanni Battista, a Canon of San Lorenzo and for thirty years the youth chaplain for Catholic Action. He struck up a very good friendship with the senator, becoming his spiritual guide as well. The future Paul VI learned of this and, on January 27, 1958, wrote to him:

> They tell me that you are counseling Senator Frassati and that he was pleased to receive a recent letter of mine. I venture, therefore, to commend him to your charitable care: I have fond memories of and great esteem for the senator, as Pier Giorgio's father and a man of great intellect and noble sentiments. I think that religious sentiment ought to be rekindled in him by a new, higher light; and to this end, some good friendship may be rather helpful to him. I do not know how his health is or whether he still travels; if he happened to be traveling through Milan some morning, I would be very glad to pay my respects to him. Tell him meanwhile, if possible, that I am praying for him.
>
> Respectfully and devotedly yours, G. B. Montini Archb.

We can infer that the future Paul VI was extremely interested in guiding Alfredo Frassati spiritually, first of all because he was "Pier Giorgio's father" and, then, because he was "a man of great intellect and noble sentiments". Montini, who was always very attentive to the spiritual recovery of ailing souls, with an altogether special interest in intellectuals, artists, and priests, had understood that the senator had in him fertile soil for the faith that could be cultivated if it was properly sown, and his recommendations to Canon Bosso are very precise in this regard. The insight of the archbishop of Milan was correct. Bosso wrote to Montini:

> As I was saying goodbye, I recommended to the housekeeper, a very fine young woman, that she help him, so that he might be able to get back to the sacraments. I found in her the same concern, accompanied by much hope.
>
> The senator approached the sacraments in Rome in 1954. Unfortunately, he did not remain content [with that decision]. This year he seemed to want to make his Easter duty, then instead. . . .
>
> I recommended that the young housekeeper watch for the opportune moment and advise him to call on whomever he trusted most. May Your Eminence obtain that grace from the Lord. That is my sole preoccupation these days. I have asked a cloistered monastery to pray for this intention, and I will ask others, too.
>
> Bless me, Your Eminence, while I respectfully kiss your Sacred Purple. Very humbly and devotedly yours, Canon Giov. Batt. Bosso.

From this document we know, therefore, that Pier Giorgio's father approached the sacraments in 1954, but was not satisfied by the experience. Nevertheless, Frassati began to attend Mass every Sunday, always instructing his grandchildren to be attentive and well-behaved in church. He spent his most peaceful moments now with them, or else amusing himself with his favorite game, *bocce* [Italian lawn bowling].

The deep tie consisting of esteem, admiration, and trust that bound him to Montini did not slacken but rather increased. On December 19, 1959, the senator wrote to the cardinal excusing himself for having been unable to go to Milan to greet the archbishop on his birthday because of an illness; on that occasion he recalled with gratitude the meeting between the two that had taken place in Turin some time earlier and hoped to be able to obtain an audience as soon as possible. Two months before that, Frassati had again approached the sacraments, this time with great joy, as Bosso reports to Montini on October 20, 1959:

Your Eminence,

I am very happy to be able to inform you that this evening His Excellency Senator Frassati went to Confession and tomorrow morning will receive Holy Communion together with his entire household.

This evening, as he welcomed me, he was weeping for joy. He told me to express to Your Eminence his most profound gratitude for the visit that you paid him in Turin. "Tell His Eminence that I am exceedingly happy. He came to call on me, and, without saying a single word to me— in perfect silence—he did me a great deal of good."

Last Sunday His Eminence Cardinal Tardini imparted to him the Holy Father's blessing, and this too greatly moved him.

He is doing well enough for a sick man. A medical consultation assured him that the pleurisy has now passed. They advise him to convalesce for seven weeks at the seaside by Naples. But I can see that he is slowly declining.

I thank Your Eminence for all that you have done for the benefit of this dear friend of ours. Be so kind as to bless me and also all the Youth [of Catholic Action] in Turin.

Bowing to kiss your Sacred Purple, I profess that I am very humbly and devotedly yours, Canon Giovanni Battista Bosso.

From Rome on March 3, 1960, Frassati again wrote to Montini in his old-style penmanship, which had been the despair of the editors of *La Stampa*, evoking the figure of Pier Giorgio, "who deserves to be remembered by everyone, even by those who did not know him during his lifetime". His unusual sympathy was abundantly shared by the prelate, who on Easter Sunday 1960 wrote to him, expressing the hope that he could "still do much good, with fortitude, in the light of faith and after the example of Pier Giorgio, for your merit and comfort and for the edification and consolation of those who wish you well".

Immediately after Pier Giorgio's death, many initiatives inspired by him began to spring up. As early as 1931, there were 250 pious works named after him, and continual pilgrimages were made to his tomb in Pollone. But the first initiative, which started between 1925 and 1926 and still exists, is the Pier Giorgio Frassati Community (now the Diocesan Pier Giorgio Frassati Institute), which was established thanks to donations from the senator and by the decision of the Diocesan Council of the Catholic Youth. It organized summer camps for boys aspiring to join Catholic Action, especially those who had to deal with difficult economic conditions and frail health. The Frassati summer camp that opened at San Pietro Vallemina in the vicinity of Pinerolo later settled permanently at Cesana Torinese, high up in the Val di Susa, and the project was carried out thanks to the commitment of Canon Giovanni Battista Bosso.

The president of the Frassati Institute was Cornelio Valetto, who in San Pietro Vallemina from 1929 to 1932 learned about and admired the example of Pier Giorgio's life through the words of Canon Silvio Murzone, the chaplain of the pious work along with Giovanni Battista Bosso. "I was one of the first campers in Vallemina," Doctor Valetto recalls, "and they explained to me who Pier Giorgio Frassati was. Three times a day we meditated on episodes from his life on the pages written by Don Cojazzi. My devotion to the Blessed continues, and for the past seventy years I have not forgotten to recite every morning the prayer to the Blessed that I learned in Catholic Action."

Alfredo Frassati's surprising and wonderful conversion ripened slowly in the light of his son, and his unchanging devotion to Montini continued until his death, which arrived peacefully at five o'clock on May 21, 1961, Pentecost Sunday. The housekeeper Borowy, who had worked for thirty-nine years in the Frassati household, had asked him in alarm several minutes previously: "Do you recognize who is giving you a drink?" And he replied: "Good heavens!" Then he coughed and expired. At his viewing, there were no flowers around the body, at his request, and between his lifeless hands he wanted there to be a crucifix and a photograph of his beloved Pier Giorgio, one of those at which Alfredo could no longer bear to look; he had gone so far as to recommend to his heirs that there should be no portraits of his son present when he went to visit them, just as he had not wanted his seven grandchildren to have his son's name as their first name: Pier Giorgio was unique, one of a kind.

News of his death was not officially announced, because the senator had expressed the preference that it should be made public only after the funeral. Montini, however, was informed the same day by Canon Bosso in a telegram: "I inform Your Eminence rather unexpected death Senator Frassati this morning. Letter follows. Filial respects."

In Turin there was no funeral ceremony. The last will and testament expressed the desire to bequeath 700 million lire (this was in 1961) to "a single work" in his son's name.

Unfortunately his wishes were not respected, and the ECA [bureau for public assistance] intervened and took the legacy after a judicial ruling: the 700 million were divided between the two claimants, the municipality of Turin and that of Pollone. In Pollone, they decided to build a useless gymnasium, and the 380 million that went to Turin ended inauspiciously: one hundred were distributed among the lawyers of the two municipal boards, and the rest vanished between construction schemes and Communist cooperatives. In recent years, a contrast has come about between the father and the daughter; proof of this is what Luciana wrote, referring to Pier Giorgio: "Along with his poor people, I would be his only heir. The thought of leaving 25,000 lire to me[13] seemed to signify that his dear protection should never cease, even mitigating the later humiliation of the inheritance from my father that I missed. My brother's affection, indeed, never failed me."[14]

When Frassati was about to live out his final days on earth, Montini asked the archbishop of Turin to be at the sick man's side, and Cardinal Maurilio Fossati remained for a long time with the senator, calmly conversing. They also called a missionary returning from China, from whom the senator, with great emotion, received the sacraments, "manifesting", Don Massetti explains, "his most lively gratitude toward those who had worked to procure for him the happiness of that encounter with the Lord". Brother Filiberto Guala, a friend of Pier Giorgio, who earned a degree in engineering and then donned the Trappist habit, explained in a letter to Don Massetti: "The father's 'complete' conversion is a fruit of Pier Giorgio, which we have seen ripen

[13] The insurance policy that Pier Giorgio had taken out in case of a mountain-climbing accident.

[14] L. Frassati, *Il cammino di Pier Giorgio* (Milan: Rizzoli, 1990), 259.

slowly. After the visit we paid him together in 1959, inviting him to make his confession, I had three precious meetings with him at the Frattocchie.[15] He had been one of my friends who most 'rejoiced' over my entering the monastery —he, too, would have come, if he had been younger!— What progress. . . ."[16]

The desire for peace, to encounter the light of faith, became ever more urgent for Alfredo, causing him at the end of his days to make peace with himself because he was at peace with God. There is no faith without a miracle, and this, in our judgment, was Pier Giorgio's first miracle. The very long spiritual travail caused his soul to arrive at its final moorings in the light of grace. With the following very moving and touching words of his last will and testament,[17] a father who anxiously looked forward to being reunited with the creature he loved most took leave of this world:

> When these lines are read I will be where I have wanted to be since July 4, 1925. It seems to me unnecessary to recall that I wish to be buried close to him, to my Dearly Beloved, to the best little son who ever existed in the world: I was proud of him while he was alive: and no one will ever be lamented again and again more than he, because no one ever was or ever will be like him.
>
> Close to him, forever: if possible without a wall between the two coffins, so that they touch, eternally united to compensate for the distressing separation for so many years. If I should be so unfortunate to have to die at sea or in any place where my corpse cannot be found, I also wish that what ought to have been my tomb should remain empty: if I die in Pollone, may it be in the room that was his. Furthermore, I wish that upon my body should be placed, together

---

[15] A Trappist monastery in the vicinity of Rome.

[16] Massetti, *Pier Giorgio Frassati nel ricordo di un amico*, 104.

[17] The last will and testament had been drawn up on October 10, 1947.

with the crucifix, a portrait of Pier Giorgio, and so, too, that the room where I shall be laid out for the last twenty-four hours should be full of portraits of him, all those you have at hand, pictures that even today I cannot see without affliction. May the memory of him that is so alive in thousands of hearts never fade among all my heirs, who must seek to imitate him: in sorrowful hours may they invoke him, and may he be their companion in hours of gladness. I want flowers to be at his tomb always.

How I would have liked for you to me near me at the hour of my death, and how happy I would have been if I could have lived with you throughout these very long years.

I wept for him every day, even when it seemed that sometime I might be less sad. I wept for him, and I will weep for him until my final hour. Farewell, my Giorgetto: when my last testament is opened, I will be with you forever.

APPENDIX

CORRESPONDENCE BETWEEN CARDINAL GIOVANNI BATTISTA MONTINI AND SENATOR ALFREDO FRASSATI

Turin, December 20, 1957

Your Excellency,

Accept from a very humble admirer of yours the warmest greetings for the upcoming holidays. I follow your brilliant career with joy, and a thousand times I have planned to tell you in person all these sentiments of mine. But I am, as Your Eminence knows, a solitary who is condemned increasingly each day to stay far away even from the persons who are most dear. But one day I will conquer this fear and come to kiss your hand, bringing all my greetings.

Remember me occasionally in your prayers, and consider me always your very humble servant,

Alfredo Frassati

~

Milan, Christmas 1957

Dear Excellency!

Your note moves me because it reminds me of a very pleasant memory that I look back on with affectionate devotion.

And so I present to you my sincerest wishes and pray to God for you that he will make you strong and the harbinger of every good thing.

To see you again would be a great pleasure for me, too, but I think that right now it is not easy for you to travel. Know, in any case, that I am close to you spiritually, in the memory of your Pier Giorgio and ours and in the desire for your prosperity and peace.

Allow me to give to you, as to a revered and respected Friend, my blessing.

Giovanni Battista Montini

~

Turin, January 18, 1959

Dearest Eminence,

I am glad that an ever vaster field in which to do good has been given to Your Eminence. I cordially congratulate Y.E. on your election as cardinal, but even more than over this exalted appointment I rejoiced when during the conclave Y.E., though absent physically, was nonetheless morally the most striking figure, the most present of those present.

Everyone knows what this paradoxical case signifies.

You know that I am a misanthrope, but when you have a minute of free time, have your secretary tell me, and I will come to Milan immediately to tell you all I think.

Accept my most devoted respects.

Yours, Alfredo Frassati

~

Milan, February 3, 1959

Excellency!

I received with immense pleasure your very dear letter, even though it contains meanderings about my situation, which I am willing to ascribe to your kindness. One thing that you say pleases me and does me good, namely, the wish that I might have better hope of living up to the mission that has been given to me. At every hour, it tests the inadequacy of my strength. And I constantly practice trust in God, in which I find, in interior humility, a bit of courage and peace. Heartfelt thanks!

But your news is more urgent to me than my own: I always remember you, and I look forward to the opportunity to see you again, to pay you my respects, and to tell you things that Pier Giorgio secretly puts into my heart. If my duties were less demanding, I would come to visit you! Know, at any rate, that I keep you in my memory and in prayer.

Very devoted,
G. B. Montini

〜

Turin, March 5, 1959

Dearest Eminence,

The letter from Y.E. that I received just this moment moved me to tears.

How is it possible that Y.E., although so high-ranking, so burdened and overburdened with work, should have the time to send such an invaluable letter to an old man who has completed 90 years and already belongs more to the next world than to this one! But it is quite understandable, considering the great kindness of Y.E.

Many times, actually many, many times, Canon Bosso and I had decided to make an excursion to Milan to bring you the expression of our sentiments of affection and highest esteem. I have been the one, I specifically, to postpone this deep pleasure, because I always thought and still fear that it would rob precious time from your many weighty occupations.

But now, as soon as the weather is a little bit milder, I ask Y.E. to set a date and time when you will be able to receive me.

I still have before my mind's eye your glance during our meeting at Saint John Lateran: in that glance there was a whole agenda; what . . . maintained was not true, that the blame for what happened should be assigned to the poor people. In that glance there was the agenda that you always carry out and have always carried out and will carry out in all the offices that God has destined to entrust to Y. E.

Devotedly yours,
Alfredo Frassati

~

Turin, September 1, 1959

Dearest Eminence,

I will never forget this day. I know for Whom you came to visit me, though performing an act of humility. Thank you, thank you. I kiss your ring; pray for me, I need it so much.

Yours very devotedly,
Alfredo Frassati

Turin, October 2, 1959

Excellency!

Let the Rev. Canon Bosso convey to you the greetings, wishes, and respects that I hoped to express to you personally today, although your indisposition prevented me from doing so. Take care of yourself; do not think about me. You are not obliged by any duty toward me: I, rather, if I have the opportunity to return to Turin (but when?), will take the liberty again of paying you a little visit.

Know that I, along with many people who wish you well, am near you with my wishes and prayers.

With cordial respects, Very devotedly yours,
Giovanni Battista Cardinal Montini

⁓

Turin, December 19, 1959

Your Eminence,

An illness that lasted a month and a half prevented me from procuring for myself the honor and the great pleasure of coming personally to Milan to present to you my most fervent wishes for the approaching holidays and to thank you, ever mindful of the great benefit that Y.E. procured for me by your visit to Turin, a visit that will never be forgotten by me. I hope to be restored to health soon and to be able to ask Y.E. for an audience, even a brief one, given your endless duties, so as to express to you personally and completely my profound gratitude.

Accept my greeting for the upcoming holidays, and be assured of my unchanging devotion.

Rome, March 3, 1960

Your Eminence,

Your letter dated January 29 arrived today at the housing complex of my grandson around 15 miles from Rome. I reply immediately, thanking Y. E. profoundly for your willingness to devote a bit of time to my nothingness, and I still ask myself how you ever remember a poor man like me, and I realize with tears in my eyes that I ought to know the reason why. The reason is my dear son, Pier Giorgio, who deserves to be remembered by everyone, even by those who did not know him during his lifetime.

I kiss your hands, most grateful for your moving words to me.

Very devotedly,
Alfredo Frassati

~

Milan, Easter 1960

Excellency,

Thank you, thank you for your courteous note, which brings me your greetings and gives me proof of your faithful memory. Be assured that mine is equally diligent and devoted! For Easter, then, which always puts great thoughts in our hearts, I remembered you in a special way: I prayed to the Lord for you and for your family, and I formulated the wish that I now express to you: "that you may still do much good, with fortitude, in the light of faith and after the example of Pier Giorgio, for your merit and comfort and for the edification and consolation of those who wish you well!"

With cordial respects,
G. B. Card. Montini

Pollone, December 22, 1960

Accept, Your Eminence, my devoted wishes at Christmas and for the turn of the New Year.

Devotedly yours,
Alfredo Frassati

~

Milan, January 23, 1961

Excellency!

I cherished your greetings for Christmas and the New Year, and I reciprocate with all my heart, glad to learn that you are well and active and still wishing every good thing for you and for your concerns. I pray that the Lord may always revive in your spirit the light of better memories and of higher hopes and zeal for good works.

Yes, may you still have the courage to do great and beneficent things, as you had the opportunity to mention to me during your last visit, which I still cherish. It will give your life a fullness of merits that will not be forgotten! Pier Giorgio will bless. I greet you cordially.

Giovanni Battista Montini,
Archbishop

~

Rome, March 31, 1961

Your Eminence,

I ask you to accept my wish for a Happy Easter that comes right from the heart, hoping that time will confirm what I think about Cardinal Montini.

Alfredo Frassati

Telegram from Milan, May 22, 1961

Sadly and pensively I express condolences [on the] death [of] Senator Frassati and commend to the Lord his soul [which was] strong and sensitive [to] Christian and human values.

Cardinal Montini

~

BIBLIOGRAPHY

Antonioli, F. *Pier Giorgio Frassati: Il borghese delle otto beatitudini*. Milan: Edizioni Paoline, 1989.

————. *Pier Giorgio Frassati: Il giovane delle otto beatitudini*. Milan: Paoline Editoriale Libri, 1994.

————, R. Falviola, and A. Labanca. *Pier Giorgio Frassati*. Introduction by Giuseppe Lazzati. Rome: AVE, 1985.

Atti del Processo apostolico di beatificazione e canonizzazione del servo di Dio Pier Giorgio Frassati (1980–1981). Vols. 1–3.

Biffi, G. *Il mistero di Benedetta Bianchi Porro*. Casale Monferrato [AL]: Piemme, 1994.

Casalegno, C. *Pier Giorgio Frassati: Una vita di preghiera*. Introduction by Cardinal Anastasio Ballestrero. Casale Monferrato: Piemme, 1988.

————. *Pier Giorgio Frassati: Una vita di carità*. Introduction by Cardinal Giovanni Saldarini. Casale Monferrato: Piemme, 1990.

————. *Pier Giorgio Frassati*. Casale Monferrato: Piemme, 1993.

Castronovo, Valerio, ed. *Storia illustrata di Torino*. Vol. 5: *Torino nell'Italia unita*. Milan: Elio Sellino Editore, 1993.

————. *Storia illustrata di Torino*. Vol. 6: *Torino nell'età giolittiana*. Milan: Elio Sellino Editore, 1993.

———. *Storia illustrata di Torino*. Vol. 7: *Torino dal fascismo alla repubblica*. Milan: Elio Sellino Editore, 1993.

Claude, R. *Frassati parmi nous*. Tournai: Casterman, 1957.

Codi, M. *Pier Giorgio Frassati: Una valanga di vita*. Casale Monferrato [AL]: Portalupi, 2001.

Cojazzi, A. *Pier Giorgio Frassati: Testimonianze*. Turin: SEI, 1928. New revised edition with introduction by Piero Bargellini. Turin: SEI, 1977. Latest edition with preface by Francesco Traniello. Turin: SEI, 1990.

Congregatio pro Causis Sanctorum. *Canonizationis Servi Dei Petri Georgii Frassati: Positio super miraculo*. Rome: Tipografia Guerra, 1989.

———. *Canonizationis Servi Dei Petri Georgii Frassati: Positio super virtutibus*. Rome: Tipografia Guerra, 1987.

———. *Canonizationis Servi Dei Petri Georgii Frassati: Relatio et vota; Congressus Peculiaris super virtutibus*. Rome: Tipografia Guerra, 1987.

———. *Decretum Canonizationis Servi Dei Petri Georgii Frassati*. Rome: October 23, 1987.

De Felcourt, M. *Santi fanciulli*. Milan: Mursia, 1968.

Di Lorenzo, M. *Pier Giorgio Frassati: L'amore non dice mai "basta"*. Milan: Paoline Editoriale Libri, 2002.

Falciola, R., and A. Labanca. *Conosci Pier Giorgio Frassati*. Rome: Fondazione Apostolicam Actuositatem, 1998.

Frassati, L. *Antologia di una vita*. Preface by Carlo Bo. Parma: Guanda, 1992.

———. *Calendario di una vita: 1901–1925: Pier Giorgio Frassati*. Turin: Istituto La Salle, 1981.

———. *Il cammino di Pier Giorgio*. Milan: Rizzoli, 1990.

————. *La carità di Pier Giorgio.* Preface by Luigi Gedda. Rome: Edizioni Paoline, 1951. Second expanded edition, Turin: SEI, 1957.

————. *Pier Giorgio Frassati: I giorni della sua vita.* Introduction by Karl Rahner. Third edition. Rome: Edizioni Studium, 1990. Translated by Dinah Livingstone as *A Man of the Beatitudes: Pier Giorgio Frassati*, edited and adapted by Patricia O'Rourke (San Francisco: Ignatius Press, 2000).

————. *Mio fratello Pier Giorgio: La fede.* Preface by Cardinal Giacomo Lercaro. Rome: Edizioni Paoline, 1954.

————. *Mio fratello Pier Giorgio: L'impegno sociale e giudizi sul carattere.* Preface by Giorgio La Pira. Rome: Edizioni Paoline, 1953. New edition, *L'impegno sociale e politico di Pier Giorgio.* Introduction by Carlo Trabucco. Rome: AVE, 1978.

————. *Mio fratello Pier Giorgio: La morte.* Preface by Giovanni Papini. Rome: Edizioni Paoline, 1952. New edition, *Mio fratello Pier Giorgio: Gli ultimi giorni (29 giugno–4 luglio 1925).* Reggio Emilia: Città Armoniosa, 1982. Most recent edition, *Una vita mai spenta.* Preface by Renato Romanelli. Turin: Editrice La Stampa, 1992.

————. *Mio fratello Pier Giorgio: Vita e immagini*, with contributions by Francesco Olgiati, Luigi Ambrosini, Filippo Turati, Ennio de Concini, Mario Soldati, Guido Piovene, Silvio Negro. Genoa: Edizioni Siglaeffe, 1959.

————. *La piccozza di Pier Giorgio.* Turin: SEI, 1995.

————. *Sole in miniera.* Introduction by Carlo Bo. Genoa: Marietti, 1988.

————. *Un uomo, un giornale: Alfredo Frassati.* 3 vols. Rome: Edizioni di Storia e Letteratura, 1978–1982.

————, ed. *Pier Giorgio Frassati: Echi di memorie*. Genoa: Marietti, 1989.

Frassati, P. G. *Lettere*. Edited by Luciana Frassati. Preface by Luigi Sturzo. Rome: Editrice Studium, 1950; Brescia: Queriniana, 1976.

————. *Lettere 1906–1925*. Milan: Vita e Pensiero, 1995.

Gariglio, B. *Cattolici democratici e clerico-fascisti: Il mondo cattolico torinese alla prova del fascismo*. Bologna: Il Mulino, 1976.

Giuntella, M. C. *La Fuci tra modernismo, Partito Popolare e Fascismo*. Rome: Edizioni Studium, 2000.

Landi, G. *Teresio Olivelli: Un progetto di vita*. Milan: Massimo, 1983.

Marcucci Fanello, G. *Storia della F.U.C.I.* Rome: Editrice Studium, 1971.

Massetti, F. V. *Pier Giorgio Frassati nel ricordo di un amico: Testimonianze riflessioni lettere*. Milan: Edizioni O.R., 1976. New edition, Castelmaggiore [BO]: Tip. Tipocolor, 1984.

Molinari, F., and V. Neri. *Olio Santo e olio di ricino: Rapporto su Chiesa e fascismo*. Second edition. Turin: Marietti, 1976.

Monaci mercanti & cow-boy: Il borgo della Crocetta tra storia e vita quotidiana. Turin: Opera, 2002.

Monti, A. *Il mestiere di insegnare: Scritti sulla scuola 1909–1965*. Cuneo: Araba Fenice, 1994.

Pier Giorgio Frassati Terziario Domenicano: ricordi, testimonianze e studi . . . Bologna: Edizioni Studio Domenicano, 1985.

Pierazzi, M. R., *Così ho visto Pier Giorgio: ricordi e testimonianze*. Brescia: Queriniana, 1955. New edition, Sofia Scavia, 1976.

————. *Pier Giorgio Frassati: storia vera di un bambino vero.* Brescia: La Scuola, 1957.

Risso, P. *Pier Giorgio Frassati: Il giovane ricco che disse "sì".* Leumann [TO]: Elle Di Ci, 1989.

Ruiz De Cardenas, L. *Giovani anime sante: Profili.* Turin: Edizioni Colle San Giovanni Bosco, 1942.

Scaltriti, G. A. *Pier Giorgio Frassati e il suo Savonarola.* Rome: Edizioni Paoline, 1979.

Soldi, P. *Verso l'assoluto: Pier Giorgio Frassati.* Milan: Jaca Book, 1991.

Staglieno, M. *Un santo borghese: Pier Giorgio Frassati.* Milan: Bompiani, 1988.

Tranfaglia, Nicola, ed. *Storia di Torino: Gli anni della Repubblica.* Turin: Einaudi, 1999.

Tuninetti, G., and G. D'Antino. *Il cardinale Domenico Della Rovere, costruttore della cattedrale, e gli arcivescovi di Torino dal 1515 al 2000: Stemmi, alberi genealogici e profili biografici.* Cantalupa [TO]: Effatà Editrice, 2000.